Ken Hom's
Hot Wok

Over 150 One-pan Wonders

Photographs by
Philip Webb

WEST
175
Publishing

DEDICATION

For Sue Burke, for her indispensable support, and
Michael Levene, who made it all possible.

West 175 Publishing
P. O. Box 84848
Seattle, WA 98124

Web site: www.greatfoodtv.com

Credits
Publishing Team

Publisher	Greg Sharp
Americanization Editor	Alison Leach
Editor	Chris Rylko
Culinary Director	Jenny Steinle
Production Coordinator	Kate Terhaar
Design Modification	Kay Green
Proofreader	Mary Rose Sliwoski

This book is published to accompany the television series entitled Great Food which was first broadcast in 1998.

UK Version
Home Economist Sarah Ramsbottom
Designed by Mason Linklater
Illustrations by Graham Rosewarne
Photographs and Styling by Philip Webb
First published to accompany the BBC television series entitled Ken Hom's Hot Wok
which was first broadcast in 1996.
First Published by BBC Worldwide 1996
Reprinted 1996 (eleven times)
(c) Taurom Incorporated 1996

Library of Congress Cataloging-in-Publication Data
Ken Hom's Hot Wok, over 150 one-pan wonders, photographs by Philip Webb - 1st U.S. ed.
p. cm.
Includes index.
Published to accompany the television series entitled Great Food.
ISBN 1-884656-08-0
1. Wok cookery. 2. Quick and easy cookery. 3. Cookery, Chinese. I. Title II. Title: Hot Wok.
TX840.W65H66 1999 98-37627
641.7'7-dc21   CIP

West 175 Publishing is a division of West 175 Enterprises, Inc.

Printed in Hong Kong
1 2 3 4 5 6 7 8 9 10

First U.S. Version

DISTRIBUTED BY PUBLISHERS GROUP WEST

Ken Hom's
Hot Wok

West 175 Publishing

CONTENTS

ACKNOWLEDGMENTS

The inspiration for this book came from Heather Holden-Brown, Senior Commissioning Editor at BBC Books, who worked hard to persuade me to take on this project, a task which I am most grateful she undertook. I must thank her first.

Next, thanks to all the hardworking editors at BBC Books who made this book a reality: Charlotte Lochhead, for her careful supervision; Wendy Hobson, for her meticulous editing; Doug Young for his constant support throughout the writing of this book.

I am, of course, deeply appreciative of the beautiful photographs which grace this book. For those I must thank Philip Webb and his stylist Sarah Ramsbottom. And thanks as well to Frank Phillips and Bill Mason for their handsome design.

And thanks to my own personal circle of supportive friends who worked as hard as I did on this book. First, as always, to Gordon Wing who assisted me in testing and questioning every recipe. This book would not be complete without his fine-tuning. Second, to Gerry Cavanaugh for his observant editing and research. And finally to Andrew Walton Smith (Drew) for his copy-editing of the manuscript. His editorial comments certainly were an asset to the final manuscript.

And finally, to my literary agents, Carole Blake and Julian Friedmann. I am eternally grateful for their affection, their guidance, and their wise counsel. Thank you both, and one and all.

NOTES ON THE RECIPES

Eggs are large.

•

Wash all fresh produce before preparation.

•

Spoon measurements are level.

•

Conversions are approximate and have been rounded up or down.
In a few recipes it has been necessary to modify them very slightly.
Follow one set of measurements only; do not mix
metric and imperial in the same recipe.

•

The symbol Ⓥ appearing after a recipe title indicates that it is suitable
for vegetarians. Some dairy products have been used in these recipes,
and sometimes it may be necessary to use alternative ingredients, such
as vegetable stock for chicken stock.

INTRODUCTION

The wok has been central to my life as a professional chef and food writer. But it was central to my childhood and youth as well. To grow up Chinese means enjoying wonderful foods prepared in the wok. It also means learning how essential the wok is in the Chinese idiom. Terms such as "stir-frying the real estate," to engage in land speculation, and "breaking the wok," to divorce or to break up the home, indicate how deeply the wok and its telling metaphors have penetrated the language. The wok and its applications dominate the Chinese kitchen and it is well embedded in our expressive understanding of all other aspects of life. Only a devoted Jungian psychologist could exhaust the rich contents of its symbolism.

My mother put together three- or four-course meals every night in a tiny kitchen, ill-equipped by modern Western standards. In my eyes, she did this quickly and smoothly. I never heard her complain of any technical problems. Our dinner was on the table within an hour of her coming home from work.

Usually, the dishes were simple: a soup, which we consumed as a beverage; one or two stir-fried dishes, either pork, chicken or seafood with vegetables, a simple vegetable dish; and, of course, rice. The tool at the center of this culinary creativity was the richly blackened, perfectly seasoned family wok, expertly manipulated by my mother. It was and remains the indispensable tool in the making of such wonderful foods. There were also a few steamers and pots for soup and rice, but the wok was the rightful ruling monarch of the *batterie de cuisine*.

Today, the wok still commands pride of place in my own professional kitchen. And increasingly, it is becoming central in many Western kitchens. My mother never would have predicted such a development among the non-Chinese. But the wok remains what it has always been, an extremely versatile, reliable and easily mastered implement. Its enduring and endearing qualities are such that it needed only to be discovered to be loved and adopted. With today's hectic lifestyle, in which time in the kitchen is limited and yet people are so mindful of health and nutrition, the wok is something of a wonder. With the wok, the harried cook can prepare nutritious, delectable and satisfying meals in a very short time, just as my mother did so many years ago.

Now, the wok did not just come into being. Chinese cuisine has accurately been defined as a "cookery of scarcity." In a geographic situation of limited arable land and even more limited forests, providing food and firewood for a population of so many millions was an enormous challenge. Over the centuries, the Chinese learned how to extract from nature the maximum of edible ingredients and to prepare them tastefully with a minimum of cooking oil and fuel. Out of these necessities, stir-fry cookery and the wok were conceived and fashioned.

Archeological evidence indicates that the wok came into wide use about 2000 years ago and its appearance coincides with the progression of China's Iron Age, which came much later than Europe's. The word "wok" is Cantonese. In Mandarin or pin yin Chinese, the word used is "guo." While cooking in a wok is common throughout the whole of China, it is the Cantonese who are the great travelers among the Chinese and thus it is their pronunciation of the term that has won world-wide acceptance.

Today traditional Chinese kitchens are sparsely furnished. The substantial kitchen stove is usually in the shape of a large rectangle, with two openings above the fire chamber. Large, round-bottomed, cast-iron woks fit tightly on these openings so that all the heat is transferred to the wok and none is lost so the proper cooking temperatures are quickly attained. Every tool in the kitchen is versatile, every technique extracts the full nutritional value and flavor from ingredients, the foods themselves are prepared so that they cook quickly in a little oil, and don't waste heat. The wok evolved to its perfection in this environment, a warm stove and versatile wok becoming synonymous with heart and home at the center of Chinese family life.

There are many types of wok on the market today. I highly recommend the one-handled, heavy carbon steel model with a slightly flattened bottom (made for all types of stove tops). This wok offers maximum efficiency and effectiveness in creating the authentic textures and flavors, most particularly the smoky flavors characteristic of wok cookery.

Information in other chapters of the book will describe and clarify in more detail the various uses of the wok, with suggestions on how to get the most out of this venerable kitchen tool. I am sure that with good woks your efforts will be rewarded.

All that remains is to wish you good wokery and delicious enjoyment.

WOK TALK

In over 20 years of demonstrating and writing about cooking with the wok, I have been impressed by how people everywhere tend to ask the same questions. Everyone is fascinated by wok cookery but they often feel intimidated. To calm such anxieties and to facilitate the use of this book, I list here the most frequently asked questions about the wok, to dispel any concerns you may have.

1 Must I use a special spatula/turner to cook in the wok?
No. However, there are special spatulas/turners whose shapes are specifically designed to help turn the food more easily in the hot wok.

2 How do I know when the vegetables are cooked?
Pierce the thickest part of the vegetable with the tip of a small, sharp knife. If it goes through easily, the vegetables are cooked. If the knife meets some resistance, it needs a little more cooking.

3 How can you tell if the meat is cooked?
This is tricky and subject to many considerations. Most meats are cooked when they are slightly firm to the touch. But, as with vegetables, some meats take longer than others. Experience and your own preferences will guide you. My own advice: don't overcook any food. And remember, food removed from a very hot wok continues to cook.

4 Is there any vegetable or food I can't cook in the wok, like, for example, soup?
It depends on the type of wok you have. In a carbon steel wok, certain types of acidic fruits like lemons or pineapple will remove some of the wok's seasoning. This is not harmful to the wok but it does not look attractive. Also, a very strong vinegar sauce may remove the seasoning in a carbon steel wok. Other than these cases, you can cook almost anything in a wok and it is ideal for making soups too. Its wide surface allows the soup to simmer slowly and to be skimmed efficiently.

5 Why do my vegetables come out soggy?
Sometimes vegetables come out soggy when they are thrown in all at once, regardless of the water content. For example, if you add spinach with asparagus, cabbage, etc., all at once, the water from the spinach and cabbage will make the other vegetables soggy. Vary the quantity of cooking water you add according to how much natural water is in the vegetable you are cooking.

If you are using the wok covered, make sure you have a minimum amount of water in the wok when you cook your vegetables, otherwise the vegetables will oversteam and become soggy.

Soggy vegetables may simply be caused by too many types of vegetables being cooked at once. There should be no more than four to five types of vegetable at the most, some crisper, like green beans, others leafier, such as spinach. They should never be added at the same time. Give the tougher, more textured vegetables a head start.

6 How do you season the wok?
Only carbon steel woks need seasoning. The best way to season it is to scrub it clean with cleanser or detergent the first time you get it. Wipe it dry. Heat it over medium heat, and add about 2 tablespoons of vegetable oil (not olive oil). With a clean paper towel, rub the oil over the surface of the wok and repeat this rubbing every 5 minutes for about 20 minutes until the

paper towel comes out clean. You now have a seasoned wok.

7 *How do you wash the wok?*
In warm water with a soft sponge. Do not scrub it or use soap or detergent. To avoid rust, dry it quickly over heat or wipe it dry with paper towels or a cloth.

8 *My wok is rusty, should I throw it out?*
No. If it is a good carbon steel wok, simply scrub the rust out with an abrasive cleaner, wipe it clean, and re-season it.

9 *Why does my food stick to the wok when I'm cooking in it?*
It could mean that your wok has not been seasoned properly or that you are using detergent to clean the wok each time which wipes off the seasoned surface. Or you may not be cooking properly in it, heating the wok first and getting it hot before you add the oil. Most commonly, food sticking means the wok isn't hot enough.

10 *How do I clean the wok with soap if the food is stuck in it?*
Simply soak it in warm water and wipe it with a soft sponge. This should work unless the food has really been burnt in the wok. In that case, use the professional Chinese chef method. Heat the wok with any oil and burn the food until it flakes off. Rinse it in warm water. Dry it over high heat and re-season the surface of the wok by adding oil to the surface and rubbing it into the surface of the wok. Then, heat it gently for about 25 minutes.

11 *What is the difference between carbon steel and non-stick woks?*
I am partial to carbon steel woks because I think that they capture the more authentic flavors of wok cooking. This is because the wok is seasoned and can be heated to a very high temperature, the secret of wok cooking. However, I understand the need for convenience and today there are now good carbon steel, non-stick, woks which are effective.

One great difference is that non-stick woks are non-reactive. This means you can use them with a lemon sauce, or with acidic fruits, and you do not have to worry about re-seasoning the wok.

12 *Can I use the wok on an electric/ceramic/halogen/induction surface?*
A wok can be used on almost any element, as long as it is hot. The best woks to use with those surfaces are the ones with a slightly flattened bottom so that some of the wok surface comes in contact with the fiercest heat.

13 *Why shouldn't I use an electric or stainless steel wok?*
Unfortunately, electric woks do not maintain the high heat needed for successful wok cookery. The temperature drops as soon as food is added and it takes a while before it can reach a high heat again. Also, electric woks are quite expensive, as are stainless steel woks. And stainless steel woks have hot spots and when heated to very hot, food can burn very easily. They are therefore not appropriate for good wok cooking.

14 *When do you put in the sauces?*
That, of course, depends on the recipes. However, a general principle to remember is that you stir-fry food to a certain stage and then it begins to get dry. This is usually the time to add the sauces.

15 *How do you cook egg noodles or rice noodles without them sticking in the wok?*
Egg noodles should be blanched first, drained and then tossed in sesame oil and cooled before being added to the wok. Hot or wet noodles will stick to the wok.

16 How do you steam foods in the wok?
Simply add 2 inches (5 cm) of hot water to the wok. Then place either a bamboo steamer or a rack on top of the wok. (It must be set so as to allow the cover to fit snugly.) Place the food to be steamed on a heatproof plate, place the plate on the steamer or rack, cover, and steam according to the recipe.

17 How do you make fried rice?
First, you must have already cooked some long-grain white rice, and left it to go cold. Make sure the wok is heated to very hot, add the oil and when the oil is smoking, add the rice. Keep stir-frying until the rice is heated through but not to the point of being crispy. Then add whatever ingredients you want to your fried rice.

18 Why is Chinese cooking so healthy in the wok?
Because of the small amount of oil that is used and because high heat tends to cook food rapidly, preserving its nutritional value; very few nutrients are lost or destroyed in proper wok cookery. However, it is important to follow the instructions of the recipes, for example, to drain the meat, etc.

19 Do you have to use a wok for stir-frying?
A wok is not absolutely necessary for stir-frying. However, you will find that if you do stir-fry in a flat pan, the food doesn't stay in the pan when you stir it, making the procedure messy, awkward and wasteful.

20 When do you use the lid on a wok?
The lid or cover is useful when you are steaming, smoking or braising food in the wok. It can also help you to speed up the cooking of vegetables.

21 How many portions of food can you make in a wok?
It is best to make a recipe for four in a wok about 12-14 inches (30-35 cm) in diameter. If you need to make more, simply cook a second batch. But do not attempt to put a double portion of a recipe into a wok. You will wind up with food that is steamed instead of stir-fried.

22 When should you turn down the heat on a wok?
If the oil is smoking too much, turn down the heat. Sometimes, adding a touch of rice wine or water can rapidly cool the wok down. A good way to cool frying oil immediately is to plunge a cold stainless steel spatula into the oil. This heat transfer method will bring down the temperature substantially.

23 Why doesn't my food cooked in the wok taste the same as food from a Chinese restaurant? What am I doing wrong?
Chinese restaurants tend to cook their food in very hot woks. If you are not getting the same taste, it could be because you are not getting your wok hot enough. It is also important to get the right ingredients and sauces.

24 What is wrong with using a cheaper wok?
Many Chinese shops sell very cheap woks that are thin-gauge steel, which means they will have a hard time maintaining their seasoning. They can also easily burn through, making them rather dangerous. Invest in a better-grade, heavy-gauge wok.

25 How should I store my wok if I don't use it a lot?
Store a seasoned carbon steel wok by rubbing the surface with vegetable oil and then covering the wok with a plastic bag. Store it in a dry place. I hope, however, that you will use your wok often!

INGREDIENTS

Techniques can be learned, implements can be obtained or fashioned, but authentic ingredients can sometimes be elusive. Fortunately, events of the past decades have opened up the kitchens of the world to Asia's many products. This is especially true of Chinese ingredients. In the West today, many of the most exotic foods are readily available. The recipes in this book were all tested with easily obtainable ingredients.

The following is a brief guide to authentic ingredients which I have used in this book. One ingredient commonly used throughout Asia and in China which you will not find mentioned here is monosodium glutamate (also known as MSG, Ve tsin, Accent, seasoning or taste powder). This is a white crystalline extract of grains and vegetables widely used to tenderize and enhance the natural flavor of certain food and some people have an adverse reaction to it. I believe that the natural flavors of the freshest and finest ingredients need no enhancing and I therefore never use MSG.

BAMBOO SHOOTS

Bamboo shoots are the young edible shoots of some kinds of bamboo. Fresh bamboo shoots are the best, canned are an acceptable substitute. Pale yellow with a crunchy texture, they come peeled and either whole or thickly sliced. Rinse them thoroughly before use and transfer any unused shoots to a jar, cover them with fresh water and keep in the refrigerator. If the water is changed daily, they will keep for up to a week.

BEAN SPROUTS

Now widely available, these are the sprouts of the green mung bean, although some Chinese markets also stock yellow soybean sprouts, which are much larger. Bean sprouts should always be very fresh and crunchy. They will keep for several days when loosely wrapped in a paper towel inside a plastic bag in the vegetable crisper of a refrigerator.

BLACK BEANS

These small black soybeans, also known as salted black beans, are preserved by being fermented with salt and spices. They have a distinctive, slightly salty taste and a rich pleasant aroma. Thus prepared, they are a tasty seasoning, especially when used in conjunction with garlic or fresh gingerroot.

Black beans are inexpensive and can be obtained from Chinese grocers, usually in cans labeled "Black Beans in Salted Sauce," but you may also see them packed in plastic bags. These should be rinsed before use; I prefer to chop them slightly, too, as it helps to release their pungent flavor. Transfer any unused canned beans and liquid to a sealed jar and the beans will keep indefinitely if stored in the refrigerator.

BOK CHOY

Although there are many varieties, the most common bok choy is the one with a long, smooth, milky-white stem and large, crinkly, dark green leaves. Bok choy has a light, fresh, slightly mustardy taste and requires little cooking. Look for firm crisp stalks and unblemished leaves, the smaller the better. Store bok choy in the vegetable crisper of your refrigerator.

CAUL FAT

Caul fat is the lower stomach of a pig or cow used by cooks to encase stuffings and to keep food moist while cooking. It is highly perishable so buy it in small quantities and use it quickly. For longer storage, wrap the caul fat carefully and freeze it. To defrost, rinse in cold water to separate the fat without tearing its lacy and fragile webs. You can order caul fat from your local butcher.

CHILI BEAN SAUCE *(see Sauces and Pastes, p.21)*

CHILI POWDER

Chili powder or cayenne pepper is made from dried red chilies. It is pungent, aromatic and ranges from hot to very hot. Your own palate will determine how much you use.

CHILI OIL/CHILI DIPPING SAUCE

Chili oil is sometimes used as a dipping condiment as well as a seasoning and varies in strength and flavor. The Thai and Malaysian versions are especially hot; the Taiwanese and Chinese versions are more subtle. Chili oil is too dramatic to be used as the sole cooking oil, so combine it with other milder oils. I include pepper and black beans in this recipe for additional flavors so that I can also use it as a dipping sauce. Once made, put the chili oil in a tightly sealed glass jar and store in a cool dark place where it will keep for months.

⅔ cup oil, preferably peanut
1 tablespoon chopped dried red chilies
2 teaspoons unroasted Szechuan
   peppercorns
2 tablespoons whole black beans

Heat a wok or frying pan over a high heat and add the oil. Continue to heat until the oil begins to smoke. Remove the wok or pan from the heat and add the chilies and peppercorns. Allow the mixture to cool undisturbed and then pour it into a jar. Let the mixture sit for 2 days, and then strain the oil.

CHILIES

Chilies are the seed pods of the capsicum plant and can be obtained fresh, dried or ground. One must differentiate between the various types because they vary greatly in taste and pungency.

Fresh chilies
Fresh chilies can be distinguished by their small size and elongated shape. They should look bright with no brown patches or black spots. There are several varieties. Red chilies are generally milder than green ones because they sweeten as they ripen. To prepare fresh chilies, rinse them in cold water and slit them lengthwise. Remove and discard the seeds. Rinse under cold running water, and then follow recipe directions. Wash your hands, knife and chopping board before preparing other foods, and do not touch your eyes.

Dried Red Chilies
Dried red chilies are small, thin and about ½ inch (1 cm) long, and used to season oil used in stir-fried dishes, in sauces and in braising. They are normally left whole or cut in half lengthwise with the seeds left in and can be left

in the dish during cooking, but, as they are extremely hot and spicy, you may choose just to flavor the cooking oil. They can be kept indefinitely in a tightly covered jar.

CHINESE BROCCOLI

Chinese broccoli is very crunchy, slightly bitter, and has an earthy, "green" taste. It has deep olive-green leaves and is sometimes sprinkled with white flowers. When selecting it, look for stems that are firm and leaves which look fresh and green. It is prepared in exactly the same way as ordinary broccoli. Where Chinese broccoli is not to be found, substitute regular broccoli.

CHINESE CHIVES

The taste of Chinese chives is much stronger and more garlic-like than common chives; their flowers can be used as well as the blades. They have an earthy, onion taste and can be substituted in smaller quantities for common chives.

Rinse and dry the chives, store them in a plastic bag with a slightly damp paper towel in the refrigerator and use as soon as possible.

Chinese yellow chives are Chinese chives which have been grown in the dark and are pale yellow in color with a more subtle flavor. Select the freshest leaves possible. Trim off any discolored parts. They are highly perishable and will only keep for one or two days.

CHINESE FLOWERING CABBAGE

Chinese flowering cabbage, or choi sum, is part of the wide mustard green cabbage family. This cabbage has green leaves and may have small yellow flowers which are to be eaten along with the leaves and stems.

CHINESE LONG BEANS

These beans are also known as yard-long beans because they can grow to a yard (meter) in length. There are two varieties: the pale green ones and the dark green, thinner ones. Buy beans that are fresh and bright green, with no dark marks. There is no need to string them before cooking. They have a crunchy taste and texture like string beans but cook faster. Store the fresh beans in a plastic bag in the refrigerator and use within four days.

CHINESE WHITE RADISH (MOOLI)

Also known as Chinese icicle radish or daikon, it is long and white and rather like a carrot in shape but usually much larger. It is a winter radish or root and can withstand long cooking without disintegrating. It thus absorbs the flavors of other foods while retaining its distinctive radish taste and texture. Look for firm, heavy, solid, unblemished ones. They should be slightly translucent inside, solid and not fibrous. Always peel before use. Store the radishes in a plastic bag in the vegetable crisper of your refrigerator where they will keep for over a week.

CILANTRO

Cilantro is one of the relatively few herbs used in Chinese cookery. It looks like flat-leaf parsley but its pungent, musky, citrus-like flavor gives it a distinctive character which is unmistakable. Often used as a garnish, or chopped and mixed into sauces and stuffings, look for deep green, fresh-looking leaves and substitute with parsley if unavailable. Store cilantro by washing, draining, wrapping it in paper towels and keeping it in the refrigerator for several days.

INGREDIENTS

CINNAMON STICKS OR BARK

Cinnamon sticks are curled, paper-thin pieces of the bark of the cinnamon tree. Chinese cinnamon is thicker, highly aromatic and more pungent than the regular variety. Either adds a refreshing taste to braised dishes and it is an important ingredient of five-spice powder. Store cinnamon in a tightly sealed jar. Ground cinnamon is not a satisfactory substitute.

CITRUS PEEL

Dried citrus peel is usually made from tangerines or oranges and used to flavor braised, smoked and stir-fried dishes. Drying the peel concentrates the flavor, but you can use fresh peel if necessary. Chinese dried citrus peel can be found in Cellophane or plastic packets. Soak the required amount of peel in warm water until it softens, then chop or slice it according to the recipe.

CORNSTARCH

In China there are many flours and types of starch, such as water chestnut powder, taro starch and arrowroot. They are primarily used to bind ingredients, to thicken sauces and to make batter. These exotic starches and flours are difficult to obtain, but I have found cornstarch works just as well in my recipes. As part of a marinade, it helps to coat the food properly and it gives dishes a velvety texture. It also protects food during deep-frying by helping to seal in the juices, and it can be used as a binder for minced stuffings. Cornstarch is blended with cold water until it forms a smooth paste before it is used in sauces. During the cooking process, the cornstarch turns clear and shiny.

EGGPLANTS

These pleasant, purple-skinned vegetables vary in size from the larger plump ones, easy to find in supermarkets, to the small, thin variety which the Chinese prefer for their more delicate flavor. Look for those with smooth, unblemished skin. Do not peel eggplants since the skin preserves texture, taste and shape. Large eggplants should be cut, sprinkled with a little salt and left to sit for 20 minutes before rinsing and blotting dry with paper towels. This process extracts bitter juices and excess moisture from the vegetable before it is cooked. This procedure is unnecessary if you are using Chinese eggplants.

EGG WHITES

Egg whites are often used in Chinese recipes as ingredients for batters and as coatings that seal in a food's flavor and juices when the food is plunged into warm oil. One egg white from a large egg generally equals about 2 tablespoons. You can easily freeze the egg whites in tablespoon-size cubes in an ice cube tray.

FISH SAUCE

Fish sauce is also known as fish gravy or nam pla and is a thin brown sauce made from fermented, salted fresh fish. It is sold bottled and has a very fishy aroma and salty taste. However, cooking greatly diminishes the "fishy" flavor, and the sauce simply adds a special richness and quality to dishes. The Thai brands are especially good.

FIVE-SPICE POWDER

Five-spice powder, five-flavored powder or five-fragrance spice powder is a mixture of star anise, Szechuan peppercorns, fennel, cloves and cinnamon. A good blend is pungent, fragrant, spicy and slightly sweet at the same time. It keeps indefinitely in a well-sealed jar.

FLOURS

Glutinous Rice Flour
Made from glutinous rice it gives a chewy texture to dough and is used in dim sum pastries. However, it is not an acceptable substitute in recipes that call for ordinary rice flour.
Rice Flour
Made from raw rice and used to make fresh rice noodles. Store it as you would wheat flour.

GARLIC

The Chinese use garlic in numerous ways: whole, finely chopped, crushed and pickled. It is used to flavor oils as well as spicy sauces, and it is often paired with other equally pungent ingredients such as green onions, black beans and fresh gingerroot. Select fresh garlic which is firm and preferably pinkish in color. It should be stored in a cool, dry place but not in the refrigerator.

GINGERROOT

Fresh gingerroot is pungent, spicy and fresh-tasting, adding a subtle but distinctive flavor to soups, meats and vegetables. It is also an important seasoning for fish and seafood since it neutralizes fishy smells. Gingerroot can range in size and has pale brown, dry skin which is usually peeled away before use. Select fresh gingerroot which is firm with no signs of shriveling. It will keep in the refrigerator, well wrapped in plastic wrap, for up to two weeks. Dried powdered ginger has a quite different flavor and should not be substituted for fresh gingerroot.

GINGER JUICE

Ginger juice is made from fresh gingerroot and is used in marinades to give a subtle ginger taste without the bite of fresh chopped pieces. Cut unpeeled fresh gingerroot into 1-inch (2.5-cm) chunks and drop them into a food processor with the motor running. When finely chopped, squeeze out the juice by hand through a cotton or linen dish towel.

HAM

Chinese ham has a rich, salty flavor and is used primarily as a garnish or seasoning to flavor soups, sauces, stir-fried dishes, noodles and rice. A good substitute is either prosciutto or lean smoked bacon.

LEEKS

Leeks found in China are large and cylindrical and resemble a giant green onion with a white garlic-like husk. Leeks found in the West are a good substitute with their mild, slightly sweet, onion flavor. To prepare them, cut off and discard the green tops and roots and slice the leek in half lengthwise. Wash them well, and store them in a plastic bag in the vegetable crisper of your refrigerator.

LEMON GRASS *(CYMBOPOGON CITRATUS)*

This Southeast Asian original has a subtle lemony fragrance and flavor. Fresh lemon grass is sold in stalks that can be 24 inches (60 cm) long – it looks like a very long green onion. It is fibrous and lemon grass pieces are always removed after the dish is cooked. Some recipes may call for lemon grass to be finely chopped or pounded into a paste, in which case it becomes an integral aspect of the dish. Avoid dried lemon grass, as it is mostly used for herbal tea purposes. Fresh lemon grass can be kept, loosely wrapped, in the bottom part of your refrigerator for up to one week. Neither fresh lemon nor citronella grass should be used as a substitute for the unique flavors of lemon grass.

LILY BUDS

Also known as tiger lily buds, golden needles, or lily stems, dried lily buds are an ingredient in muxi (mu shu) dishes and hot and sour soups. They provide texture as well as an earthy taste to any dish. Soak the buds in hot water for about 30 minutes or until they are soft. Cut off the hard ends and shred or cut in half according to the recipe directions. They are quite inexpensive and can be found in Chinese markets. Store them in a jar in a dry place.

MALTOSE SUGAR, *see also Sugar*

This type of malt sugar is a liquid syrup that adds a wonderful richness to stews and sauces without a cloying sweetness. It is found only in Chinese markets and may be stored at room temperature. Honey may be used as a substitute.

MUSHROOMS

Chinese Dried Mushrooms or shiitake
There are many varieties, black or brown in color. The very large ones with a lighter color and a cracked surface are the best. They are usually the most expensive so use them with a light touch. They can be bought in boxes or plastic bags from Chinese grocers. Store them in an airtight jar. To use, soak the mushrooms in a bowl of warm water for about 20 minutes until soft and pliable. Squeeze out the excess water and cut off and discard the wood stems. Only the caps are used. The soaking water can be saved and used in soups and as rice water.

Strain the liquid through a fine sieve to discard any sand or residue from the dried mushrooms.

Chinese Cloud Ear Fungus
These tiny, black, dried leaves are also known as cloud ears; when soaked, they puff up to look like little clouds. Soak the dried fungus in hot water for 20-30 minutes until soft. Rinse well, cutting away any hard portions. These fungi are valued for their crunchy texture and slightly smoky flavor. You can find them at Chinese markets, usually wrapped in plastic or Cellophane bags. They keep indefinitely in a jar stored in a cool dry place.

Chinese Wood Ear Fungus
These fungi are the larger variety of the Chinese tree fungi described above. Prepare, soak and trim them in the same manner. In soaking, they will swell up to four or five times their size. Sold in Chinese markets, they keep indefinitely when stored in a jar in a cool dry place.

Straw Mushrooms
These are among the tastiest mushrooms found in China. When fresh they have deep brown caps which are molded around the stem. In the West they are only available in cans. They can be bought in Chinese grocers and in some supermarkets and delicatessens. Drain them and rinse in cold water before use.

NAPA CABBAGE (CHINESE LEAVES)

Napa cabbage comes in various sizes from long, compact barrel-shaped ones to short, squat-looking types. They are also tightly packed with firm, pale green (or in some cases slightly yellow), crinkled leaves.

This versatile vegetable is used for soups and added to stir-fried meat dishes. Its sponge-like ability to absorb flavors and its sweet pleasant taste and texture make it a favorite of chefs, who match it with rich foods. This is a delicious crunchy vegetable with a mild but distinctive taste. Store it as you would regular cabbage.

NOODLES OR PASTA

Beanthread (Transparent) Noodles

Also called Cellophane noodles, these are made from ground mung beans and not from a grain flour. They are available dried, are very fine and white and are packed in neat, plastic-wrapped bundles. They are never served on their own, instead being added to soups or braised dishes or deep-fried and used as a garnish. They must be soaked in warm water for about 5 minutes before use. As they are rather long, you might find it easier to cut them into shorter lengths after soaking. If you are frying them, they do not need soaking beforehand, but they do need to be separated. A good technique for separating the strands is to pull them apart in a large paper bag which stops them from flying all over the place.

Egg Noodles and Wheat Noodles

These are made from hard or soft wheat flour and water. If egg has been added, the noodles are usually labeled as egg noodles. Supermarkets and delicatessens also carry both the dried and fresh varieties. Flat noodles are usually used in soups, and rounded noodles are best for stir-frying or pan-frying. The fresh ones freeze nicely if they are well wrapped. Thaw them thoroughly before cooking.

Rice Noodles

These dried noodles are opaque white and come in a variety of shapes. One of the most common examples is rice stick noodles which are flat and about the length of a chopstick. They can also vary in thickness. Use the type

called for in each recipe. Rice noodles are very easy to prepare. Simply soak them in warm water for 20 minutes until they are soft. Drain them in a colander or a sieve, and then they are ready to be used in soups or to be stir-fried.

To Cook Wheat and Egg Noodles

8 oz (225 g) fresh or dried Chinese egg or wheat noodles

If you are using fresh noodles, immerse them in a pan of boiling water and cook them for 3-5 minutes or until you find their texture done to your taste. If you are using dried noodles, either cook them according to the directions on the package, or cook them in boiling water for 4-5 minutes. Drain and serve.

If you are cooking noodles in advance or before stir-frying them, toss the cooked and drained noodles in 2 teaspoons of sesame oil and put them into a bowl. Cover this with plastic wrap and chill. The cooked noodles will remain usable for about 2 hours.

OILS

Corn Oil

Corn or maize oil has a high heating point although I find it to be rather bland and with a slightly disagreeable smell. It is high in polyunsaturates and is therefore one of the healthier oils.

Other Vegetable Oils

Some of the cheaper vegetable oils available include soybean, safflower and sunflower oils. They are light in color and taste, and can also be used in Chinese cooking, but they smoke and burn at lower temperatures than peanut oil, and therefore care must be taken when cooking with them.

Peanut Oil

Peanut oil or arachide oil is the most commonly used oil in Chinese cookery. It has a pleasant, unobtrusive taste and its ability to be heated to a high temperature without burning makes it perfect for stir-frying and deep-frying. Corn oil can be used instead if peanut oil is unavailable.

Sesame Oil

This thick, rich golden brown oil made from sesame seeds has a distinctive, nutty flavor and aroma. It is widely used as a seasoning but is not normally used as a cooking oil because it heats rapidly and burns easily. It is often added at the last minute to finish a dish. Sold in bottles, it can be obtained in Chinese grocers and many supermarkets.

OYSTERS, DRIED

Dried oysters are frequently used in finely minced form to enhance dishes. Use them carefully because they can overwhelm a dish with their assertive flavors. Soak them until soft in a bowl of warm water for anywhere between an hour and overnight. If you wish, you may substitute canned smoked oysters for the dried variety.

PEANUTS

Raw peanuts add flavor and a crunchy texture; they are especially good when marinated or added to stir-fry dishes. The thin red skins need to be removed before you use the nuts. To do this simply immerse them in a pan of boiling water for about 2 minutes. Drain them and let them cool; then the skins will come off easily

RICE

Glutinous Rice

Glutinous rice is also known as sweet rice or sticky rice. It is short, round and pearl-like and has a higher gluten content than other rices. The Chinese use it in stuffings, rice pudding and pastries. It is used for rice dishes, sometimes wrapped in lotus leaves, and served after Chinese banquets. It is also used for making Chinese rice wine and vinegar. Most Chinese markets and supermarkets stock it. Glutinous rice must be soaked for at least 2 hours (preferably overnight) before cooking. You may cook it in the same way as long-grain rice *(see p. 210)*.

Long-grain Rice

This is the most popular rice for cooking in China where there are many different varieties. Although the Chinese go through the ritual of washing it in cold water and rinsing it repeatedly, rice purchased at supermarkets doesn't require this step.

Short-grain Rice

Short-grain rice is most frequently found in northern China and is used for making rice porridge, a popular morning meal.

RICE PAPER (BÁNH TRÁNG)

Made from a mixture of rice flour, water and salt, and rolled out by a machine to paper thinness, it is then dried hard and flat on bamboo mats in the sun, giving them their beautiful cross-hatch imprint or pattern. It is available only in dried form and is used extensively for wrapping Vietnamese spring rolls. You can buy rice paper in many Chinese grocers and supermarkets in packages of 50-100 sheets but avoid yellowish papers, which may be too old. Store them in a dry cool place. After use, wrap the remaining rice papers carefully in the package they came in and put this in another plastic bag and seal well before storing.

SAUCES AND PASTES

Chinese and Asian cookery involves a number of thick, tasty sauces and pastes. They are essential to the authentic taste of Chinese cooking, and it is well worth making the effort to obtain them. Most are sold in bottles or cans by Chinese grocers and some supermarkets. Canned sauces, once opened, should be transferred to screw-top glass jars and kept in the refrigerator where they will last indefinitely.

Chili Bean Sauce

This thick, dark sauce or paste which is made from soybeans, chilies and other seasonings, is very hot and spicy. It is usually available in jars in Chinese grocers. Be sure to seal the jar tightly after use and store in the larder or refrigerator. Do not confuse it with chili sauce *(see below)* which is a hotter, redder, thinner sauce made without beans and used mainly as a dipping sauce for cooked dishes.

Chili Sauce

Chili sauce is a bright red, hot sauce which is made from chilies, vinegar, sugar and salt. It is sometimes used for cooking, but is mainly used as a dipping sauce. There are various brands available in Chinese grocers and many supermarkets, and you should experiment with them until you find the one you like best.

If you find your chili sauce is too strong, dilute it with a little hot water. Do not confuse this sauce with the chili bean sauce *(see above)* which is a much thicker and darker sauce used for cooking not dipping.

Hoisin Sauce

This is a thick, dark, brownish red sauce which is made from soybeans, vinegar, sugar, spices and other flavorings. It is sweet and spicy. Hoisin sauce is sold in cans and jars (it is sometimes also called barbecue sauce) and is available in Chinese grocers and supermarkets. If refrigerated, it can keep indefinitely.

Oyster Sauce

This thick, brown sauce is made from a concentrate of oysters cooked in soy sauce and brine. Despite its name, oyster sauce does not taste fishy. It has a rich flavor and is used not only in cooking but also as a condiment, diluted with a little oil, for vegetables, poultry and meats. It is usually sold in bottles and can be bought in Chinese grocers and supermarkets. I find it keeps best in the refrigerator.

Sesame Paste

This rich, thick, creamy brown paste is made from sesame seeds. It is used in both hot and cold dishes. It is sold in jars at Chinese grocers. If you cannot obtain it, use peanut butter which resembles it in texture.

Soy Sauces

Soy sauce is an essential ingredient in Chinese cooking. It is made from a mixture of soybeans, flour and water, which is then fermented naturally and aged for some months. The liquid which is finally distilled is soy sauce. Most soy sauce sold in supermarkets is dark soy. Be sure you buy the correct one as there are two main types.

LIGHT SOY SAUCE is light in color, but full of flavor, this is the better one to use for cooking. It is saltier than dark soy sauce. It is known in Chinese grocers as Superior Soy.

DARK SOY SAUCE is aged for much longer than light soy sauce, hence its darker, almost black color. It is slightly thicker and stronger than light soy sauce and is more suitable for stews. I prefer it to light soy as a dipping sauce. It is known in Chinese grocers as Soy Superior Sauce.

Whole Yellow Bean Sauce

This thick, spicy, aromatic sauce is made of yellow beans, flour and salt which are fermented together. It is quite salty, but it adds a distinctive flavor to Chinese sauces. There are two forms: whole beans in a thick sauce and mashed or puréed beans (sold as crushed yellow bean sauce). I prefer the whole bean variety because it is slightly less salty and has a better texture.

SAUSAGES, CHINESE

Chinese sausages look exactly like thin salami and are about 6 inches (5 cm) long. They are made from cured duck liver, pork liver or pork meat. They are dark red in color with white flecks of fat. Their tasty flavor varies according to type, but they are sweet rather than spicy. They must be cooked before they can be eaten and are most commonly used to season chicken and rice dishes. If they are unobtainable from Chinese grocers, ham can be substituted.

SESAME SEEDS

These are dried seeds of the sesame herb. Unhulled, the seeds range from grayish white to black in color, and hulled seeds are tiny, somewhat flattened, cream-colored, and pointed at one end. Keep them in a glass jar in a cool dry place; they will last indefinitely.

To Make Toasted Sesame Seeds

Heat a frying pan over a burner until hot. Add the sesame seeds and stir occasionally. Watch them closely, and when they begin to brown lightly, about 3-5 minutes, stir them again and pour them onto a plate. When thoroughly cool, store in a jar in a cool, dark place.

Alternatively, you could pre-heat the oven to 325°F/160°C. Spread the sesame seeds on a baking sheet, and roast them in the oven for about 10-15 minutes until they are nicely toasted and lightly browned. Leave them to cool, then place in a glass jar until you are ready to use them.

SHALLOTS

Shallots are mild-flavored members of the onion family. They are small — about the size of pickling onions — with copper-red skins. They have a distinctive onion taste without being as strong or as overpowering as regular onions.

Readily available in all supermarkets, they make an excellent substitute for Chinese shallots, which are difficult to find. In China, you will find them fresh or pickled as a snack. Shallots can be expensive but their sweet flavor permeates food and a few go a long way. Keep them in a cool, dry place (not the refrigerator) and peel, slice or chop them as you would an onion.

SHAOXING RICE WINE

Rice wine is used extensively for cooking and drinking throughout all of China, but I believe the finest of its many varieties to be from Shaoxing in Zhejiang Province in eastern China. It is made from glutinous rice, yeast and spring water. Chefs use it for cooking as well as in marinades and sauces. Now readily available in Chinese markets and in some wine shops in the West, it should be kept tightly corked at room temperature. A good-quality, dry pale sherry can be substituted but cannot equal its rich, mellow taste. Do not confuse this wine with sake, which is the Japanese version of rice wine and quite different. Western grape wines are not an adequate substitute either.

SHERRY

It you cannot obtain rice wine, you can use a good-quality, dry, pale sherry instead. Do not use sweet or cream sherries.

SHRIMP PASTE

This ingredient adds an exotic flavor and fragrance to dishes. Made from shrimps which are ground and fermented, it has an odor before cooking much stronger than its actual taste. It is like anchovy paste in texture. It can be found in Chinese markets, usually in glass jars. Refrigerated, it will keep indefinitely.

SHRIMPS, DRIED

Dried shrimps are used to perk up fried rice or mixed with meat dishes to give an added dimension. They are sold in packages and may be found in Chinese and Asian specialty markets.

Look for the brands with the pinkest color and avoid grayish ones. Dried shrimps will keep indefinitely when sealed in a glass container and stored in a cool dry place. When cooked, the dried shrimps' strong odor is moderated, and they add a delicate taste to sauces.

SILK SQUASH (CHINESE OKRA)

This is a long, thin, cylindrical squash with deep narrow ridges and one tapered end. Choose firm, unblemished, dark green ones and peel the ridges.

If the vegetable is young, you can leave on some of the green; if older, it is best to peel away all the skin. The inside flesh turns soft and tender as it cooks, tasting like a cross between a cucumber and zucchini. Absorbent, it readily picks up flavors of the sauce or food it is cooked with.

SNOW PEAS

This familiar vegetable combines a tender, crunchy texture and a sweet, fresh flavor. Look for pods that are firm with very small peas, which means they are tender and young. Snowpeas will keep for at least a week in the vegetable crisper of the refrigerator.

SPINACH

Western varieties of spinach are quite different from those used in China. Nevertheless, they make satisfactory substitutes for the Chinese variety. Spinach is most commonly stir-fried, so frozen spinach is unsuitable. Chinese water spinach is available in Chinese markets and has hollow stems and delicate, green, pointed leaves; it is also lighter in color than common spinach and has a milder taste. It should be cooked when it is very fresh, preferably on the day it is bought.

SPRING ROLL SKINS

These are the paper-thin pastry wrappers which are filled with bean sprouts and other vegetables to make spring rolls. They are about 6 inches (15 cm) square, are white, and are made from a soft flour and water dough. As they are very thin and probably too tricky to make at home, I suggest you buy them frozen in packages from Chinese grocers. They keep well in the freezer when wrapped in plastic wrap.

STAR ANISE

The star anise is a hard, star-shaped spice and is the seedpod of an attractive bush. It is similar in flavor and fragrance to common anise, but it is more robust and licorice-like. Star anise is an essential ingredient of five-spice powder and is widely used in braised dishes to which it imparts a rich taste and fragrance. It is sold in plastic packs by Chinese grocers, and should be stored in an airtight jar in a cool, dry place.

SUGAR

Chinese sugar comes in several forms: as rock or yellow lump sugar, as brown sugar slabs, and as maltose or malt sugar (see p. 18). I particularly like to use rock sugar which is rich and has a more subtle flavor than that of the refined granulated sugar. It also gives a good luster or glaze to braised dishes and sauces. You can buy it in Chinese grocers where it is usually sold in packages. You may need to break the lumps into smaller pieces with a wooden mallet or rolling pin. If you cannot find it, use white sugar or coffee sugar crystals (the amber, chunky kind) instead.

SZECHUAN PEPPERCORNS

Also known as peppers because they look like flower buds opening and are reddish brown with a strong, pungent aroma which distinguishes them from the hotter black peppercorns. They are the dried berries of a shrub which is a member of the citrus family. Their taste is sharp and mildly spicy. They can be ground in a conventional peppermill and are very often roasted before they are ground to bring out their full flavor. They are inexpensive and sold wrapped in Cellophane or plastic bags in Chinese grocers. They will keep indefinitely if stored in a well-sealed container.

To Roast Szechuan Peppercorns
Heat a wok or heavy frying pan to a medium heat. Add the peppercorns (you can cook about 1 cup at a time) and stir-fry them for about 5 minutes until they brown slightly and start to smoke. Remove the pan from the heat and let

them cool. Grind the peppercorns in a peppermill, clean coffee grinder or with a mortar and pestle. Seal the mixture tightly in a screw-top jar until you need some. Alternatively keep the whole roasted peppercorns in a well-sealed container and grind them when required.

SZECHUAN PRESERVED VEGETABLE

The root of the mustard green, pickled in salt and hot chilies. Sold in cans in Chinese grocers, it gives a pleasantly crunchy texture and spicy taste to dishes. Before using it, rinse in cold water and then slice or chop as required. Any unused vegetable should be transferred to a covered jar and stored in the refrigerator where it will keep indefinitely.

TEA, CHINESE BLACK

Chinese black tea is a full-bodied, fragrant and smooth tea with a rich aroma and a superb bouquet. There are various kinds, of which Keemun is one of the most well known. Tea is used in smoked dishes or for simmering. You can purchase Chinese black teas in Chinese grocers, delicatessens and in many supermarkets. I prefer to store tea in cans since these keep it in the freshest possible condition.

TOFU (BEANCURD)

Tofu is also known as beancurd. It is highly nutritious and rich in protein and has a distinctive texture, but a bland taste. It is made from yellow soybeans, which are soaked, ground, mixed with water and then cooked briefly before being solidified.

Tofu is usually sold in two forms: cakes, suitable for stir-frying, braising and poaching, and as a thickish junket called silken tofu, used in soups. Tofu may be kept in the refrigerator for up to five days, provided the water is changed daily.

VINEGAR

Vinegars are widely used in Chinese cooking. Unlike Western vinegars, they are usually made from rice. There are many varieties, ranging in flavor from the spicy and slightly tart to the sweet and pungent. All these vinegars can be bought in Chinese grocers and will keep indefinitely. If you cannot get Chinese vinegars, I suggest you use cider vinegar. Malt vinegar can be used, but its taste is stronger and more acidic.

Black Rice Vinegar
Black rice vinegar is very dark in color and rich, though mild, in taste. It is used for braised dishes, sauces, and sometimes as a dipping sauce for crab.

Red Rice Vinegar
Red rice vinegar is sweet and spicy in taste and is often used as a dipping sauce for seafood.

White Rice Vinegar
White rice vinegar is clear and mild in flavor. It has a faint taste of glutinous rice and is used for sweet and sour dishes.

WATER CHESTNUTS

Water chestnuts are a sweet root vegetable or bulb about the size of a walnut. They are white and crunchy.

Fresh water chestnuts can sometimes be obtained from Chinese grocers or good supermarkets. They are tastier than canned ones and will keep, unpeeled, in a paper bag in the refrigerator for up to two weeks. Peel them before use, and, if you have any left over, put them back in the refrigerator covered with cold water. Canned water chestnuts should be rinsed well in cold water before you use them, and any unused ones stored in a jar of cold water. They will keep for several weeks in the refrigerator if you change the water daily.

WHEAT STARCH

Wheat starch is a flour-like powder left after the protein is removed from wheat flour itself. It is commonly used as a wrapping for dumplings, especially in China. Bought in Chinese markets, wheat starch will keep indefinitely when tightly sealed and kept in a cool dry place.

WONTON SKINS

Wonton skins are made from egg and flour and can be bought fresh or frozen from Chinese grocers. They are thin pastry-like wrappings which can be stuffed with ground meat and fried, steamed or used in soups. They are normally sold in little piles of 3¼ inches (8 cm) yellowish squares and will be wrapped in plastic.

Fresh wonton skins will keep for about five days if stored in plastic wrap or a plastic bag in the refrigerator.

If you are using frozen wonton skins, just peel off the number you require and thaw them thoroughly before you use them.

EQUIPMENT

Traditional Asian and Chinese cooking equipment is not essential for the preparation of Asian food, but there are some tools which will make it very much easier.

WOK

All your enthusiasm for wok cookery and your own skills will come to naught without a good wok! The wok may be used for stir-frying, blanching, deep-frying and steaming foods. Its shape allows for fuel-efficient, quick and even heating and cooking. In the stir-frying technique, the deep sides prevent the food and oils from spilling over; in deep-frying, much less oil is required because of the shaped concentration of the heat and ingredients at the wok's base.

There are two basic wok types: the traditional Cantonese version, with short, rounded handles on either side of the edge or lip of the wok; and the pau or Peking wok, which has one long handle 12–14 inches (30–35 cm) long. The long-handled wok keeps you more safely distanced from the possibility of splashing yourself with hot oils or water.

You should know that the round-bottomed wok may only be used on gas stove tops. Woks are now available with flatter bottoms designed especially for electric stove tops, although this shape really defeats the purpose of the traditional design, which is to concentrate intense heat at the center, it does have the advantage over ordinary frying pans of having deeper sides.

Choosing a Wok
Choose a large wok – preferably about 12–14 inches (30–35 cm) in diameter, with deep sides. It is easier, and safer, to cook a small batch of food in a large wok than a large quantity in a small one. Be aware that some modernized woks are too shallow or too flat-bottomed and thus no better than a frying pan. A heavier wok, preferably made of carbon steel, is superior to the lighter stainless steel or aluminum types, which cannot take very high heat and tend to blacken as well as scorch the food. There are now on the market, good non-stick carbon steel woks that maintain the heat without sticking. However, these woks need special care to prevent scratching. In recent years, the non-stick technology has improved vastly, so that now they can be safely recommended. They are especially useful when cooking foods that have a high acid level such as lemons.

Wok Stand
This is a metal ring or frame designed to keep a conventionally shaped wok steady on the stove top, and it is essential if you want to use your wok for steaming, deep-frying or braising. Stands come in two designs. One is a solid metal ring punched with about six ventilation holes. The other is like a circular thin wire frame. If you have a gas range or stove, use only the latter type as the more solid design does not allow for sufficient ventilation and may lead to a build-up of gas which could put the flame out completely.

Wok Lid
This light and inexpensive, domed cover, usually made from aluminum, is used for steaming. The lid normally comes with the wok, but if not, it may be purchased at a Chinese or Asian market, or you may use any domed pan lid that fits snugly.

SPATULA

A long-handled metal spatula shaped rather like a small shovel is ideal for scooping and tossing food in a wok. Alternatively any good long-handled spoon can be used.

RACK

When steaming foods in your wok, you will need a wooden or metal rack or trivet to raise the food to be cooked above the water level. Wok sets usually include a rack, but if not, Asian and Chinese grocers sell them separately. Department stores and kitchen suppliers also sell wooden and metal stands which can serve the same purpose. Any rack, improvised or not, that keeps the food above the water so that it is steamed and not boiled will suffice.

BAMBOO BRUSH

This bundle of stiff, split bamboo is used for cleaning a wok without scrubbing off the seasoned surface. It is an attractive, inexpensive implement but not essential. A soft washing-up brush will do just as well.

STEAMERS

Steaming is the best method for preparing many foods of delicate taste and texture, such as fish and vegetables. Bamboo steamers come in several sizes, of which the 10 inches (25 cm) one is the most suitable for home use. A tight-fitting bamboo lid prevents the steam escaping; several steamers, stacked one above the other, may be utilized at once. Of course, any kind of wide metal steamer may be used if you prefer. Before using a bamboo steamer for the first time, wash it and then steam it empty for about 5 minutes.

CLAY OR SAND POTS

For braised dishes, soups and rice cooking, the Chinese rely upon these lightweight clay pots, the design of which allows for the infusion of aromas and tastes into food. Their unglazed exteriors have a sandy texture, hence their other name. Clay pots are available in many sizes, with matching lids, and, being quite fragile, they are often encased in a wire frame. They are to be used directly on the stove top, but never put an empty sand pot on to a heated element or place a hot sand pot on a cold surface: the shock will crack it. Clay pots should always have at least some liquid in them, and when filled with food, they can take very high heat. If you have an electric stove, use a heat-diffusing pad to insulate the pot from direct contact with the hot coils. Note that, because of the release of hot steam when you lift the lid, always lift the lid *away* from you.

WOK COOKING TECHNIQUES

The wok's versatile concave sides make it an ideal tool for multiple uses. This chapter covers the main techniques used with the wok, although you will find the wok is just as useful for cooking any type of food. For simple omelets, a well-seasoned wok is ideal. Even bacon and eggs can be made in the wok. In other words, use your wok and you will find what an essential tool it can become in your kitchen.

The preparation of foods and ingredients before cooking is more important, and time-consuming, in wok cookery than in any other type of cookery. However, once the ground-work has been done, the rest is comparatively quick and easy, and the results are always rewarding.

Because the wok must be hot when you cook, it presupposes that all the ingredients have been properly prepared for the cooking process. This means that meats and vegetables have been cut into appropriate shapes and sizes to cook quickly and evenly while retaining their natural tastes and textures. As an important by-product, such preparation enhances the visual appeal of whatever is being served.

Several different cooking techniques may be used in the preparation of a single dish. There is nothing mysterious about such techniques and mastery of them comes quickly in almost every case. When you plan your meals, be sure to select dishes that involve a range of techniques. Limit yourself to one stir-fry dish per meal until you have become accustomed to the crucial techniques that this style of cooking requires.

STIR-FRYING

Success with stir-frying depends upon having all the required ingredients prepared, measured out and immediately at hand, and on having a good source of fierce heat. Its advantage is that, properly executed, stir-fried foods can be cooked in minutes in very little oil so they retain their natural flavors and textures. It is very important that stir-fried foods not be overcooked or made greasy. Using a wok is definitely an advantage when stir-frying as its shape not only conducts the heat well but its high sides enable you to toss the ingredients rapidly, keeping them constantly moving while cooking.

Having prepared all the ingredients for stir-frying, the steps are as follows:

Heat the wok or frying pan until it is very hot before adding the oil. Add the oil and, using a metal spatula or long-handled spoon, distribute it evenly over the surface. When flavoring oil, you will need to work very quickly so that the ingredients will not burn and become bitter. Toss them quickly in the oil for a few seconds. In some recipes these flavorings will then be removed and discarded before cooking proceeds.

Then add the ingredients as described in the recipe and proceed to stir-fry by tossing them over the surface of the wok or pan with the metal spatula or long-handled spoon. If you are stir-frying meat, let each side rest for just a few seconds before continuing to stir. Keep moving the food from the center of the wok to the sides. Stir-frying is a noisy business and is usually accompanied by quite a lot of splattering because of the high temperature at which the food must be cooked, hence my preference for the long-handled wok.

Some stir-fried dishes are thickened with a mixture of cornstarch and cold water. To avoid getting a lumpy sauce, be sure to blend the mixture thoroughly, and remove the wok or pan from the heat for a minute before you add the cornstarch mixture. The sauce can then be returned to the heat and thickened.

BLANCHING

Putting food into a wok filled with hot water or into moderately hot oil for a few minutes will cook it briefly but not entirely. It is a sort of softening-up process to prepare the food for final cooking. Chicken is often blanched in oil or water after being "velveted" (that is, coated in egg white and cornstarch). Meat is sometimes blanched to rid it of unwanted gristle and fat and in order to ensure a clean taste and appearance. Blanching in water is common with hard vegetables such as broccoli or carrots. The vegetable is plunged into boiling water for several minutes, then drained and plunged into cold water to arrest the cooking process. In such cases, blanching usually precedes stir-frying, which finishes the cooking. You must always avoid overcooking your foods at the blanching stage.

POACHING

This is a method of simmering food gently in the wok until it is partially cooked. Poached food is then put into soup or combined with a sauce and the cooking process continued. Delicately flavored and textured foods such as eggs and chicken are often simmered.

DEEP-FRYING

This is one of the most important techniques in Chinese cooking. The trick is to regulate the heat so that the surface of the food is sealed and doesn't become greasy but does not brown so fast that the food is uncooked inside. Some points to bear in mind when deep-frying are as follows.

Wait for the oil to get hot enough before adding the food to be fried. The oil should give off a haze and almost produce little wisps of smoke when it is the right temperature, but you can test it by dropping in a small piece of food. If it bubbles all over, then the oil is sufficiently hot. Adjust the heat as necessary to prevent the oil from actually smoking or overheating.

To prevent splattering, use paper towels to dry the food thoroughly before cooking. If the food is first steeped in a marinade, remove it with a slotted spoon and let it drain before putting it into the oil. If you are using a batter, make sure all the excess batter drips off before adding the food to the hot oil.

SHALLOW-FRYING

This wok technique is similar to sautéing in a frying pan and is just as effective. It involves more oil than stir-frying but less than for deep-frying. Food is fried first on one side and then on the other. Sometimes the excess oil is then drained off and a sauce added to complete the dish.

SLOW-SIMMERING AND STEEPING

These processes are quite similar. In slow-simmering, food is immersed in liquid which is brought almost to the boil and then the temperature is reduced so that it simmers, cooking the food to the desired degree. This is the technique used for making stock.

In steeping, food is similarly immersed in liquid (usually stock) and simmered for a time. The heat is then turned off and the remaining heat of the liquid finishes off the cooking process.

BRAISING AND RED-BRAISING

This wok technique is most often applied to tougher cuts of meat and certain vegetables. The food is usually browned and then put into stock which has been flavored with seasonings and spices. The stock is brought to the boil, the heat reduced and the food simmered gently until it is cooked. Red-braising is simply the technique by which food is braised in a dark liquid such as soy sauce. This gives food a reddish-brown color, hence the name. This type of braising sauce can be saved and frozen for re-use. It can be re-used many times and becomes rich in flavor.

STEAMING

Steamed foods are cooked by a gentle moist heat which must circulate freely in order to cook the food. It is an excellent method of bringing out subtle flavors and so is particularly appropriate for fish. Bamboo steamers can be used over water in a wok to steam food, but you could use any one of several utensils.

Put about 2 inches (5 cm) of water into a wok, then put a metal or wooden rack into the wok. Bring the water to a simmer, and put the food to be steamed on a heatproof plate. Lower the plate onto the rack and cover the wok tightly with a wok lid. Check the water level from time to time and replenish it with hot water as necessary. The water should never make direct contact with the food.

If you do not have a metal or wooden rack you could use a small empty can to support the plate of food. Remember that the food needs to remain above the water level and must not get wet. The water should be at least 1 inch (2.5 cm) below the edge of the heatproof plate *(see note on Steamers p.27)*.

TWICE-COOKING

As the name implies, this is a two-step process involving two quite different techniques, such as simmering and stir-frying. It is used to change the texture of food, to infuse it with flavor, and to render foods which are difficult to cook into a more manageable state. It is especially useful for removing fat from meat before final cooking.

REHEATING FOODS

Steaming in the wok is one of the best methods of reheating food since it warms it without cooking it further and without drying it out. To reheat soups and braised dishes, bring the liquid slowly to a simmer but do not boil. Remove it from the heat as soon as it is hot to prevent overcooking.

SMOKING

The wok is also useful for smoking foods. Simply line the inside of the wok with aluminum foil. Add the smoking ingredients (in Chinese cooking, it is usually black tea leaves, sugar and spices). Place your marinated food on an oiled rack. Slowly heat the ingredients and when they begin to burn and smoke, cover the wok tightly. Turn the heat down to low and slowly smoke according to the directions in the recipe.

APPETIZERS

The wok is an ideal cooking utensil for preparing appetizers because they can almost always be prepared as your guests gather around the dining room and kitchen. Food for thought is generated as the food for the palate is being prepared.

Many of the appetizers in this chapter, such as Thai Crispy Prawn-Coconut Treats *or* Parchment Paper Fish, *should be prepared and served immediately for the best effect. Hot from the wok, the appetizers stimulate the appetite and offer a perfect start to a festive evening. Other appetizers like* Savory Stuffed Orange Slices *are deliciously unusual: the stuffing is made in the wok and then paired with fresh orange slices for a refreshing starter.*

VIETNAMESE-STYLE SPRING ROLLS

I have long been an admirer and consumer of Vietnamese spring rolls. Their crackling rice paper skin with their savory filling, all eaten in a leaf of fresh lettuce with either mint or basil, dipped in sauce, is an ideal appetizer. Here I have taken the classic Vietnamese spring roll recipe and have modified it to my own taste. I think you will find it as tasty and fun to eat.

Although they can be made in advance, it is best to deep-fry them at the last minute. They are terrific treats to go with drinks or make a lovely first course for a dinner party when served with the Dipping Sauce (see p. 33).

The rice paper wrappers can be found at Chinese or Southeast Asian grocers. They are dry and must be gently soaked before using them. Handle them with care as they are quite fragile. When deep-frying them, do not crowd them in the pan as they tend to stick. If they stick don't separate them as you may risk breaking them.

MAKES ABOUT 25 SMALL SPRING ROLLS

FOR THE FILLING

1 oz (25 g) beanthread (transparent) noodles

½ oz (15 g) Chinese dried wood ears

1 tablespoon peanut oil

1 small onion, finely chopped

2 tablespoons coarsely chopped garlic

2 tablespoons finely chopped green onions

2 tablespoons finely chopped shallots

2 cups ground pork

1½ teaspoons salt

½ teaspoon freshly ground black pepper

6 oz (175 g) cooked fresh crabmeat

5 tablespoons all-purpose flour

5 tablespoons water

1 package rice paper wrappers

2 cups oil, preferably peanut

8 oz (225 g) iceberg lettuce

Assorted sprigs of fresh basil, mint or
  cilantro, or a combination of all three

Soak the noodles in a large bowl of warm water for 15 minutes. When they are soft, drain them and discard the water. Cut them into 3 inch (7.5 cm) lengths using scissors or a knife. Soak the wood ears in warm water for about 20 minutes until soft. Rinse well in cold water and squeeze the excess liquid from the wood ears. Remove any hard stems and shred the caps finely.

Heat a wok or large frying pan over high heat until it is hot. Add the oil, and when it is very hot and slightly smoking, add the onion, garlic, green onions and shallots and stir-fry for 3 minutes. Add the pork, salt and pepper and continue to stir-fry for 5 minutes. Drain the pork in a colander and allow it to cool.

When the pork is cool, combine it in a large bowl with the beanthread noodles, wood ears and cooked crabmeat. In a small bowl, mix the flour and water together into a paste.

When you are ready to make the spring rolls, fill a large bowl with warm water. Dip one of the rice paper rounds in the water and let it soften. Remove and drain it on a linen dish towel. Put about 2 tablespoons of the filling on each softened rice paper wrapper. Fold in each side and then roll it up tightly. Seal the ends with a little of the flour paste mixture. You should have a roll about 3 inches (7.5 cm) long, a little like a small sausage. Repeat the procedure until you have used up all the filling.

Heat the oil in a deep-fat fryer or a large wok until it is hot. Deep-fry the spring rolls, a few at a time, until they are golden brown.

They have a tendency to stick to each other at the beginning of the frying, so only fry a few at a time. Do not attempt to break them apart should they stick together. You can do this after they have been removed from the oil. Drain them on paper towels.

Serve at once with lettuce leaves, herb sprigs and dipping sauce.

DIPPING SAUCE

This sauce can be made well in advance.

SERVES 4

4 tablespoons Thai fish sauce
1 teaspoon dried chili powder or flakes
1 tablespoon finely chopped garlic
1 tablespoon lime juice
4 tablespoons water
1 tablespoon sugar

Combine all the ingredients together in a blender, mixing them thoroughly. Let the mixture sit for at least 10 minutes before using.

THAI CRISPY PRAWN-COCONUT TREATS

O n my frequent visits to Bangkok, I often cook at the famous Oriental Hotel kitchen.
Whenever I get the chance, I observe the excellent chefs in the Thai food section of the kitchen.
I have discovered that there are many similarities between Chinese and Thai cuisine, but the addition
of certain Thai ingredients adds another depth or dimension to Chinese food.

Here is a simple Thai appetizer which would be quite Chinese but for the added twist of coconut
and curry paste. These touches turn the dish into a wonderful party treat or a splendid opener for
any dinner.

The filling can be made in advance, but the actual stuffing should be done at the last moment,
otherwise the pasta will become soggy. These treats should not be frozen.

SERVES 4

FOR THE FILLING

12 oz (350 g) raw prawns, peeled and coarsely
chopped

1 cup ground pork

1 teaspoon salt

½ teaspoon freshly ground black pepper

4 tablespoons finely chopped green onions

3 tablespoons dried coconut

2 teaspoons light soy sauce

2 tablespoons oyster sauce

1½ tablespoons finely chopped orange zest

1 teaspoon Madras curry paste

1 teaspoon sugar

9 oz (250 g) wonton skins

2½ cups peanut or vegetable oil for deep-
frying

Put the prawns and pork in a large bowl, add
the salt and pepper and mix well, either by
kneading with your hand or by stirring with a
wooden spoon. Then add the rest of the filling
ingredients and stir them well into the prawn
and pork mixture. Cover the bowl with plastic
wrap and chill it for at least 20 minutes.

When you are ready to stuff the packages,
put 1 tablespoon of the filling in the center of
the first wonton skin. Dampen the edges with a
little water and bring up the sides of the skin
around the filling. Pinch the edges together at
the top so that the wonton is sealed; it should
look like a small, filled bag.

Heat a wok or large frying pan over high
heat until it is hot. Add the oil, and when it is
very hot and slightly smoking, add a handful of
wontons and deep-fry for 3 minutes until
golden and crispy. If the oil gets too hot, turn
down the heat slightly. Drain the wontons well
on paper towels. Continue to fry the wontons
until they are all cooked.

CRISPY THAI-STYLE WONTONS

Here is my interpretation of the familiar crispy wontons, but with a touch of various typically Thai flavors. The wontons are easily prepared and their crisp, dry texture goes down well as an appetizer or with drinks. Wonton skins can be bought fresh or frozen from Chinese grocers. (Be sure to defrost them thoroughly if they are frozen.)

SERVES 4-6

FOR THE FILLING

12 oz (350 g) cooked fresh crabmeat

1 cup ground pork

1 tablespoon finely chopped garlic

2 teaspoons salt

¼ teaspoon freshly ground black pepper

2 teaspoons Madras curry powder

1½ tablespoons finely chopped fresh cilantro

3 tablespoons finely chopped green onions

2 teaspoons Shaoxing rice wine or dry sherry

1 teaspoon sugar

1 teaspoon sesame oil

FOR THE SWEET AND SOUR DIPPING SAUCE

⅔ cup water

2 tablespoons sugar

3 tablespoons Chinese white rice vinegar or
  cider vinegar

3 tablespoons tomato paste or tomato
  ketchup

1 teaspoon salt

½ teaspoon freshly ground white pepper

1 teaspoon cornstarch mixed with 2
  teaspoons water

9 oz (250 g) wonton skins

2½ cups peanut or vegetable oil for
  deep-frying

Put the crabmeat and pork in a large bowl. Add the garlic, salt and pepper and mix well, either by kneading with your hand or by stirring with a wooden spoon. Add rest of the filling ingredients and stir them well into the crabmeat and pork mixture. Cover the bowl with plastic wrap and chill it for at least 20 minutes.

In a small pan, combine all the ingredients for the sweet and sour sauce, except the cornstarch mixture. Bring the ingredients to the boil, stir in the cornstarch mixture and cook for 1 minute. Leave to cool.

When you are ready to stuff the wontons, put 1 tablespoon of the filling in the center of the first wonton skin. Dampen the edges with a little water and bring up the sides of the skin around the filling. Pinch the edges together at the top so that the wonton is sealed. It should look like a small, filled bag.

Heat a wok or large frying pan over high heat until it is hot. Add the oil, and when it is very hot and slightly smoking, add a handful of wontons and deep-fry for 3 minutes until golden and crispy. If the oil gets too hot, turn down the heat slightly. Drain them well on paper towels. Continue to fry the wontons until they are all cooked. Serve immediately with the sweet and sour sauce.

CRISPY PRAWN AND HAM BALLS

*T*he magic of the wok makes this delightful treat easy to prepare and to serve. It performs *admirably as a delicious starter, but it can as easily be served by itself or with a salad as a light lunch. Inspired by the prawn appetizers served in dim sum specialty restaurants, I have added here a touch of ham and lemon zest for an East-West variation. For maximum enjoyment, these easy-to-make treats should be cooked at the last minute and served immediately.*

If you use fresh water chestnuts, you will need about 8 oz (225 g) unpeeled weight.

SERVES 4-6

FOR THE PRAWN MIXTURE

12 oz (350 g) raw prawns

4 oz (100 g) canned water chestnuts, coarsely chopped

4 oz (100 g) prosciutto ham, finely chopped

2 teaspoons finely chopped lemon zest

1 teaspoon salt

½ teaspoon freshly ground white pepper

1 egg white

1 teaspoon sesame oil

2 tablespoons green onions, white part only, finely chopped

2 teaspoons cornstarch

1 teaspoon sugar

Cornstarch, for dusting

2½ cups peanut oil

Peel the prawns and, if you are using large, uncooked ones, remove the fine digestive cord. Wash the prawns and pat them dry with a paper towel. Using a cleaver or sharp knife, chop the prawns coarsely and then grind them finely into a paste. Put the paste into a bowl and mix in the rest of the ingredients for the prawn mixture. Alternatively, you could do this in a food processor. This step can be done hours in advance, but you should then wrap the paste well in plastic wrap and put it into the refrigerator until you need it.

Using your hands, form the mixture into 1½ inch (4 cm) balls—about the size of a golf ball. Continue until you have used up all the paste. Dust the balls in cornstarch, shaking off any excess.

Heat the oil in a deep-fat fryer or wok to a moderate heat. Deep-fry several prawn balls at a time for about 3–5 minutes or until they are golden. Repeat the process until they are all cooked. Remove with a slotted spoon, drain on paper towels and serve at once.

TASTY STIR-FRIED FAVA BEANS

Stir-fried fava beans are an unusual and exotic food to Western eyes. As such, they can make delicious starter to go with drinks (on toothpicks) or they can be served as a simple vegetarian first course. They are, of course, most delicious when they are as fresh as can be, but they are also quite acceptable in frozen form. Here they are simply stir-fried in the wok, the various seasonings giving the beans a richness of taste.

SERVES 4

2 lb (900 g) fresh fava beans (unshelled) or
   12 oz (350 g) frozen fava beans
1 tablespoon peanut oil
1 teaspoon salt
¼ teaspoon freshly ground black pepper
1 teaspoon sugar
2 teaspoons water or *Vegetable Stock (see p.60)*
1 tablespoon Shaoxing rice wine or dry
   sherry
1 teaspoon sesame oil

If you are using fresh fava beans, shell them and blanch them for 2 minutes in boiling salted water. Drain them thoroughly and refresh them in cold water. When cool, slip off the skins. If you are using the frozen beans, simply defrost them.

Heat a wok or large frying pan over high heat until it is hot. Add the oil and, when it is very hot and slightly smoking, add the salt, pepper and fava beans. Stir-fry for 1 minute. Then add the sugar, water or stock, and Shaoxing rice wine or dry sherry and continue to stir-fry over high heat for 2 minutes. Finally, stir in the sesame oil, give the mixture two turns and serve at once.

Alternatively, you can leave the dish to cool and serve it at room temperature.

PARCHMENT PAPER FISH

This delightful appetizer is as delicious as it is cleverly contrived: a thin slice of fish is sandwiched between delicate, flavorful ingredients, then wrapped in parchment or wax paper and finally deep-fried. As the package cooks, the mixture steams and the flavors marry, the happy result being a uniquely tasty starter.

In the preparation, the package must be wrapped carefully so the oil does not seep in. Although this recipe takes a little more work than others, the outcome is well worth the effort.

SERVES 8 AS A STARTER

9 oz (250 g) firm white boneless fish fillet, such as cod, sea bass or halibut, skinned

FOR THE MARINADE

1 tablespoon Shaoxing rice wine or dry sherry

1 teaspoon sesame oil

½ teaspoon salt

¼ teaspoon freshly ground black pepper

3 tablespoons finely chopped green onions

3 tablespoons finely shredded fresh gingerroot

1 oz (25 g) prosciutto ham, finely chopped

5 cups peanut oil

Cut the fish into 1½ inch x ¼ inch (4 cm x 5 mm) pieces and combine it with the Shaoxing rice wine or dry sherry, sesame oil, salt and pepper in a glass bowl. Let it marinate in the refrigerator for at least 1 hour.

Cut 30 pieces of parchment or wax paper, each 6 inches (15 cm) square. Place one square of parchment with a corner towards you and fold the tip in slightly. Put in the center of the square the following: a piece of fish, a bit of green onion, 2 shreds of gingerroot and a bit of ham. Bring the first corner over the ingredients, then fold in the two sides. Now fold the entire package in half, leaving a flap at the farthest corner from you. Finally tuck this flap in to secure the package. Repeat until all the packages have been filled.

Heat a wok over high heat until it is hot, then add the oil. When the oil is hot and slightly smoking, add about 10 packages and deep-fry for about 3 minutes. Remove them with a slotted spoon and drain well. Deep-fry the rest of the packages in batches in the same manner. When they are completely finished, arrange them on a platter and let each of your guests unwrap their own packages.

SAVORY STUFFED ORANGE SLICES

I *like to begin a dinner party with something elegant and unusual that delights the eye and gets the conversation started. At the same time, I want something that is fairly easy to make which will allow me to spend time with my guests. These orange slices certainly fulfill that need. They are light and refreshing with a unique bite. You can assemble them at least an hour before serving.*

SERVES 4-6

1 cup ground pork
2 teaspoons light soy sauce
1 teaspoon Shaoxing rice wine or dry sherry
½ teaspoon sesame oil
4 large oranges
1 tablespoon peanut oil
2 tablespoons sugar
½ cup peanuts, roasted and crushed
½ teaspoon salt
A pinch of freshly ground black pepper
Fresh cilantro leaves

Combine the pork with the soy sauce, Shaoxing rice wine or dry sherry and sesame oil.

Peel the oranges and, with a small sharp knife, slice them horizontally into ¼ inch (5 mm) thick pieces.

Heat a wok or large frying pan over high heat until it is hot. Add the oil and, when it is very hot and slightly smoking, add the pork and stir-fry for 4 minutes or until it is cooked through. Drain any fat off the pork, then return it to the wok. Add the sugar and continue to stir-fry for 3 minutes or until the mixture begins to dry out. Then add the peanuts and continue to stir-fry for another 2 minutes. Transfer the pork mixture to a bowl, season with salt and pepper, mix well and leave the mixture to cool.

When the mixture has cooled, place a cilantro leaf on each orange slice. Fill each slice with 2 teaspoons of the pork, then fold it over. Continue to fill them until you have used up all the mixture. Arrange on a serving dish.

CORN PORK FRITTERS WITH CILANTRO

Here is an engaging starter, an enticingly delicious mixture of corn and pork fried to a crispy morsel. You may partially fry them beforehand and then later plunge them into hot oil again just before serving. The pork adds richness and deep flavor to the fritters. This treat works nicely with Sweet and Sour Dipping Sauce *(see p. 35).*

SERVES 4-6

1 lb (450 g) fresh corn on a cob,
  or 1 (10 oz) (275 g) can corn, drained
1½ cups ground pork
1 tablespoon finely chopped fresh cilantro
2 tablespoons finely chopped green onions
2 tablespoons finely chopped garlic
1 tablespoon Shaoxing rice wine or dry
  sherry
1 tablespoon Thai fish sauce
1 teaspoon salt
½ teaspoon freshly ground white pepper
1 teaspoon sugar
1 tablespoon all-purpose flour
1 teaspoon baking powder
2 eggs, beaten
2½ cups peanut oil, for frying

FOR THE GARNISH

2 tablespoons finely chopped fresh cilantro

Clean the corn and remove the kernels with a sharp knife or cleaver. You should end up with about 1½ cups. If you are using canned corn, drain it, empty the contents into a bowl and set it aside. In a blender or food processor, combine half of the corn with the pork and the rest of the ingredients, except the oil, and purée. Pour this mixture into a bowl and mix in the rest of the corn.

Heat a wok or large frying pan over high heat until it is hot. Add the oil, and when it is very hot and slightly smoking, spoon a ladleful of mixture into the wok. Continue to spoon ladle-sized fritters into the wok until it is full. Turn the heat to low and cook until they are brown. Turn the fritters over and fry on the other side. Remove them with a slotted spoon and drain on paper towels. Continue to fry until all the mixture has been used. Arrange the fritters on a warm platter, garnish with the cilantro and serve at once.

CRISPY BEGGAR'S PURSE

The sweet and sour sauce can be made a day in advance, chilled and brought to room temperature before serving. Wrappers are now widely available, making this treat even easier to prepare. There are two types of wrappers. The Cantonese-style uses a smooth noodle-type dough and results in a heavier wrapper, while the Shanghai-style, which I prefer, is more like rice paper, translucent and lighter.

SERVES 6-8

1 package spring roll skins, preferably the Shanghai-type

1 oz (25 g) cloud ear fungus (see p. 18) or dried shiitake mushrooms

4 oz (100 g) beanthread (transparent) noodles

12 oz (350 g) raw prawns, peeled and coarsely ground

1 cup ground pork

2 teaspoons salt

1 teaspoon freshly ground black pepper

4 tablespoons finely chopped green onions

3 tablespoons finely chopped garlic

2 tablespoons finely chopped fresh cilantro

2 teaspoons Shaoxing rice wine or dry sherry

1 teaspoon sugar

2 teaspoons sesame oil

1 egg white, lightly beaten

FOR THE SWEET AND SOUR DIPPING SAUCE

⅔ cup water

2 tablespoons sugar

3 tablespoons Chinese white rice vinegar or cider vinegar

3 tablespoons tomato paste or tomato ketchup

1 teaspoon salt

½ teaspoon freshly ground white pepper

1 teaspoon cornstarch mixed with 2 teaspoons water

2 teaspoons chili flakes or powder

8 green onions, green parts only, blanched or microwaved on full power for 15 seconds

2½ cups peanut or vegetable oil for deep-frying

If frozen, defrost the spring roll skins thoroughly. Soak the fungus or mushrooms in warm water for 20 minutes. If using the fungus, finely shred, cutting off and discarding any hard ends. If using the shiitake mushrooms, squeeze out the excess liquid. Remove and discard the stems and finely chop the caps. Soak the noodles in a large bowl of warm water for 15 minutes. When soft, drain and discard the water. Cut into 3 inch (7.5 cm) lengths.

Put the prawns and pork in a large bowl, add salt and pepper and mix well. Then add the rest of the ingredients, noodles and fungus or mushrooms and stir them well into the prawn and pork mixture. Wrap the bowl with plastic wrap and chill it for at least 20 minutes.

Place all the ingredients for the sweet and sour sauce, except the cornstarch mixture and chili in a pan. Bring to the boil, stir in the cornstarch mixture and cook for 1 minute. Stir in the chili flakes. Let cool and set aside.

When you are ready to stuff the wontons, put 2 tablespoons of the filling in the center of each spring roll skin. Dampen the edges with a little water and bring up the sides of the skin around the filling. Pinch the edges together at the top so the dumpling looks like a small, filled bag. Tie with a green onion. Continue, to use up all the filling.

Heat a wok over high heat. Add the oil and, when it is moderately hot, add a handful of dumplings and deep-fry for 3 minutes until golden and crispy. If the oil get too hot, turn the heat down slightly. Drain on paper towels and fry the remaining dumplings. Serve immediately with the sweet and sour sauce.

VEGETARIAN CRISPY BEGGAR'S PURSES

I was invited to cook at John Cleese's final cast party for his film Fierce Creatures. *He requested a vegetarian treat, so I adapted my* Crispy Beggar's Purses *into something fiery and fierce, but without any creatures!*

SERVES 6-8

1 package spring roll skins, preferably Shanghai-type

1 oz (25 g) cloud ear fungus (see p. 18) or dried shiitake mushrooms

4 oz (100 g) beanthread (transparent) noodles

1 cup coarsely grated carrots

4 oz (100 g) snow peas, finely shredded

1 cup coarsely chopped celery

½ cup seeded and finely shredded fresh red chilies

2 teaspoons salt

1 teaspoon freshly ground black pepper

4 tablespoons finely chopped green onions

1 tablespoon finely chopped fresh gingerroot

1 tablespoon finely chopped garlic

3 tablespoons finely chopped fresh cilantro

1 teaspoon Shaoxing rice wine or dry sherry

1 teaspoon sugar

1 teaspoon sesame oil

8 green onions, green parts only, blanched

SWEET AND SOUR DIPPING SAUCE

⅔ cup water

2 tablespoons sugar

3 tablespoons Chinese white rice vinegar or cider vinegar

3 tablespoons tomato paste or tomato ketchup

1 teaspoon salt

½ teaspoon freshly ground white pepper

1 teaspoon cornstarch with 2 teaspoons water

1 teaspoon chili flakes or powder

½ teaspoon chili oil

2½ cups peanut or vegetable oil, for deep-frying

If frozen, defrost the spring roll skins throughly. Soak the fungus or mushrooms in warm water for 20 minutes. If using the fungus, finely shred, cutting off and discarding any hard ends. If using the shiitake mushrooms, squeeze out the excess liquid. Remove and discard the stems and finely chop the caps. Soak the noodles in a large bowl of warm water for 15 minutes. When soft, drain and discard the water. Cut into 3 inch (7.5 cm) lengths.

In a large bowl, combine the carrots, snow peas, celery and chilies, add the salt and pepper and mix well. Add the rest of the ingredients, noodles and fungus or mushrooms (except the green onions) and stir them to mix well. Wrap the bowl with plastic wrap and chill for at least 20 minutes.

Place all the ingredients for the sweet and sour sauce, except the cornstarch mixture, chili and chili oil in a pan. Bring to the boil, stir in the cornstarch mixture and cook for 1 minute. Stir in the chili flakes and oil. Cool and set aside.

When you are ready to stuff the wontons, put 2 tablespoons of the filling in the center of each spring roll skin. Bring up the sides of the skin around the filling. Pinch the edges together at the top so the dumpling looks like a small filled bag. Tie with a green onion. Continue until you have used up all the filling.

Heat a wok or large frying pan over high heat. Add the oil and when it is moderately hot, add a handful of dumplings and deep-fry for 3 minutes, until golden and crispy. If the oil gets too hot turn the heat down slightly. Drain well on paper towels. Continue to fry the dumplings until you have finished with all of them. Serve them immediately with the sweet and sour sauce.

CRACKLING RICE CAKE WITH DIPPING SAUCE

I was delighted to discover how the Thais use fried bits of dried rice as a starter. They simply fry the dried rice in the wok until it is toasty and crackling and then serve it like chips along with a savory dip. This is a simple dish to make and is an ideal treat when entertaining because the rice cake can be made days ahead. However, it should be fried at the last minute.

SERVES 4-6

FOR THE RICE CAKE

1¼ cups long-grain white rice
2½ cups water
2 teaspoons peanut oil
5 cups peanut oil

FOR THE DIPPING SAUCE

1½ tablespoons peanut oil
6 tablespoons finely sliced shallots
3 tablespoons coarsely chopped garlic
1 tablespoon chili bean sauce
1 teaspoon dried chili powder or flakes
2 teaspoons sugar
3 tablespoons lime juice
2 tablespoons Thai fish sauce
2 tablespoons coconut milk
1 tablespoon finely chopped fresh cilantro

NOTE

The oil used for deep-frying the rice cake can be saved and reused once it has cooled. Filter it through coffee filter papers before storing it.

Wash the rice and put it in a 9 inch (23 cm) wide, heavy pan with the water. Bring to the boil, then turn the heat down as low as possible, cover the pan and let the rice cook for about 45 minutes. The rice should form a heavy crust on the bottom. Remove all the loose rice, leaving the heavy crust. The loose rice can be used for making any of the fried rice dishes in the Rice, Noodles and Pasta chapter (*see p. 185*).

Drizzle the 2 teaspoons of oil evenly over the top of the crust and let it cook over a very low heat for 5 minutes. The crust should lift off easily at this point. If it is still sticky, add another teaspoon of oil and continue to cook until it comes loose. Place crust on a plate and set aside. Once cooked, it can be left at room temperature for several days. Don't cover it, or moisture will form and make the cake moldy. Let the rice cake dry out before using.

Heat a wok over high heat until hot. Add the 1½ tablespoons of oil and, when it is very hot and slightly smoking, add the shallots and garlic. Stir-fry for 30 seconds. Turn the heat down and stir-fry until golden brown. Combine the garlic and shallots with the rest of the sauce ingredients and purée in a blender. Set aside.

Just before serving, heat a wok over high heat until it is hot. Add the 5 cups of oil and, when very hot and slightly smoking, drop in a small piece of the dried rice cake to test the heat. It should bubble and immediately come to the top. Now deep-fry pieces of rice cake for about 1–2 minutes until they puff up and brown slightly. Remove immediately with a slotted spoon and drain on paper towels. Quickly transfer the pieces of hot rice cake to a platter and serve immediately with the dipping sauce.

SOUPS

Soups are easily made in the wok. Heat is distributed evenly throughout the wok while its large, open surface allows for quick skimming. Some of the soup recipes call for a brisk stir-frying of the ingredients beforehand. This will give the ensemble a wonderful, smoky flavor that adds depth to the soup. The Spicy Soup with Green Onions, *for example, benefits greatly when the ingredients are stir-fried first.*

Other hearty soups, like the Succulent Meatball Noodle Soup, *demonstrate the ability of the wok to make a delicious, wholesome one-dish meal. The wok's rapid heating capability helps ease the pressures of today's lifestyle, when time is at such a premium.*

With the proper stocks at hand, the wok is clearly an asset in the final preparation of this refreshing food. Everybody enjoys a good soup.

SPICY SOUP WITH GREEN ONIONS

The chefs at the Hyatt Regency in Adelaide, Australia, developed this inspired soup as a daily special. I found it simple but classic in its clarity and subtle taste. They combined modest ingredients — vegetables, seasonings, stock — into a most satisfying treat.

The vegetables are first stir-fried in the wok. This imparts a lovely smoky flavor to the dish. Chicken or vegetable stock is then added and, as with any soup, a good stock is essential to its final flavor. The Chinese or Napa cabbage leaves bring a gentle sweetness.

To make a more substantial one-dish meal of this soup, just add cooked rice or wheat noodles or serve it with rice. The soup can thus be a perfect opener for any meal, or it may be a meal in itself. Use vegetable stock for a vegetarian version.

SERVES 4

8 oz (225 g) Chinese or Napa cabbage

4 oz (100 g) button mushrooms

1 tablespoon peanut oil

1 teaspooon salt

¼ teaspoon freshly ground black pepper

1 tablespoon light soy sauce

5 cups *Chicken Stock (see p.56)*
  or *Vegetable Stock (see p.60)*

2 fresh red or green chilies, seeded and finely
  shredded

4 whole green onions, finely shredded

5 sprigs of fresh cilantro

Cut the cabbage leaves into fine shreds. Finely slice the mushrooms.

Heat a wok or large frying pan over high heat until it is hot. Add the oil and, when it is very hot and slightly smoking, add the cabbage leaves and stir-fry for 1 minute. Then add the mushrooms, salt, pepper and soy sauce and continue to stir-fry for 2 minutes. Add the stock, turn the heat to low, cover and cook for 10 minutes or until the cabbage is very tender.

Stir in the chilies and green onions and continue to simmer for 2 minutes. Turn off the heat and stir in the cilantro sprigs.

Ladle into a large soup tureen and serve immediately.

REFRESHING CUCUMBER SOUP

*I*n the West, cucumber is most often eaten raw or in salads. In Chinese cuisine, however, cucumbers enjoy higher status. Chinese chefs strive to maintain the cool crispness and varied green colors of this prosaic food. We love to eat it stir-fried, braised, pickled and even stuffed.

When cucumber is used in soup, as in this recipe, it keeps its refreshing cool crunch, which makes a nice contrast to the hot soup. The versatility of the wok is such that it can be used even to make this soup. Once the stock is made, the rest is quickly assembled and on the table in a matter of minutes. It is a sparkling starter for any meal and quite economical as well. The beef in this version of the soup adds richness. If you prefer a delicious vegetarian alternative, however, simply omit the beef and use vegetable stock.

SERVES 4

1 lb (450 g) cucumbers

2 teaspoons salt

1 cup lean ground beef

1 teaspoon light soy sauce

1 teaspoon Shaoxing rice wine or dry sherry

½ teaspoon sesame oil

1 teaspoon cornstarch

¼ teaspoon freshly ground black pepper

5 cups *Chicken Stock (see p.56)* or *Vegetable Stock (see p.60)*

2 tablespoons light soy sauce

1 whole green onion, finely shredded

1 teaspoon sugar

1 teaspoon sesame oil

Cut the unpeeled cucumbers into 1 inch (2.5 cm) slices, sprinkle with salt and put them into a colander to drain for 20 minutes. Squeeze the cucumber slices in a linen dish towel to remove any excess moisture and liquid. Blot them dry with paper towels.

Combine the beef with the soy sauce, Shaoxing rice wine or dry sherry, sesame oil, cornstarch and black pepper.

Heat the stock in a wok, add the beef and stir to break up any lumps. Simmer for 3 minutes. Then stir in the soy sauce, green onion, sugar and sesame oil. Turn off the heat and stir in the cucumber slices and let them sit in the hot stock for 2 minutes.

Ladle into a large soup tureen and serve immediately.

CHINESE-STYLE FISH SOUP

Chinese fish soups are simple affairs that rely on using the freshest possible fish, quickly cooked in a way that enhances its taste.

Easily made in the wok, this soup is also versatile: you can supplement the fish and the broth with a wide variety of complementary ingredients and seasonings. Adding leftovers can turn this soup into a substantial one-dish meal. I add a bit of chili oil and a touch of vinegar to give the soup real zest.

SERVES 2-4

1 lb (450 g) fresh, firm white fish fillets, such as cod, sea bass or halibut

1 egg white

2 teaspoons salt

1 teaspoon freshly ground white pepper

1 teaspoon sesame oil

2 teaspoons cornstarch

5 cups *Chicken Stock (see p.56)*, *Vegetable Stock (see p.60)* or fish stock

2 tablespoons light soy sauce

2 teaspoons Shaoxing rice wine or dry sherry

2 teaspoons finely shredded fresh gingerroot

2 tablespoons finely chopped green onions

1 teaspoon chili oil

2 teaspoons black or red rice vinegar

FOR THE GARNISH

1 tablespoon finely chopped fresh cilantro

Remove the skin from the fish fillets and then cut them into small pieces, about 1 inch (2.5 cm) square. Combine the fish, egg white, salt, pepper, sesame oil and cornstarch and mix well. Refrigerate this for at least 20 minutes.

Pour the stock into a wok and bring it to a simmer. Add the soy sauce, Shaoxing rice wine or dry sherry, gingerroot and green onions and simmer for 30 seconds. Then add the fish and stir gently for 1 minute. As soon as the fish turns white, immediately turn off the heat. Add the chili oil and vinegar. Ladle the soup into individual bowls or a soup tureen, garnish with the cilantro and serve immediately.

VIETNAMESE-STYLE NOODLE SOUP

*W*hen I travel, good food is always foremost on my agenda. As Napoleon said, "An army marches on its stomach."

When I can't spare the time for a whole meal, I look for Asian-style fast food. I am very rarely disappointed when I find a good Vietnamese restaurant and order home-style noodle dishes flavored with lemon grass, ginger and garlic.

Here is a tasty soup with my own embellishments. It is a delicious, quick and easy, one-dish meal that is ideal for today's hectic and hurried lifestyle. This fragrant dish is at once pleasing and nutritious. The rice noodles give the soup a delicate and light touch. If they are unavailable, dried egg noodles may be substituted. Feel free to add your own touches. Once the broth is made, the rest is assembled very quickly.

SERVES 2-4

2 oz (50 g) thin rice noodles

8 oz (225 g) Chinese or Napa cabbage

4 oz (100 g) boneless, skinless chicken breasts

1 stalk fresh lemon grass

1 tablespoon peanut oil

2 garlic cloves, lightly crushed

2 thin slices of fresh gingerroot

1 fresh red or green chili, seeded and finely
  shredded

1 teaspooon salt

¼ teaspoon freshly ground black pepper

1 tablespoon light soy sauce

5 cups *Chicken Stock (see p.56)* or *Vegetable
  Stock (see p.60)*

4 whole green onions, finely shredded

FOR THE SAUCE

4 tablespoons Thai fish sauce

1 teaspoon dried chili powder or flakes

1 tablespoon finely chopped garlic

1 tablespoon lime juice

4 tablespoons water

1 tablespoon sugar

FOR THE GARNISH

Handful of sprigs of fresh cilantro

Soak the rice noodles in a bowl of warm water for 25 minutes, then drain them in a colander or sieve. (If you are using dried egg noodles, cook them for 3-5 minutes in boiling water, plunge them in cold water, drain them thoroughly and toss them in peanut oil.) Set them aside.

Combine all the sauce ingredients in a blender, mixing them thoroughly. Let the mixture sit at least 10 minutes before using.

Cut the cabbage leaves into fine shreds, finely slicing them widthwise. Then, finely shred the chicken. Peel the lemon grass stalk to reveal the tender, whitish center and crush it with the flat of a knife. Then cut it into 3 inch (7.5 cm) pieces.

Heat a wok or large frying pan over high heat until it is hot. Add the oil and, when it is very hot and slightly smoking, add the cabbage leaves and stir-fry for 1 minute. Then add the lemon grass, garlic, gingerroot, chili, salt, pepper and soy sauce and continue to stir-fry for 2 minutes. Add the stock, turn the heat to low, cover and cook for 5 minutes. Add the noodles and cook for another 5 minutes or until the leaves are very tender.

Stir in the green onions and chicken and continue to simmer for 2 minutes. Turn off the heat and stir in the cilantro. Stir in the sauce, ladle into a large soup tureen and serve immediately.

Vietnamese-style Noodle Soup

SUCCULENT MEATBALL NOODLE SOUP

This is a substantial one-dish meal my mother would serve on the cold winter nights of my childhood in Chicago.

Once the meatballs are made, the rest is easily assembled. You can, of course, add any vegetable in season to supplement the soup. This is characteristic Chinese family cooking: simple, but solid, nutritious and tasty.

SERVES 4

2 oz (50 g) beanthread (transparent) noodles

FOR THE MEATBALLS

10 oz (275 g) fresh water chestnuts or
  6 oz (175 g) canned water chestnuts
2 cups ground pork
½ egg white
2 tablespoons cold water
1 tablespoon light soy sauce
2 teaspoons dark soy sauce
1 tablespoon Shaoxing rice wine or dry
  sherry
2 teaspoons sesame oil
2 teaspoons sugar
1 teaspoon salt
¼ teaspoon freshly ground black pepper
1 teaspoon cornstarch
5 cups *Chicken Stock (see p.56)* or *Vegetable
  Stock (see p.60)*
1½ tablespoons light soy sauce
2 teaspoons sesame oil

Soak the noodles in warm water for 15 minutes. Drain well.

If you are using fresh water chestnuts, peel them and coarsely chop them. If you are using canned ones, rinse them well and coarsely chop them. Mix the pork with the egg white and cold water by hand. The mixture should be light and fluffy. Do not use a blender as it would make the mixture too dense. Then add the water chestnuts, soy sauces, Shaoxing rice wine or dry sherry, sesame oil, sugar, salt, pepper and cornstarch and mix thoroughly. Divide the mixture into 12 equal parts and roll each part into a meatball.

Heat a wok until it is hot. Add the stock, turn the heat down to a simmer, add the meatballs and stir slowly. Simmer gently for about 5 minutes, then add the noodles and soy sauce and continue to cook for another 5 minutes. Now add the sesame oil and give the soup several good stirs. Ladle the soup into a tureen and serve at once.

CREAMY CORN AND CRAB SOUP

This is a popular East-West dish that has found its way on to Chinese restaurant menus all over the world. I suspect that it was invented by Chinese-American Cantonese cooks, who then transported it back to Hong Kong and southern China. It eventually went to the Britain, as well as Australia where it continues to be a standard item on many menus. Rather than use canned creamed corn, I prefer to make it with fresh corn and to get the creaminess from the starch of the corn. It is a bit thinner than the version you find in Chinese restaurants, but I think, better-tasting. Use the best, freshest crabmeat you can find for this rather lusty dish.

SERVES 4

1 lb (450 g) fresh corn on a cob, or
  1 (10 oz) (275 g) can plain corn
5 cups *Chicken Stock (see p.56)*
2 tablespoons finely chopped green onions
1 teaspoon finely chopped fresh gingerroot
1 tablespoon Shaoxing rice wine or dry
  sherry
1 tablespoon light soy sauce
1 teaspoon salt
¼ teaspoon freshly ground white pepper
1 teaspoon sugar
2 teaspoons cornstarch blended with
  2 teaspoons water
8 oz (225 g) fresh crabmeat
1 egg
1 teaspoon sesame oil
½ teaspoon salt

FOR THE GARNISH

2 tablespoons finely chopped fresh cilantro

Clean the corn and remove the kernels with a sharp knife or cleaver. You should end up with about 1½ cups. If you are using canned corn, drain the contents into a bowl and set the kernels aside.

In a blender, combine half of the chicken stock with the corn and purée. Pour this mixture into the wok with the remaining stock and bring the soup to a simmer. Simmer for 10 minutes, uncovered, then add the green onions, gingerroot, Shaoxing rice wine or dry sherry, soy sauce, salt, pepper and sugar. Now add the cornstarch mixture. Bring it back to the boil, then lower the heat and simmer for another 5 minutes. Add the crabmeat to the soup and stir slowly to mix well.

In a small bowl, combine the egg with the sesame oil and salt. Slowly pour the egg, salt and sesame oil mixture in a steady stream into the wok, stirring all the time, pulling the strands slowly as they cook. Ladle the soup into a tureen, garnish with cilantro and serve.

WINTER MELON SOUP

Winter melon, despite the name, grows in tropical climates and is harvested in the summer. The unripe melons are green in color, but the mature melons develop a blotchy white skin that appears to be a light dusting of snow, hence the name "winter melon." Moreover, the melon keeps well in cold storage (as in a potato cellar) and is most often eaten in the winter months, other melons having long since been consumed.

Winter melon can grow to weigh as much as 110 lb (50 kg). These giants are usually reserved for elaborate banquets, at which they are carved and served whole as an organic tureen filled with broth and other ingredients. Such huge tureens are called "winter melon ponds." The melon is steamed whole and the soup is scooped out with some of the tender flesh of the melon. It has a subtle soft taste that complements the seasonings in the broth.

The version I remember the most is the one made by my mother. Chinese grocers will cut the melons into variously sized pieces and my mother would buy a small piece and simply simmer it in broth and toss in whatever appropriate meats or ingredients she had left in the refrigerator. Her family-style winter melon soup was just as delicious as any "winter melon pond" soup.

If you are unable to obtain winter melon, you can easily substitute zucchini. This is a delicious substantial soup that is almost a meal in itself. It also reheats well.

SERVES 4-6

1 lb (450 g) Chinese winter melon or zucchini

2 oz (50 g) dried shiitake mushrooms

6 oz (175 g) boneless, skinless chicken breasts

2 teaspoons egg white, beaten

1 teaspoon cornstarch

¼ teaspoon salt

5 cups *Chicken Stock (see p. 56)* or *Vegetable Stock (see p. 60)*

¾ cup frozen peas

6 oz (175 g) prosciutto, finely shredded

2 tablespoons finely chopped green onions

1 teaspoon finely chopped fresh gingerroot

2 teaspoons light soy sauce

Peel off the hard skin of the winter melon and scoop out all the soft, pulpy interior together with any seeds. Cut the winter melon or zucchini into 1 inch (2.5 cm) pieces. Bring a large pan of salted water to the boil, blanch the melon or zucchini for 5 minutes and drain.

Soak the mushrooms in warm water for 20 minutes. Then drain them and squeeze out the excess liquid. Remove and discard the stems and cut the caps into 1 inch (2.5 cm) pieces.

Cut the chicken into 1 inch (2.5 cm) pieces. Combine them with the egg white, cornstarch and salt and mix well. Chill for 20 minutes.

Bring a medium-sized pan of water to a boil, then remove it from the heat and immediately add the chicken pieces, stirring vigorously to keep them from sticking. When the chicken turns white (about 2 minutes), quickly drain it.

Bring the stock to a simmer in a wok, add the blanched winter melon or zucchini and mushrooms and simmer for 15 minutes or until the melon or zucchini are soft. Then add the peas, prosciutto, green onions, gingerroot, soy sauce and chicken. Simmer for another 5 minutes, then serve at once.

CHICKEN STOCK

C hicken stock is an all-purpose base for soups and sauces. Its chief ingredient is inexpensive, it is light and delicious and it marries well with other foods, enhancing and sustaining them. Small wonder, then that from the Imperial kitchens to the most humble food stalls, good stock is a basic ingredient. The usual Chinese chicken stock is precisely that: the essence of chicken, with complements of ginger and green onions often added. Combined with the condiments that give Chinese food its distinctive flavor, good stock captures the essential taste of China.

Many of the most famous recipes in the Chinese repertoire require stock. There are two basic types. One is a clear stock made from chicken bones and meat; the other is a richer stock that uses ham and pork bones as well. Different recipes call for one or other of these stocks but both types make a solid base for soups and sauces.

During the Qing dynasty, the last Imperial dynasty (1644-1911), Chinese cuisine reached its peak of classic perfection. One of the most highly prized dishes featured in the Imperial banquets was a bowl of clear soup, a consommé of chicken stock, much appreciated for its subtle, light, flavorful elegance.

This serves as a reminder that stock can also be used as a clear soup. I find that the richer stocks made with ham or pork bones are heavier and not quite suited to my tastes. The following simple recipe for stock therefore reflects what I believe works best for any Chinese dish.

There are commercially prepared canned or cubed (dried) stocks but many of them are of inferior quality, being either too salty or containing additives and colorings that adversely affect your health as well as the natural taste of good foods. Stock does take time to prepare but it is easy to make your own — and when homemade, it is the best. I prefer to make large quantities of it at a time and freeze it. Once you have a supply of stock available, you will be able to prepare any number of soups or sauces very quickly. Here are several important points to keep in mind when making stock:

- good stock requires meat to give it richness and flavor, so it is necessary to use at least some chicken meat, if not a whole bird
- the stock should never boil — if it does, it will be undesirably cloudy and the fat will be incorporated into the liquid; flavors and digestibility come with a clear stock
- use a tall, heavy-based pan so the liquid covers all the solids and evaporation is slow
- simmer slowly and skim the stock regularly — be patient and you will reap the rewards each time you prepare a Chinese dish
- strain the finished stock well through several layers of cheesecloth or a fine mesh sieve
- let the stock cool completely, chill and remove any fat before freezing it

The classic Chinese method for ensuring a clear stock is to blanch the meat and bones before simmering. I find this unnecessary. My method of careful skimming achieves the same result with far less work.

Remember to save all your uncooked chicken bones and carcasses for stock. They can be frozen until you are ready to make it. You can halve the quantities given in the recipes if it makes too much for your needs.

4½ lb (2 kg) uncooked chicken bones, such as
    backs, feet, wings, etc.
1¾ lb (750 g) chicken pieces, such as wings,
    thighs, drumsticks, etc.
8¾ pints cold water
6 slices fresh gingerroot
9 green onions
6 whole garlic cloves, unpeeled
2 teaspoons salt
1 teaspoon whole black peppercorns

Put the chicken bones and chicken pieces into a very large pan. (The bones can be put in either frozen or defrosted.) Cover them with the cold water and bring it to a simmer. Meanwhile cut the gingerroot into diagonal slices, 2 inches x ½ inch (5 cm x 1 cm). Remove the green tops of the green onions. Lightly crush the garlic cloves, leaving the skins on.

Using a large, flat spoon, skim off the scum as it rises from the bones. Watch the heat as the stock should never boil. Keep skimming until the stock looks clear. This can take from 20 to 40 minutes. Do not stir or disturb the stock.

Now turn the heat down to a low simmer. Add the ginger, green onions, garlic cloves, salt and peppercorns. Simmer the stock on a very low heat for 2-4 hours, skimming any fat off the top at least twice during this time. The stock should be rich and full-bodied which is why it needs to be simmered for such a long time. This way the stock (and any dishes you make with it) will have plenty of flavor.

Strain the stock through several layers of dampened cheesecloth or through a very fine meshed sieve, then let it cool thoroughly. Remove any fat which has risen to the top. It is now ready to be used or transferred to containers and frozen for future use.

DOUBLE-STEAMED CHINESE CABBAGE SOUP

Yet another wok-friendly soup, the unusual technique for making this soup is not difficult to master. Double-steaming is a process in which rich ingredients are steamed for hours in a covered casserole filled with soup. This diffuses and marries all the flavors of the different ingredients. It is a technique often used for making the classic Shark's Fin and Bird's Nest Soups.

The result is a distinctive consommé, clear and rich but also light. Here the delicate sweet flavor of the cabbage plays gently with the subtle taste of the ham. This elegant soup is a refreshing starter for any dinner party. It can be made in advance and frozen, as it reheats well.

SERVES 4

1 lb (450 g) Chinese or Napa cabbage

1 oz (25 g) Chinese dried mushrooms or dried shiitake mushrooms

2 oz (50 g) prosciutto or lean smoked bacon

4 slices fresh gingerroot

5 cups *Chicken Stock (see p.56)*

4 whole green onions

2 tablespoons Shaoxing rice wine or dry sherry

½ teaspoon salt

¼ teaspoon freshly ground white pepper

2 teaspoons sesame oil

Using a sharp, heavy knife or cleaver, cut the cabbage leaves in half lengthwise, then into 2 inch (5 cm) segments. Soak the mushrooms in warm water for 20 minutes. Drain them and squeeze out the excess liquid. Remove and discard the stems and finely shred the caps into thin strips. Cut the prosciutto or bacon into very fine shreds and cut the gingerroot into slices 2 x ¼ inch (5 cm x 5 mm).

Next set up a steamer or put a rack into a wok or deep pan and fill it with 2 inches (5 cm) of water. Bring the water to the boil.

Meanwhile, bring the stock to the boil in another large pan and then pour it into a heat-proof glass or china casserole. Add the cabbage leaves, prosciutto, gingerroot, green onions, Shaoxing rice wine or dry sherry, salt, pepper and sesame oil to the casserole and cover it with a lid or foil. Put the casserole on the rack and cover the wok or deep pan tightly with a lid or aluminum foil. You now have a casserole within a steamer, hence the term "double-steaming." Turn the heat down and steam gently for 1½ hours. Replenish the hot water from time to time. An alternative method is simply to simmer the soup very slowly in a conventional pan, but the resulting taste will be quite different.

When the soup is cooked, place the contents into a large soup tureen. The soup can be served immediately or cooled and stored in the refrigerator or freezer to be reheated when required.

VEGETABLE STOCK

*V*egetable stock can be tasty and light. Stir-frying vegetables in the wok with oil before simmering helps to impart a wonderful smoky flavor to the stock. Use the recipe as it is or, by all means, experiment and suit your own taste. You can cut the quantities in half if the recipe makes too much for your needs.

MAKES ABOUT 5 QUARTS

1 oz (25 g) dried shiitake mushrooms
2 lb (900 g) carrots
2 lb (900 g) Chinese leaves or Napa cabbage
4 celery stalks
2 lb (900 g) onions
4 leeks
8 oz (225 g) shallots
2 tablespoons peanut oil
6 green onions
6 slices fresh gingerroot
8 garlic cloves, crushed
1 tablespoon whole black peppercorns
1 tablespoon whole Szechuan peppercorns
4 bay leaves
2 tablespoons salt
2 tablespoons Shoaxing rice wine or dry sherry
5 quarts water
3 tablespoons light soy sauce

Soak the dried mushrooms in warm water for 20 minutes, drain them, squeeze out any excess liquid and coarsely chop the caps and stems. Strain and reserve the mushroom liquid. Coarsely chop the carrots, cabbage leaves, celery and onions. Wash, cut and discard the green part of the leeks and coarsely chop the white portion. Peel the shallots but leave them whole.

Heat a large pan or wok over a moderate heat. Add the oil, green onions, gingerroot, garlic and shallots and stir-fry for 1 minute. Then add the carrots, celery, leeks and onions and continue to cook for 5 minutes. Put all the vegetables and the rest of the ingredients into a very large pan. Cover them with the reserved mushroom liquid and cold water and bring it to a simmer. Using a large, flat spoon, skim off the foam as it rises to the top – this will take about 5 minutes. Bring the stock to a boil. Now turn the heat down to a moderate simmer and cook for about 2 hours.

Strain the stock through a large colander and then through a very fine-meshed sieve, and then let it cool thoroughly. It is now ready to be used or transferred to containers and frozen for future use.

SIZZLING RICE SOUP

There are few ingredients which complement and enhance the natural flavor of a good home-made rich chicken stock better than a crispy rice crust. When this simple dish comes to the dining table and the hot toasty crust meets the liquid soup, it all sizzles and steams dramatically.

You need first to make the rice cake as directed for Crackling Rice Cake with Dipping Sauce on p. 45. Do not use "easy-cook" rice for this dish because it does not have enough starch to form a crust; use long-grain white rice. If you use vegetable stock, you can turn this soup into a spectacular vegetarian treat.

SERVES 4-6

1 quantity rice cake *(see p.45)*
5 cups peanut oil

FOR THE SOUP

1 oz (25 g) Chinese dried black mushrooms
8 oz (225 g) firm tofu
5 cups *Chicken Stock (see p.56)* or *Vegetable Stock (see p.60)*
⅔ cup frozen peas
3 tablespoons finely shredded green onions
1½ tablespoons light soy sauce
½ teaspoon salt
¼ teaspoon freshly ground white pepper

FOR THE GARNISH

1 tablespoon finely chopped green onions, green tops only
2 teaspoons sesame oil

After making the rice cake (as directed on p. 45), soak the mushrooms in warm water for 20 minutes. Then drain them and squeeze out the excess liquid. Remove and discard the stems and finely shred the caps into thin strips. Rinse the tofu well in cold water and blot dry with a paper towel. Cut the tofu into ½ inch (1 cm) pieces.

Bring the stock to a simmer in a large pan, add the mushrooms and tofu and simmer gently for 10 minutes. Then add the peas, green onions, soy sauce, salt and pepper. Allow to simmer for another 5 minutes. Stir in the garnishing green onions and sesame oil and ladle the soup into a large tureen.

Now you are ready to fry the rice cake. Heat a wok or deep-fryer until it is hot. Add the 5 cups of oil and, when it is very hot and slightly smoking, drop in a small piece of the dried rice cake to test the heat. It should bubble all over and immediately come up to the surface. Now deep-fry the pieces of rice cake for about 1-2 minutes until they puff up and brown slightly. Remove them immediately with a slotted spoon and drain on a plate lined with paper towels. Then quickly transfer the pieces of hot rice cake to a warm platter and drop them into the soup. They should sizzle dramatically. Once you are skilled at preparing this dish, you can attempt to perform this trick at the dinner table. (The oil used for deep-frying the rice cake can be saved and reused once it has cooled. Filter it through coffee filter papers before storing it.)

HEARTY MEATBALL VEGETABLE SOUP

I have always loved those hearty soups which are a meal in themselves. Combined with Chinese flowering cabbage and beanthread noodles, the meatballs make this a rich and savory soup that is perfect for a cool fall or rainy evening. It is easy to make, once you have the stock.

The soup can be cooled and reheated. You can, of course, use any vegetables instead of the Chinese flowering cabbage. This soup is delicious with Chinese greens, spinach, even cabbage. Serve it with a good bread or with rice if you have some.

SERVES 4

12 oz (350 g) Chinese greens, such as Chinese flowering cabbage or bok choy
2 oz (50 g) beanthread (transparent) noodles
5 cups *Chicken Stock (see p.56)* or *Vegetable Stock (see p.60)*
1 tablespoon light soy sauce
2 teaspoons Shaoxing rice wine or dry sherry
½ teaspoon salt
2 teaspoons sesame oil

FOR THE MEATBALL MIXTURE

12 oz (350 g) ground beef
1 egg white
3 tablespoons very cold water
1 teaspoon salt
1½ tablespoons light soy sauce
1 teaspoon freshly ground black pepper
1 tablespoon sesame oil
1 teaspoon finely chopped fresh gingerroot
3 tablespoons finely chopped fresh cilantro
3 tablespoons finely chopped green onions
1 teaspoon cornstarch
2 teaspoons sugar

Cut the Chinese greens into 2 inch (5 cm) pieces. Peel the stalks and cut them at a slight diagonal into 2 inch (5 cm) pieces. Soak the noodles in a large bowl of warm water for 15 minutes. When soft, drain and discard the water. Cut into 3 inch (7.5 cm) lengths using scissors or a knife.

Whiz the beef in a food processor for a few seconds. Slowly add the egg white and cold water and mix them for a few more seconds until they are fully incorporated into the meat. Then add the rest of the meatball ingredients and mix for about 1 minute until the meat mixture has become a light paste. Using your hands, form the mixture into about 12 (1½ inch) (4 cm) balls–about the size of a golf ball.

Bring a large pan of water to the boil, gently drop in the meatballs and simmer for 5 minutes or until the meatballs float to the top. Remove them immediately with a slotted spoon and drain well.

In a large pan, bring the stock to a simmer, then add the beanthread noodles, soy sauce, Shaoxing rice wine or dry sherry and salt. Add the Chinese greens and simmer gently for 5 minutes. Return the meatballs to the simmering stock and cook for another 5 minutes. Add the sesame oil and give the soup several good stirs. Ladle into a soup tureen or individual bowls and serve at once.

FISH AND SHELLFISH

The wok's versatility is highlighted by the different ways in which it can be used to cook fish and shellfish. The wok's range is demonstrated as it is used in a simple stir-fried dish, such as Stir-fried Fish with Black Bean Sauce, and in the more complex preparations of Deep-fried Salt and Pepper Oysters. The wok can be most gentle, as it cooks the delicate Steamed Scallops with warm hot vapors, or as it infuses Singaporean-style Curry Crab with exotic spices and savory flavors.

But the wok can also be dramatically assertive, as in deep-frying techniques, where the wok's excellence is unbeatable. Its depth allows for proper deep-frying without using a great deal of oil. The wide surface allows for easy removal of deep-fried foods, and it is simple to adjust the heat if the wok gets too hot. In fact, you will find the wok indispensable when preparing fish and shellfish.

The recipes here are derived from the cuisines of China and Southeast Asia, with a few "East meets West" touches of my own.

LILLIAN'S BEIJING-STYLE SWEET AND SOUR FISH

L illian Robayn was born in Beijing and grew up in Taipei, Taiwan. She later married an American and moved to California – a wonderful marriage of East and West. Her Chinese cultural heritage remains a vibrant part of her life, and she is an expert in Chinese cuisine.

I enjoyed this particular dish one evening in her home and I immediately set out to duplicate it. Well, not quite; her recipe calls for raw garlic and I have altered it ever so slightly by browning the garlic.

SERVES 2-4

1 lb (450 g) fresh, firm fish fillets, such as
   cod, halibut or sea bass

1 teaspoon salt

¼ teaspoon freshly ground black pepper

Potato flour or cornstarch, for dusting

⅔ cup plus 1 tablespoon peanut oil

2 tablespoons thinly sliced garlic

FOR THE SWEET AND SOUR SAUCE

3 tablespoons Chinese black vinegar or cider
   vinegar

2 tablespoons sugar

1 tablespoon light soy sauce

FOR THE GARNISH

3 tablespoons finely shredded green onions

Pat the fish fillets dry using a paper towel, then cut them into 2 inch (5 cm) pieces. In a medium-sized bowl, combine the fish with the salt and pepper, mixing well. Coat the fish well with potato flour or cornstarch, shaking off any excess.

To make the sauce, combine the vinegar, sugar and soy sauce in a small bowl.

Heat the wok or large frying pan over a high heat until it is hot. Add the ⅔ cup of oil and, when it is very hot and slightly smoking, lower the heat and pan-fry the fish for 2 minutes or until it is browned. Turn it over and brown the other side for 2 minutes. Remove and drain on paper towels. You may have to do this in two batches. Place on a warm platter.

Drain all the oil from the wok, wipe clean and reheat. When it is hot again, add the 1 tablespoon of oil and the garlic. Stir-fry for 45 seconds or until it is brown. Remove and scatter this over the fish. Now pour the vinegar mixture over the fish, garnish with the green onions and serve at once.

AROMATIC FIVE-SPICE TROUT

Fresh trout makes an elegant centerpiece for lunch or dinner. With its clean and delicate taste and texture, it is a foundation course in any meal, a light and wholesome treat.

All that it needs is a touch of seasoning to complement its own unique flavor. Here I have dusted it with aromatic five-spice powder, the subtle flavors of which enhance the special qualities of trout.

This is an easy dish to put together; it browns quickly and perfectly in the wok.

SERVES 4

4 small trout, cleaned
2 tablespoons potato flour or cornstarch
1 teaspoon salt
1 teaspoon five-spice powder
3 tablespoons peanut oil
1 tablespoon finely chopped garlic
2 teaspoons finely chopped fresh gingerroot
3 tablespoons finely chopped green onions
1 lemon, quartered

FOR THE GARNISH

Sprigs of fresh cilantro

Blot the trout dry inside and out with a paper towel. Combine the potato flour or cornstarch with the salt and five-spice powder. Dust the trout on the outside thoroughly with this mixture.

Heat a wok or large frying pan over a high heat until it is hot. Add 2 tablespoons of the oil and, when it is very hot and slightly smoking, turn the heat down to medium and pan-fry the trout. You may have to do this in two batches, depending on the size of your wok or pan. When the fish is brown and crispy, turn it over and pan-fry the other side for about 4 minutes. When the fish is cooked, transfer it to a warm platter.

Reheat the wok with the remaining oil. When it is hot, add the garlic, gingerroot and green onions and stir-fry for 2 minutes. Pour this mixture on top of the trout, arrange the lemon wedges on the platter and garnish with cilantro. Serve at once.

SPICY FISH CURRY

I have eaten this wonderful fish curry many times in Singapore and Malaysia. In those countries, surrounded as they are by water, fresh fish is a standard staple in every home and on every menu. This recipe is a simplified version of the original. Most fish have a delicate taste and texture and one must be careful in applying any seasoning or spice. I have found Madras curry paste a great convenience; it works almost as well as the time-consuming hand-made curry paste. Added to a firm white fish fillet, it makes a fragrant, savory, delectable treat that goes perfectly with plain rice.

SERVES 2-4

1 lb (450 g) fresh boneless, skinless, firm
    white fish fillets, such as cod, halibut
    or sea bass
1 egg white
1 teaspoon salt
½ teaspoon freshly ground black pepper
2 teaspoons cornstarch
2½ cups peanut oil or
    4½ cups water
1 small onion, coarsely chopped
1½ tablespoons finely chopped fresh
    gingerroot
1 tablespoon finely chopped garlic
3 tablespoons Madras curry paste
1 tablespoon light soy sauce
1 teaspoon salt
1 teaspoon sugar
⅔ cup canned coconut milk

FOR THE GARNISH

2 tablespoons finely chopped green onions

Cut the fish into 2 inch (5 cm) pieces and then combine them with the egg white, salt, pepper and cornstarch in a medium-sized bowl. Mix well and chill for 20 minutes.

Heat a wok until it is very hot, then add the oil. When the oil is very hot, remove the wok from the heat and immediately add the fish pieces, stirring vigorously to prevent them from sticking. When the fish pieces turn white (about 2 minutes), quickly drain the fish and all the oil in a stainless steel colander set in a bowl. Reserve 2 tablespoons of the oil and discard the rest.

If you choose to use water instead of oil, bring it to the boil in a pan. Remove the pan from the heat and immediately add the fish pieces, stirring vigorously to keep them from sticking. When the fish pieces turn white (about 2 minutes), quickly drain the fish in a stainless steel colander.

Reheat the wok, add 2 tablespoons of the reserved oil (if you used the water method, add 2 tablespoons of fresh oil), and when it is hot, add the onion, gingerroot and garlic and stir-fry for 3 minutes. Then add the curry paste, soy sauce, salt, sugar and coconut milk. Bring the mixture to a simmer and cook for 5 minutes. Add the fish pieces and heat for 3 minutes. Garnish with the green onions and serve at once.

SINGAPORE-STYLE OYSTER OMELET

I first tasted this treat, not in Singapore but in London, England. A close friend of mine, Jenny Lo, took me to dinner at the Singapore Garden restaurant, near Swiss Cottage in northwest London. The experience was a revelation to me. Jenny hails from Malaysia, so she knows where Singapore-style cooking at its best is to be had in England.

This recipe is derived from the standard Singapore fish hawker's version. With such an origin, you can expect a flavorful, satisfying and easy-to-make dish — and so it is. Oysters are mild, eggs are mild, so they need a little spice and seasonings; the ones in the Singapore Garden's recipe work perfectly. The use of sweet potato flour gives the omelet a delightful, slightly chewy texture and a quite unusual flavor. The flour may be obtained at a Chinese grocer.

Serve this omelet as a main course or as an entrée for a special meal.

SERVES 4

1 dozen small oysters, shelled

1 cup sweet potato flour

2 cups water

2 teaspoons salt

2 teaspoons Shaoxing rice wine or dry sherry

4 eggs, beaten

2 tablespoons peanut oil

3 tablespoons finely chopped garlic

3 tablespoons finely chopped green onions

1½ tablespoons chili bean sauce

Drain the oysters in a colander and then pat them dry with paper towels.

Make a batter by mixing the sweet potato flour with the water, salt and Shaoxing rice wine or dry sherry. Now combine it with the eggs.

Heat a wok or large frying pan over high heat until it is hot. Add the oil and, when it is very hot and slightly smoking, pour in the egg mixture and stir quickly for 30 seconds. Then add the garlic, green onions and chili bean sauce and stir-fry for 1 minute. Now add the oysters and continue cooking until the egg has set. Reduce the heat and cook for another 3 minutes. Serve at once.

FRAGRANT PRAWN CURRY

*T*his is a delightful stir-fry dish. I enjoyed it for the first time in Singapore some time ago. The aromatic lemon grass gives it a unique fragrance. Prawns have a distinct but delicate taste and the clean, mildly citrus touch of the lemon grass is a perfect counterpart. The quick cooking style of the wok ensures that the two main ingredients are at their best.

Use fresh lemon grass whenever possible – in a dish like this it is worth a detour to obtain it. If your search is fruitless, you may substitute 2 tablespoons of lemon zest.

SERVES 2-4

1 lb (450 g) raw prawns
½ teaspoon salt
1 stalk fresh lemon grass
1 fresh red or green chili
2 tablespoons peanut oil
⅔ cup coarsely chopped onions
2 tablespoons finely chopped garlic
2 teaspoons finely chopped fresh gingerroot
2 teaspoons Madras curry paste
1 teaspoon chili bean sauce
1 teaspoon sugar
2 tablespoons water
1 tablespoon Shaoxing rice wine or dry
   sherry
2 teaspoons light soy sauce
¼ teaspoon freshly ground black pepper

FOR THE GARNISH

Sprigs of fresh cilantro

Peel the prawns and discard the shells. Using a small sharp knife, remove the fine digestive cord. Wash the prawns in cold water with the salt, rinse well and pat them dry with paper towels.

Remove the outer layer of the lemon grass until you get to the tender, whitish core. Chop the lemon grass core finely. Split the chili in half and carefully remove and discard the seeds. Chop the chili finely and combine it with the lemon grass.

Heat a wok or large frying pan over high heat until it is hot. Add the oil and, when it is very hot and slightly smoking, add the onions, garlic, gingerroot, lemon grass and chili and stir-fry for 1 minute. Then add the prawns and continue to stir-fry for 1 minute. Now add the rest of the ingredients and continue to stir-fry for 4 minutes or until the prawns are firm and cooked. Turn the mixture onto a warm serving platter, garnish with the cilantro and serve at once.

PRAWN AND PORK STIR-FRY

The Chinese combine foods in an unusual way, sometimes mixing seafood with meats, especially pork. The result is delicious, savory and quite tasty. Here ground pork is used to extend the more expensive prawns.

The best prawns to use are the uncooked variety. Although they often come frozen, a rinse in cold water with a tablespoon of salt is a technique used by Chinese cooks to refresh them. This recipe is equally good with fresh scallops.

SERVES 4

8 oz (225 g) raw prawns

1 egg white

2 teaspoons cornstarch

1 teaspoon salt

1 teaspoon sesame oil

¼ teaspoon freshly ground white pepper

2 cups peanut oil or water

1 tablespoon peanut oil

2 tablespoons coarsely chopped black beans

1½ tablespoons finely chopped fresh
   gingerroot

2 teaspoons finely chopped garlic

4 cups ground pork

1 tablespoon dark soy sauce

2 teaspoons light soy sauce

1 tablespoon Shaoxing rice wine or dry
   sherry

½ teaspoon salt

¼ teaspoon freshly ground white pepper

½ teaspoon sugar

2 teaspoons sesame oil

FOR THE GARNISH

2 tablespoons finely chopped green onions

Peel the prawns and, if you are using large uncooked ones, cut them to remove the fine digestive cord. Wash them and pat them dry with paper towels. Combine the prawns with the egg white, cornstarch, salt, sesame oil and pepper. Mix well and leave in the refrigerator for 20 minutes.

Heat a wok until it is very hot, then add the 2 cups of oil. When the oil is very hot, remove the wok from the heat and immediately add the prawns, stirring vigorously to keep them from sticking. When the prawns turn white (about 2 minutes), quickly drain them, discarding the oil.

If you choose to use water instead of oil, bring it to the boil in a pan. Remove the pan from the heat and immediately add the prawns, stirring vigorously to keep them from sticking. When the prawns turn white (about 2 minutes), quickly drain them.

Reheat the wok or large frying pan over high heat until it is hot. Add the 1 tablespoon of oil and, when it is very hot and slightly smoking, add the black beans, gingerroot and garlic and stir-fry for 10 seconds. Add the pork and stir-fry for 5 minutes. Drain the pork of any excess oil and return the pork to the wok. Then add the prawns to the wok, together with the soy sauces, Shaoxing rice wine or dry sherry, salt, pepper and sugar. Stir-fry the mixture for 1 minute. Stir in the sesame oil. Turn onto a warm platter, garnish with green onions and serve at once.

DEEP-FRIED SALT AND PEPPER OYSTERS

A popular Hong Kong-style of cooking seafood is to deep-fry it quickly in hot oil, then drain and stir-fry again in a spicy salt and pepper mixture. I have found this style especially delicious when used for oysters. Here they are dipped and then fried in a crispy batter. The soft, briny oysters make a wonderful contrast to the batter and the spices. This dish makes a delicious opener for any dinner party or can be served as a simple appetizer with drinks.

SERVES 4

1 lb (450 g) oysters, shelled

2 cups peanut oil

1 tablespoon finely chopped garlic

1 teaspoon salt

½ teaspoon ground, roasted Szechuan
   peppercorns

½ teaspoon five-spice powder

½ teaspoon freshly ground black pepper

FOR THE BATTER

½ cup potato flour or cornstarch

¼ cup all-purpose flour

1 teaspoon baking powder

1 teaspoon baking soda

A pinch of salt and pepper

2 teaspoons sesame oil

⅔ cup water

FOR THE GARNISH

2 tablespoons finely chopped green onions

1 lemon, cut into wedges

Drain the oysters in a colander and pat them dry with paper towels.

Prepare the batter by mixing the potato flour or cornstarch, flour, baking powder, baking soda, salt, pepper, sesame oil and water together in a small bowl until smooth. Let the mixture stand for about 20 minutes.

Heat a wok or large frying pan over a high heat until it is hot. Add the oil and, when it is very hot and slightly smoking, turn the heat down to medium. Dip some of the oysters into the batter and deep-fry them until they are golden brown. This should take just a few minutes. Drain them on paper towels and repeat the process until you have cooked all the oysters.

Drain off all but 1 tablespoon of the oil. Reheat the wok until it is hot. Add the garlic, salt, Szechuan peppercorns, five-spice powder and black pepper and stir-fry for 10 seconds. Then return the oysters to the wok and stir-fry for 1 minute or until the oysters are coated with this mixture. Transfer to a warm platter. Garnish with the green onions and lemon wedges and serve at once.

STIR-FRIED FISH WITH BLACK BEAN SAUCE

My mother loved making this dish because it was quick, easy and delicious. The pungency of the black beans, garlic and ginger turn an ordinary fish into a gourmet's delight. When served with vegetables and rice, it becomes the type of light, wholesome, satisfying meal that is the hallmark of the best Chinese home cooking.

SERVES 4

1 lb (450 g) fresh, firm white fish fillets, such as cod, halibut or sea bass

2 teaspoons salt

3 tablespoons peanut oil

1½ tablespoons coarsely chopped salted black beans

1 tablespoon finely chopped garlic

2 teaspoons finely chopped fresh gingerroot

3 tablespoons finely chopped green onions

1 tablespoon light soy sauce

1 teaspoon dark soy sauce

1 tablespoon Shaoxing rice wine or dry sherry

1 teaspoon sugar

1 tablespoon water

2 teaspoons sesame oil

FOR THE GARNISH

3 tablespoons finely shredded green onions

Cut the fish fillets into strips 1 inch (2.5 cm) wide and sprinkle the salt evenly over them. Let them stand for 20 minutes.

Heat a wok or large frying pan over high heat until it is hot. Add the oil and, when it is very hot and slightly smoking, turn the heat down to medium and add the fish strips. Stir-fry these gently for about 2 minutes or until they are brown on both sides, taking care not to break them up. Remove them with a slotted spoon and drain on paper towels. Drain off all but 1½ tablespoons of the oil.

Reheat the wok. When it is hot, add the black beans, garlic, gingerroot and green onions and stir-fry for 30 seconds. Then add the soy sauces, Shaoxing rice wine or dry sherry, sugar and water and bring to a simmer. Return the fish to the wok and gently finish cooking in the sauce for about 1 minute. Then add the sesame oil and give the mixture a good stir. Using a slotted spoon, arrange the fish on a warm serving platter, garnish with the green onions and serve at once.

SAVORY CLAMS AND PORK IN LETTUCE CUPS

This recipe is typical of Chinese dishes, where cooks often stir-fry seafood combined with a small amount of ground pork. The result is a rich savory mixture that is extremely tasty. Only the freshest, preferably live, clams should be used.

Here the mixture is served with fresh lettuce leaves, which provide a crisp contrast to the soft clam and pork mixture. Each guest puts a portion of the mixture into a hollow lettuce leaf and then eats it with their fingers.

This dish makes an unusual, delicious first course.

SERVES 4

2 cups ground pork

1 teaspoon light soy sauce

1 teaspoon plus 2 tablespoons Shaoxing rice
  wine or dry sherry

1 teaspoon sesame oil

1 teaspoon cornstarch

⅔ cup water

2¼ lb (1 kg) fresh live clams, well scrubbed

8 oz (225 g) iceberg lettuce

1½ tablespoons peanut oil

1 tablespoon finely chopped fresh gingerroot

1 tablespoon coarsely chopped garlic

2 tablespoons finely chopped shallots

3 tablespoons finely chopped green onions

1 tablespoon oyster sauce

½ teaspoon freshly ground white pepper

1 teaspoon sugar

Put the ground pork into a bowl together with the soy sauce, the teaspoon of Shaoxing rice wine or dry sherry, sesame oil and cornstarch and mix well. Leave to marinate for about 20 minutes.

Bring the water to the boil in a large pan and add the clams. Remove them as soon as they begin to open. Finish opening them by hand and remove them from their shells. Discard the shells. Set the clam meat aside.

Separate and wash the lettuce leaves and set them aside, wiping off any excess water.

Heat a wok or large frying pan over high heat until it is hot. Add the oil and, when it is very hot and slightly smoking, add the gingerroot, garlic and shallots and stir-fry for 20 seconds. Then add the pork and continue to stir-fry for 3 minutes. Then add the green onions, the 2 tablespoons of Shaoxing rice wine or dry sherry, the oyster sauce, pepper and sugar and continue to stir-fry for 2 minutes. Finally return the clam meat to the wok and stir-fry for 1 minute to reheat. Turn onto a warm serving platter. Arrange the lettuce on a separate platter and serve at once.

STIR-FRIED PRAWNS WITH WATER CHESTNUTS

This was a favorite of our customers in the restaurant I worked in when I was young. It is easy to see why. Rich, tasty prawns are paired with crispy water chestnuts and sweet green peas. It really is a most appealing dish, light and delectable.

This recipe makes a good starter for any dinner party, or a delicious main course for a light meal, where it would go nicely with plain rice and a vegetable dish.

SERVES 4

1 lb (450 g) raw prawns

1 egg white

2 teaspoons cornstarch

1 teaspoon salt

1 teaspoon sesame oil

½ teaspoon freshly ground white pepper

8 oz (225 g) fresh or canned (drained weight) water chestnuts

1 cup frozen small garden peas

2 cups peanut oil or water

1 tablespoon peanut oil

1½ tablespoons finely chopped fresh gingerroot

1 tablespoon finely chopped garlic

½ small onion, thinly sliced

1 tablespoon Shaoxing rice wine or dry sherry

1 teaspoon salt

½ teaspoon freshly ground white pepper

½ teaspoon sugar

2 teaspoons sesame oil

FOR THE GARNISH

2 tablespoons finely chopped green onions

Peel the prawns and, if you are using large uncooked ones, cut them to remove the fine digestive cord. Wash them and pat them dry with paper towels. Combine the prawns with the egg white, cornstarch, salt, sesame oil and pepper. Mix well and place in the refrigerator for 20 minutes. Peel the water chestnuts if fresh, or rinse if canned, and slice. Put the peas in a small bowl and let them thaw.

Heat a wok until it is very hot and then add the 2 cups of oil. When the oil is very hot, remove the wok from the heat and immediately add the prawns, stirring vigorously to keep them from sticking. When the prawns turn white (about 2 minutes), quickly drain them.

If you choose to use water instead of oil, bring it to a boil in a pan. Remove the pan from the heat and immediately add the prawns, stirring vigorously to keep them from sticking. When the prawns turn white (about 2 minutes), quickly drain them.

Reheat the wok or large frying pan over high heat until it is hot. Add the 1 tablespoon of oil and, when it is very hot and slightly smoking, add the gingerroot and garlic and stir-fry for 10 seconds. Add the onion and continue to stir-fry for 2 minutes. Then return the prawns to the wok, together with the water chestnuts, peas, Shaoxing rice wine or dry sherry, salt, pepper and sugar. Stir-fry the mixture for 3 minutes. Stir in the sesame oil. Turn onto a platter, garnish with green onions and serve at once.

STIR-FRIED SCALLOPS WITH SNOW PEAS

The delicate scallop is a perfect seafood to prepare in the wok. It requires little cooking to bring out its naturally sweet taste, and the hot wok heats it flawlessly; just enough to cook it without overcooking.

Here I have combined scallops with snow peas, a delectable and toothsome vegetable that complements the scallop's sweetness.

An easy dish to make, this can easily be a wonderful first course to any meal or a special treat as a main course with rice and another vegetable dish.

SERVES 4

2 tablespoons peanut oil
1 tablespoon finely chopped fresh gingerroot
3 tablespoons finely shredded green onions
1 lb (450 g) scallops, including the corals
2 tablespoons Shaoxing rice wine or dry sherry
2 teaspoons light soy sauce
1 teaspoon sugar
½ teaspoon salt
½ teaspoon freshly ground white pepper
8 oz (225 g) snow peas, trimmed
2 tablespoons water
2 teaspoons sesame oil

Heat a wok or large frying pan over a high heat until it is hot. Add 1 tablespoon of oil and, when it is very hot and slightly smoking, add the gingerroot and green onions and stir-fry for 10 seconds. Immediately add the scallops and stir-fry them for 1 minute. Then add 1 tablespoon of Shaoxing rice wine or dry sherry, the soy sauce, sugar, salt and pepper. Continue to stir-fry for 2 minutes. Remove the scallops to a bowl together with the sauce and set aside.

Wipe the wok clean and reheat over a high heat. When it is hot and slightly smoking, add the remaining oil and the snow peas and stir-fry for 10 seconds. Immediately add the remaining Shaoxing rice wine or dry sherry and the water and stir-fry for 2 minutes. Return the scallops to the wok and continue to stir-fry for another 2 minutes. Now add the sesame oil and stir-fry for another minute. Serve at once.

Stir-fried Scallops with Snow Peas

SINGAPOREAN-STYLE CURRY CRAB

Singapore is an Asian city rich in many different cultures. One of the joys of visiting such a fascinating city is to sample its diverse foods. The blending of disparate traditions can be seen in the street hawkers' stalls. A dish I often love to eat is Singapore's Curry Crab, which is a mixture of Chinese and Indian influences. Although the authentic recipe has ingredients which may be difficult to obtain outside Singapore, I have adapted the idea and made my own mixture with delicious results. The spices are a wonderful contrast to the sweet crabmeat. Serve it with plain rice and another vegetable dish for a complete meal. Remember, it is important to buy the freshest crab available, preferably live.

It is perfectly good manners to eat the crab with your fingers, but I suggest that you have a large bowl of water decorated with lemon slices on the table so that your guests can rinse their fingers.

SERVES 4

3 lb (1.4 kg) live or freshly cooked crab on the shell

2 stalks fresh lemon grass

2 tablespoons peanut oil

8 garlic cloves, thinly sliced

2 tablespoons finely shredded fresh gingerroot

4 tablespoons thinly sliced small onions or shallots

3 tablespoons finely shredded green onions

3 tablespoons Madras curry paste

1 (14 fl oz) (400 ml) can coconut milk

1 teaspoon salt

2 teaspoons sugar

To cook a live crab, bring a large pan of water to the boil, drop in the crab and boil until there is no movement; this will take about 2 minutes. Remove the crab and drain thoroughly.

Remove the tail-flap, push the body with legs still attached away from the shell (A) and remove the stomach sac and feathery gills from the crab (B). Using a heavy knife or cleaver, cut the crab, shell included, into large pieces.

Cut the lemon grass into 2 inch (5 cm) segments. With the flat side of a large knife or cleaver, smash the lemon grass pieces to release their aromatic oils.

Heat a wok or large frying pan over high heat until it is hot. Add the oil and, when it is

A

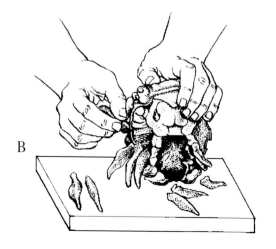

B

very hot and slightly smoking, add the lemon grass pieces, garlic, gingerroot and onions or shallots and stir-fry for 1 minute. Add the green onions and crab pieces and stir-fry for 2 minutes. Add the remaining ingredients and continue to stir-fry the mixture over a high heat for about 2 minutes. Turn the heat to low, cover and simmer for 10 minutes. Turn the curry onto a large, warm serving platter and serve.

STEAMED SCALLOPS WITH CHILI AND GINGER

Fresh scallops are sweet and rich. Perhaps the best way to preserve their qualities is the Chinese technique of steaming. Using hot, wet vapors, this method brings out the succulent texture of scallops without overcooking them. Their briny seafood taste is emphasized, and the bonus is that they are very simple to prepare and take literally minutes to cook. This dish is ideal for a quick and easy, as well as a healthy, meal and I think it makes an ideal opener for any dinner party.

SERVES 4

1 lb (450 g) fresh scallops, including the
  corals
2 fresh red chilies, seeded and chopped
2 teaspoons finely chopped fresh gingerroot
1 tablespoon Shaoxing rice wine or dry
  sherry
1 tablespoon light soy sauce
¼ teaspoon salt
¼ teaspoon freshly ground black pepper
3 tablespoons finely chopped green onions

Place the scallops evenly on a ovenproof platter. Then evenly distribute the chilies, gingerroot, Shaoxing rice wine or dry sherry, soy sauce, salt, pepper and green onions on top.

Next set up a steamer or put a rack into a wok or deep pan and fill it with 2 inches (5 cm) of water. Bring the water to the boil over a high heat. Carefully lower the platter of scallops into the steamer or onto the rack. Turn the heat to low and cover the wok or pan tightly. Steam gently for 5 minutes. Remove and serve at once.

SHAOXING RICE WINE PRAWNS

Shaoxing or yellow wine is a fragrant, mellow, rich wine that gives seafood a special taste and aromatic flavor. River prawns in Eastern China are sometimes cooked in Shaoxing rice wine in a simple recipe that produces a delicious treat.

This dish makes a good opener for any meal.

SERVES 4

1 lb (450 g) raw prawns

1 tablespoon peanut oil

2 teaspoons finely chopped garlic

2 teaspoons finely chopped fresh gingerroot

2 tablespoons finely chopped green onions

1 fresh red or green chili, seeded and finely shredded

⅔ cup Shaoxing rice wine or dry sherry

1 teaspoon salt

½ teaspoon freshly ground white pepper

FOR THE GARNISH

2 tablespoons finely chopped green onions

1 tablespoon finely chopped fresh cilantro

Peel the prawns and, if you are using large uncooked ones, cut them to remove the fine digestive cord. Wash them and pat them dry with paper towels.

Heat a wok or large frying pan over a high heat until it is hot. Add the oil and, when it is very hot and slightly smoking, add the garlic, gingerroot, green onions and chili and stir-fry for 10 seconds. Then add the prawns and continue to stir-fry for 1 minute. Then add the Shaoxing rice wine or dry sherry, salt and pepper, turn the heat down, cover and cook for 3 minutes. Place on a warm platter and garnish with green onions and cilantro and serve at once.

GINGER SCALLOPS WITH CHINESE GREENS

Almost any type of seafood tastes terrific when it has been quickly stir-fried in a hot wok. The intense heat and the little oil used gives seafood a slightly smoky flavor akin to grilled foods. In this recipe, scallops are combined with gingerroot, a classic Chinese pairing, and then mixed with fresh Chinese greens, in this case, bok choy or Chinese flowering cabbage. The sweet, rich taste of the scallops is balanced by the sharp, zesty flavor of ginger. The result is a healthy, tasty dish that is easy to make. Serve it as a first course in a multicourse meal or simply as a main course with rice and another vegetable dish for a satisfying meal.

SERVES 4

1¾ lb (750 g) Chinese greens, such as bok choy or Chinese flowering cabbage

2 tablespoons peanut oil

1½ tablespoons finely chopped fresh gingerroot

1 tablespoon finely chopped garlic

2 tablespoons finely chopped green onions

1 lb (450 g) scallops, including the corals

1 tablespoon Shaoxing rice wine or dry sherry

2 teaspoons light soy sauce

1 teaspoon sugar

½ teaspoon salt

½ teaspoon freshly ground white pepper

2 tablespoons thinly sliced garlic

2 teaspoons sesame oil

Cut the Chinese greens into 3 inch (7.5 cm) pieces.

Heat a wok or large frying pan over a high heat until it is hot. Add 1 tablespoon of oil and, when it is very hot and slightly smoking, add the gingerroot, garlic and green onions and stir-fry for 10 seconds. Immediately add the scallops and stir-fry them for 1 minute. Then add the Shaoxing rice wine or dry sherry, soy sauce, sugar, salt and pepper and continue to stir-fry for 2 minutes. Remove the scallops from the wok with any sauce and set aside.

Wipe the wok clean and reheat over a high heat. Add the remaining oil and, when it is very hot and slightly smoking, add the sliced garlic and stir-fry for 10 seconds. Then add the Chinese greens and stir-fry for 3 minutes or until the greens have wilted a little. Return the scallops to the wok and continue to stir-fry for 3 minutes more. Now add the sesame oil and stir-fry for another minute. Serve at once.

STIR-FRIED SQUID WITH PEAS

T*he Chinese love squid quickly stir-fried in a hot wok as then it is just cooked and beautifully tender. This is a subtle offering from the sea and combines well with the green peas. Once the squid is prepared, the rest of the cooking is easy. Serve it as a first course or as a main course with rice and vegetables.*

SERVES 4

1 lb (450 g) squid, fresh or frozen

1 cup fresh or frozen petit pois (peas)

1½ tablespoons peanut oil

2 tablespoons thinly sliced garlic

2 teaspoons finely chopped fresh gingerroot

5 tablespoons *Chicken Stock (see p.56)*

1 tablespoon Shaoxing rice wine or dry
   sherry

2 tablespoons oyster sauce

2 teaspoons light soy sauce

2 teaspoons cornstarch blended with
   1 tablespoon water

2 teaspoons sesame oil

The edible parts of the squid are the tentacles and the body. If it has not been cleaned by your fishmonger, you can do it yourself by washing off the purple outer skin and pulling the head and tentacles away from the body (A). Using a small sharp knife, split the body in half and remove the transparent bony section (B). Wash the halves thoroughly under cold running water. Cut the tentacles from the head, cutting just above the eye (C). (You may also have to remove the polyp or beak from the base of the ring of tentacles.) If you are using frozen squid, make sure it is properly defrosted before cooking it. Cut the squid meat into 1½ inch (4 cm) strips.

If you are using fresh peas, bring a large pan of salted water to the boil, add the peas and blanch them for 3 minutes, then drain and set aside. If you are using frozen peas, simply defrost them and set them aside.

A

B

C

Heat a wok or large frying pan over a high heat until it is hot. Add the oil and, when it is very hot and slightly smoking, add the garlic and gingerroot and stir-fry for 15 seconds. Then add the squid and stir-fry for 1 minute. Add the rest of the ingredients, except the cornstarch mixture and sesame oil, and continue to stir-fry for 3 minutes. Add the cornstarch mixture and bring the mixture to a simmer. Give it a quick stir, then add the sesame oil and mix well. Cook for 30 seconds more. Serve at once.

FRIED FISH WITH THAI DIPPING SAUCE

T*hailand's long coastline naturally means that fish have played a major role in its cuisine. Indeed, Thai cookery has made a supreme art of transforming the most common seafood and fish into glorious foods.*

Here, fish is simply pan-fried in the wok until golden brown and crispy. It is then served in a zesty sauce that can be made hours ahead. I find this dish goes very well with rice.

SERVES 2

2 (8 oz) (225 g) or 1 (1 lb) (450 g) whole flat
   white fish, such as sole or plaice
1 teaspoon salt
½ teaspoon freshly ground black pepper
Potato flour, cornstarch or plain flour, for
   dusting
1¼ cups peanut oil

FOR THE DIPPING SAUCE

2 fresh red chilies, seeded and finely
   shredded
3 tablespoons finely sliced shallots
2 teaspoons lime juice
2 tablespoons Thai fish sauce

Dry the fish well. Evenly salt and pepper each side of the fish. Dust the fish well with potato flour, cornstarch or flour, shaking off any excess.

Make the dipping sauce by combining the chilies, shallots, lime juice and fish sauce in a small bowl.

Heat a wok or large frying pan over a high heat until it is hot. Add the oil and, when it is very hot and slightly smoking, turn the heat down to moderate. Add the fish and slowly brown. Turn the fish over and cook and brown the other side. Remove the fish and drain on paper towels. Place the fish on a warm platter and serve at once with the dipping sauce.

MUSSELS IN COCONUT CURRY SAUCE

Mussels are an ideal quick and easy food and they tend to be quite economical. Once they have been scrubbed clean in cold water to remove all sand, they cook very rapidly, announcing that they are ready by opening their shells. Make sure they are firmly sealed before cooking; throw away any that do not close up when poked. Any that do not open during cooking should also be discarded.

Mussels are very much a seafood, redolent of salty tides. They are therefore prime candidates for a robust and distinctive sauce. It is an ideal dish to serve with plain steamed rice.

This simple dish can easily be increased for larger gatherings. I prefer to use smaller mussels, so if you have a choice, try them.

SERVES 4-6

1½ tablespoons peanut oil

3 tablespoons coarsely chopped garlic

2 tablespoons finely chopped fresh
  gingerroot

2 tablespoons coarsely chopped green onions

3 lb (1.4 kg) fresh mussels, well scrubbed

2 tablespoons Madras curry powder or paste

2 tablespoons Thai fish sauce

1 teaspoon sugar

1 (14 fl oz) (400 ml) can coconut milk

3 tablespoons water

Heat a wok or large frying pan over a high heat until it is hot. Add the oil and, when it is very hot and slightly smoking, add the garlic, gingerroot and green onions and stir-fry for 20 seconds, then add the mussels and stir-fry for 1 minute. Add the curry powder or paste, fish sauce, sugar, coconut milk and water, cover and continue to cook for 5 minutes or until all the mussels have opened. Discard any that do not open. Give the mixture a final stir and serve at once.

FISH WITH RAINBOW VEGETABLES

*F*resh *fish takes on added dimensions when served with colorful vegetables, as in this "rainbow" effect.*

Once the fish has been "velveted," it takes literally minutes to complete the preparations. You may substitute other vegetables, but the basic principle is the same — "velvet" the fish to keep it moist and silky. The rest of the dish is quickly assembled in the wok and an elegant meal of fresh fish with colorful vegetables is the result. Serve this with a rice dish and another vegetable dish for a wholesome, complete and tasty meal.

SERVES 2-4

2 oz (50 g) dried shiitake mushrooms

1 lb (450 g) fresh firm white fish, such as sea bass, halibut or cod

1 egg white

2 teaspoons cornstarch

1 teaspoon salt

½ teaspoon freshly ground white pepper

4 oz (100 g) snow peas

4 oz (100 g) carrots

2½ cups peanut oil or water

1 tablespoon peanut oil

1 tablespoon coarsely chopped garlic

1 tablespoon finely shredded fresh gingerroot

1 tablespoon Shaoxing rice wine or dry sherry

1 tablespoon dark soy sauce

2 teaspoons light soy sauce

1 teaspoon salt

1 tablespoon chili bean sauce

2 teaspoons rock sugar or plain sugar

6 tablespoons water

Soak the mushrooms in warm water for 20 minutes, then drain them and squeeze out the excess liquid. Remove and discard the stems and finely shred the caps into thin strips.

Cut the fish into 2 inch (5 cm) pieces and combine them with the egg white, cornstarch, salt and pepper in a medium-sized bowl. Mix well and chill for 20 minutes.

Trim the snow peas and leave whole. Cut the carrots on the diagonal into ⅛ inch (3 mm) thick slices. Blanch the carrots for 3 minutes in a large pan of boiling salted water. Drain, refresh in cold water and set aside.

Heat a wok until it is very hot and then add the oil. When the oil is very hot, remove the wok from the heat and immediately add the fish, stirring vigorously to keep the pieces from sticking. When the fish pieces turn white (about 2 minutes), quickly drain them.

If you choose to use water instead of oil, bring it to a boil in a pan. Remove the pan from the heat and immediately add the fish pieces, stirring vigorously to keep them from sticking. When the fish pieces turn white (about 2 minutes), quickly drain them.

Wipe the wok clean and reheat over a high heat. When it is hot, add the 1 tablespoon of oil, the garlic and gingerroot and stir-fry for 20 seconds. Then add the mushrooms, snow peas and carrots and stir-fry for about 2 minutes. Then add the rest of the ingredients. Now add the fish pieces and heat through. Stir several times and serve at once.

THAI-STYLE PRAWNS WITH LEMON GRASS

This is a dish inspired by one of my many visits to Bangkok where I frequently conduct food promotions for the Oriental Hotel. Working with their superb Thai chefs, I was able to learn the essentials of their rich and aromatic cuisine. One of my favorites consists of prawns and lemon grass, a very popular standard for their luncheon buffet.

Their version is made in a quite unusual brass wok. Your usual wok will do nicely, however. Note that, rather than being stir-fried, the prawns are simmered, and in coconut milk at that. The delicate taste of the prawns benefits from such tender care. The result is a hearty, satisfying main dish, redolent of chilies and ginger. It goes well with plain rice.

SERVES 4

1 lb (450 g) raw prawns

FOR THE SAUCE

2 stalks lemon grass
1 (14 fl oz) (400 ml) can coconut milk
2 tablespoons seeded and chopped fresh red chili
1 tablespoon coarsely chopped fresh cilantro
3 tablespoons coarsely chopped garlic
2 tablespoons coarsely chopped shallots
3 tablespoons water
2 tablespoons Thai fish sauce (see p. 16)
1 tablespoon sugar
2 teaspoons shrimp paste (see p. 23)

FOR THE GARNISH

A handful of fresh basil leaves

Peel the prawns and discard the shells. Using a small sharp knife, remove the fine digestive cord. Wash the prawns and pat them dry with paper towels.

Peel the lemon grass stalks to reveal the tender, whitish center and crush with flat of a knife. Cut it into 3 inch (7.5 cm) pieces.

Reserve 1 tablespoon of the coconut milk and set aside. Bring the rest of the coconut milk to a simmer in a wok. Add the lemon grass stalks and simmer for 10 minutes.

Combine the chili, cilantro, garlic and shallots in a blender or food processor with the reserved coconut milk and the water and mix well. Add this paste to the simmering coconut milk together with the fish sauce, sugar and shrimp paste. Continue simmering for 2 minutes. Now add the prawns and continue to simmer for 3 minutes or until the prawns are cooked. Toss in the basil leaves and give the mixture several good turns. Serve at once.

PAN-FRIED SALMON WITH TOMATOES

The wok is not only good for stir-frying but also for pan-frying. Not crêpes, perhaps, but it makes short work of pan-fried fish and, in this case, provides a quick and easy, as well as healthy, meal. This colorful and savory dish will go well with plain rice.

SERVES 2-4

1 lb (450 g) boneless salmon fillet, skinned and quartered

1 teaspoon salt

¼ teaspoon freshly ground white pepper

1 lb (450 g) fresh or canned tomatoes

2 tablespoons all-purpose flour, for dusting

3 tablespoons peanut oil

2 tablespoons thinly sliced garlic

2 tablespoons finely chopped shallots

2 tablespoons finely chopped green onions

1 tablespoon finely chopped fresh gingerroot

1½ tablespoons Shaoxing rice wine or dry sherry

1 tablespoon light soy sauce

2 teaspoons sugar

FOR THE GARNISH

2 tablespoons finely chopped green onions

Small handful of fresh cilantro leaves

Sprinkle the salmon pieces evenly with salt and pepper.

If you are using fresh tomatoes, drop them into boiling water for 10 seconds, remove, skin, seed and cut them into 1 inch (2.5 cm) cubes. If you are using canned tomatoes, chop them into small chunks.

Dust the salmon with the flour, shaking off any excess.

Heat a wok or large frying pan over a high heat until it is hot. Add the oil and, when it is moderately hot, add the salmon pieces and pan-fry them for 3 minutes. Turn them over and brown the other side. Remove and drain on paper towels, then arrange on a warm platter. Pour off all but 1 tablespoon of the oil, add the garlic, shallots, green onions and gingerroot and stir-fry for 1 minute. Then add the tomatoes, Shaoxing rice wine or dry sherry, soy sauce and sugar and simmer for 5 minutes. Pour this mixture over the fish, garnish with the green onions and cilantro and serve at once.

STIR-FRIED PRAWNS WITH FRESH ASPARAGUS

*A*sparagus is a relatively recent addition to the Chinese culinary repertoire. It immediately became extremely popular in Hong Kong, and its use has spread to other Asian cookery influenced by the New Hong Kong cuisine.

In any event, its popularity is well earned because this vegetable in season is colorful, crunchy and with a pleasing taste all its own. Moreover, it works well with almost all types of food. Here I have combined it with prawns. The unique tastes of these two wonderful foods is complemented by their contrasting textures — the soft prawns and the snap of the asparagus.

Once the prawns have been "velveted," the dish is put together very quickly in the versatile wok.

SERVES 4

1 lb (450 g) asparagus
1 lb (450 g) raw prawns
1 egg white
2 teaspoons cornstarch
1 teaspoon salt
1 teaspoon sesame oil
½ teaspoon freshly ground white pepper
2 cups peanut oil or water
1½ tablespoons peanut oil
1½ tablespoons finely chopped fresh
   gingerroot
3 tablespoons water
1 tablespoon Shaoxing rice wine or dry
   sherry
1 tablespoon light soy sauce
1 teaspoon salt
½ teaspoon freshly ground white pepper
2 teaspoons sesame oil

FOR THE GARNISH

2 tablespoons finely chopped green onions

Slice the asparagus thinly at a slight diagonal, discarding the tough ends. Peel the prawns and, if you are using large uncooked ones, cut them to remove the fine digestive cord. Wash them and pat them dry with paper towels.

Combine the prawns with the egg white, cornstarch, salt, sesame oil and pepper. Mix well and and let the mixture sit in the refrigerator for 20 minutes.

Heat a wok until it is very hot and then add the oil. When the oil is very hot, remove the wok from the heat and immediately add the prawns, stirring vigorously to keep them from sticking. When the prawns turn white (about 2 minutes), quickly drain them.

If you choose to use water instead of oil, bring it to a boil in a pan. Remove the pan from the heat and immediately add the prawns, stirring vigorously to keep them from sticking. When the prawns turn white (about 2 minutes), quickly drain them.

Reheat the wok or large frying pan over a high heat until it is hot. Add the 1½ tablespoons of oil and, when it is very hot and slightly smoking, add the gingerroot and stir-fry for 10 seconds. Add the asparagus and water and stir-fry for 3 minutes. Then return the prawns to the wok, together with the Shaoxing rice wine or dry sherry, soy sauce, salt and pepper. Stir-fry the mixture for 1 minute. Stir in the sesame oil and give the mixture two turns. Turn onto a platter, garnish with green onions and serve at once.

COCONUT PRAWNS

The coconut milk should alert you to the Thai origins of this recipe. It is a delicious treat that relies on the prawns marinating long enough to absorb the various aromatic flavors of the marinade. That being accomplished, the results are an extremely tasty platter that can serve as a main course or a wonderful opener. It is easy and quick to cook in the wok and makes lovely, exotic eating.

SERVES 4

1 lb (450 g) raw prawns
All-purpose flour, for dusting
2 eggs, beaten
3¾ cups peanut oil

FOR THE MARINADE

1 stalk lemon grass
2 tablespoons finely chopped garlic
2 tablespoons finely chopped shallots
1 tablespoon seeded and chopped fresh
　red chili
1 tablespoon lime juice
1 teaspoon salt
½ teaspoon freshly ground black pepper
1 (14 fl oz) (400 ml) canned coconut milk

Peel the prawns and discard the shells. Using a small sharp knife, remove the fine digestive cord. Wash the prawns and pat them dry with paper towels.

Peel the lemon grass stalk to reveal the tender, whitish center and crush it with the flat of a knife, then finely chop it. In a large bowl, combine the lemon grass, garlic, shallots, chili, lime juice, salt and pepper with the coconut milk. Mix well and add the prawns. Let the prawns marinate for 1 hour.

Lift the prawns from the marinade with a slotted spoon and dust them with flour. Dip them in the beaten egg and dust them again with flour, shaking off any excess.

Heat a wok or large frying pan over high heat until it is hot. Add the oil and, when it is very hot and slightly smoking, turn the heat to moderate and deep-fry the prawns. You may have to do this in several batches. Remove them when they are pink and crispy. Drain on paper towels and serve at once.

MEAT

The wok is a perfect implement to use when preparing meats, especially if they are to be stir-fried. The very hot temperature of the wok seals in all the juices and flavors of the meat, whether it be pork, beef or lamb. The concave sides allow the meat to be stir-fried evenly so that all the meat is sealed rapidly.

Once the meats have been browned and drained of any excess oil, other foods, such as vegetables, may be added, and thus a complete dish is prepared in no time at all.

The wok is also useful for braising dishes such as Braised Korean-style Spareribs or Savory Pork Tomato Sauce. Ordinary meats are transformed into luscious aromatic platters which tempt the palate.

In this chapter, many spices are utilized to give meats new tastes and flavors. The combinations are taken from my own personal favorites and from recipes I have gathered in my extensive travels.

HUNAN-STYLE LAMB

L amb is not a standard item on southern Chinese menus. It is much more common in northern and central China. The prejudice against lamb may be discerned in a southern proverb: "There are seventy-two ways of cooking lamb; most of them result in something quite unpalatable."

But this is unfair to lamb. As this recipe shows, it lends itself to imaginative uses. Hunan (the birth-province of Mao) is famous for its rather fiery cuisine. Chili bean and hoisin sauces, as in this recipe, are among the spices most often employed. If you prefer something a bit milder than the hot Hunanese style, simply reduce the amount of chili bean sauce.

The most tender parts of lamb, such as steaks and chops, are best for this dish. For a complete, well-balanced meal, serve it with rice and a vegetable dish.

SERVES 4

1 lb (450 g) lean lamb steak or fillet, or boned
   loin chop meat
1 tablespoon peanut oil
3 tablespoons finely chopped green onions,
   white part only
6 garlic cloves, thinly sliced
2 teaspoons finely shredded fresh gingerroot
1 tablespoon chili bean sauce
1½ tablespoons hoisin sauce
1 teaspoon sugar
1 teaspoon sesame oil

FOR THE MARINADE

1 tablespoon Shaoxing rice wine or dry
   sherry
2 teaspoons dark soy sauce
1 tablespoon light soy sauce
2 teaspoons sesame oil
1½ teaspoons cornstarch

Cut the lamb into thin slices and put it into a bowl. Mix in the marinade ingredients and leave to marinate for 20 minutes. Then drain off and reserve the marinade.

Heat a wok or large frying pan until it is hot. Add the oil and, when the oil is very hot and slightly smoking, add the marinated lamb pieces with just a little of the reserved marinade. Stir-fry for 2 minutes. Now add the green onions, garlic and gingerroot and continue to stir-fry for another 2 minutes. Add the chili bean sauce, hoisin sauce and sugar and stir-fry for 2 minutes more. Then stir in the sesame oil, turn onto a warm serving platter and serve immediately.

FRAGRANT STIR-FRIED BEEF WITH PEPPERS

My many trips to Thailand have led me to elevate the virtues of lemon grass almost to the status enjoyed by garlic and gingerroot. It has a subtle but quite distinctive flavor that adds a certain something to the most prosaic recipes.

Fortunately, it has recently become generally available in most metropolitan areas in Western countries and it is well worth searching for.

Here I have adapted the Thai version by pairing the lemon grass with sweet red bell peppers, which add color as well as contrasting tastes and texture.

SERVES 4

1 lb (450 g) lean beef steak

3 stalks fresh lemon grass

8 oz (225 g) red or green bell pepper (1 large or about 2 small)

3 tablespoons peanut oil

2 teaspoons finely chopped fresh gingerroot

4 oz (100 g) shallots, thinly sliced

3 garlic cloves, thinly sliced

1 tablespoon light soy sauce

1½ tablespoons Shaoxing rice wine or dry sherry

½ teaspoon salt

½ teaspoon freshly ground black pepper

1½ teaspoons sugar

2 teaspoons sesame oil

FOR THE MARINADE

1 tablespoon light soy sauce

1 tablespoon Shaoxing rice wine or dry sherry

2 teaspoons sesame oil

2 teaspoons cornstarch

Cut the beef into thin slices 2 inches (5 cm) long, cutting against the grain. Put the beef into a bowl together with the Marinade ingredients. Mix well, and then let the mixture marinate for about 20 minutes.

Peel the lemon grass stalks to reveal the tender, whitish center and cut into 2 inch (5 cm) pieces, then crush them with the flat of a cleaver or knife. Cut the bell peppers into 1 inch (2.5 cm) pieces.

Heat a wok or large frying pan over high heat until it is very hot. Add the oil and, when it is very hot and slightly smoking, remove the beef from the marinade with a slotted spoon. Add it to the pan and stir-fry it for 2 minutes until it browns. Remove it and leave to drain in a colander or sieve.

Pour off all but 1 tablespoon of the oil. Reheat the wok or pan over a high heat and then add the lemon grass, gingerroot, shallots and garlic slices and stir-fry for 20 seconds. Then add the peppers, soy sauce, Shaoxing rice wine or dry sherry, salt, pepper and sugar and continue to stir-fry for 3 minutes. Then return the beef to the wok and stir-fry for 4 minutes, mixing well. Drizzle in the sesame oil and give the mixture a few stirs. Transfer to a warm platter and serve at once.

CRUNCHY PEANUT BEEF

This savory recipe combines beef with crunchy peanuts. It is a delicious combination that has a wonderful texture. This dish will go well with noodles, pasta or just plain rice. Serve with a vegetable dish for a complete meal.

SERVES 4

1 tablespoon peanut oil

1½ tablespoons finely chopped garlic

1 tablespoon finely chopped fresh gingerroot

3 tablespoons finely chopped green onions

1 lb (450 g) ground beef

3 tablespoons whole yellow bean sauce

1 tablespoon chili bean sauce

1½ tablespoons Shaoxing rice wine or dry sherry

1 tablespoon dark soy sauce

1 teaspoon salt

½ teaspoon freshly ground black pepper

2 teaspoons chili bean sauce

2 teaspoons sugar

3 tablespoons *Chicken Stock (see p.56)* or water

FOR THE GARNISH

½ cup crushed roasted peanuts

3 tablespoons coarsely chopped green onions

Heat a wok or large frying pan over a high heat until it is hot. Add the oil and, when it is very hot and slightly smoking, add the garlic, gingerroot and green onions and stir-fry for 15 seconds. Add the beef, stir well to break up all the pieces and continue to stir-fry for about 2 minutes or until the beef loses its pink color. Then add the rest of the main ingredients, stirring all the time. Bring the mixture to the boil, turn the heat down to low and simmer for 5 minutes. Transfer the contents of the wok to a warm, deep-sided platter. Sprinkle on the peanuts and green onions, mix everything together well and serve at once.

SAVORY BEEF WITH ASPARAGUS

*A*sparagus is the favorite vegetable of many lovers of good food. It is easy to see why. The cooked stalks combine crunchy and soft textures, subtle and distinct flavors. And in the spring, when it is in season and readily available, it is not overly expensive.

Asparagus is congenial with almost any type of food, but it goes uncommonly well with beef. Both of these main ingredients stand up well against the hearty black beans and garlic seasonings. This is a delicious, quick, wholesome dish.

SERVES 4

1 lb (450 g) lean beef steak

1 lb (450 g) fresh asparagus

3 tablespoons peanut oil

4 oz (100 g) onions, thinly sliced

2 tablespoons coarsely chopped black beans

1½ tablespoons finely chopped garlic

2 teaspoons finely chopped fresh gingerroot

3 tablespoons *Chicken Stock (see p.56)* or water

1 tablespoon Shaoxing rice wine or dry sherry

1½ teaspoons salt

½ teaspoon freshly ground black pepper

1 teaspoon sugar

2 tablespoons oyster sauce

FOR THE MARINADE

2 teaspoons light soy sauce

2 teaspoons Shaoxing rice wine or dry sherry

2 teaspoons sesame oil

½ teaspoon salt

¼ teaspoon freshly ground black pepper

2 teaspoons cornstarch

Put the beef in the freezer for 20 minutes. This will allow the meat to harden slightly for easier cutting. Then cut it into thin slices 1½ inches (4 cm) long. Put the beef slices into a bowl and add the Marinade ingredients. Mix well and let the slices steep in the marinade for about 15 minutes.

Meanwhile, slice the asparagus on the diagonal into 3 inch (7.5 cm) pieces and set aside.

Heat a wok or large frying pan over a high heat until it is very hot. Add the oil and, when it is very hot and slightly smoking, add the beef from the marinade and stir-fry for about 2 minutes. Remove the meat and drain it in a colander. Pour off all but 1½ tablespoons of the oil and reheat it over a high heat. When it is very hot, add the onions, black beans, garlic and gingerroot and stir-fry for 1 minute. Then add the asparagus and stir-fry for 1 minute. Now add the stock or water, Shaoxing rice wine or dry sherry, salt, pepper and sugar. Continue to stir-fry for 3 minutes or until the asparagus is slightly tender. Add more water as necessary. Quickly return the meat to the wok, add the oyster sauce and stir well. Turn the mixture onto a warm platter and serve at once.

STIR-FRIED BEEF WITH CORN

*O*ften *in Thailand, beef or chicken is combined with toothsome baby corn. This Thai-inspired recipe with my own touches is easy to make and delectable.*

Often this type of corn is imported from Thailand or grown locally. It has become quite popular and is now easily found in supermarkets. It is easy to cook and, when it is stir-fried in the wok, it has a slightly smoky taste that adds to the enjoyment of this unique vegetable. Although baby corn can be found in cans, it is best fresh.

SERVES 4

1 lb (450 g) lean beef steak

3 tablespoons peanut oil

1 small onion, thinly sliced

2 tablespoons thinly sliced garlic

2 tablespoons finely chopped green onions

8 oz (225 g) fresh or canned baby corn

⅔ cup *Chicken Stock (see p.56)*

1 tablespoon Shaoxing rice wine or dry sherry

3 tablespoons oyster sauce

Handful of fresh basil leaves

FOR THE MARINADE

1 tablespoon light soy sauce

1 teaspoon five-spice powder

2 teaspoons sesame oil

1 tablespoon Shaoxing rice wine or dry sherry

2 teaspoons cornstarch

Cut the beef into thin slices 2 inches (5 cm) long and ¼ inch (5 mm) thick and put them into a bowl. Add the Marinade ingredients. Leave the mixture to marinate for 20 minutes.

Heat a wok or large frying pan until it is very hot. Add the oil and, when it is very hot and slightly smoking, add the beef slices and stir-fry for 3 minutes or until they are lightly browned. Remove them and drain them well. Discard all but 1 tablespoon of the oil.

Reheat the wok over a high heat until it is hot. Add the onion and garlic and stir-fry for 1 minute. Then add the green onions and baby corn and continue to stir-fry for 1 minute. Now add the stock and Shaoxing rice wine or dry sherry and continue to cook for 3 minutes or until the corn is tender. Then add the oyster sauce and bring it to a simmer. Return the drained beef slices and toss them thoroughly with the sauce. Add the basil leaves and give the mixture several stirs. Turn the mixture onto a warm serving platter and serve at once.

BRAISED KOREAN-STYLE SPARERIBS

Korean food is one of the least known of all the Asian cuisines. It is a cuisine that uses many of the same ingredients as Chinese cuisine but combines them in different ways. One delicious dish that I have eaten in Korean restaurants is this one with spareribs. I have added my own touches.

As it is a braised dish, it reheats well. It makes a substantial meal and is perfect for a cool evening. Serve it with rice and another vegetable dish.

SERVES 4

1¾ lb (750 g) meaty pork spareribs

1 tablespoon peanut oil

5 garlic cloves, crushed

1 tablespoon finely chopped fresh gingerroot

3 tablespoons finely chopped green onions

3 tablespoons rock or plain sugar

3 tablespoons Shaoxing rice wine or dry
  sherry

1¼ cups *Chicken Stock (see p.56)*

2 tablespoons light soy sauce

2 tablespoons sesame paste or peanut butter

Have your butcher separate the spareribs into individual ribs and then into chunks which are about 3 inches (7.5 cm) long. Alternatively, do this yourself using a heavy, sharp cleaver that can cut through the bones.

Heat a wok or large frying pan over a high heat until it is hot. Add the oil and, when it is very hot and slightly smoking, add the spareribs and stir-fry for 5 minutes or until they are brown. Remove them with a slotted spoon and discard all the oil and fat. Wipe the wok clean.

Put the rest of the ingredients into the clean wok or frying pan. Bring the mixture to the boil and then reduce the heat. Add the spareribs, cover and simmer slowly for about 45 minutes, stirring occasionally. If necessary, add a little water to the sauce to prevent the dish from drying out. Skim off any surface fat, turn onto a warm serving platter and serve immediately.

STIR-FRIED GARLIC PORK

Garlic and pork are two very familiar items in Chinese cuisine. Mainly for geographic reasons, pork is the "red meat" of Chinese cookery. The lack of grazing land and pastures make raising beef on a large scale impossible. Garlic is one of the three main spices (with gingerroot and soy sauce) in Chinese cuisine. And the two ingredients go so well together, with the garlic nicely enhancing the fine qualities of the pork.

The black beans in this recipe are also important, giving the dish its trademark salty pungency. It is altogether very much a southern Chinese concoction, balancing crisp, clean, distinct flavors. My mother often made this dish and it has always been a favorite of mine. She would vary the taste once in a while by adding a dash of spicy chili bean sauce.

An easy dish to make in the wok, it goes perfectly with plain rice and any stir-fried vegetable.

SERVES 4

1 lb (450 g) lean pork
2 tablespoons peanut oil
3 tablespoons finely chopped garlic
3 green onions, thinly sliced diagonally
2 teaspoons chili bean sauce
1 tablespoon light soy sauce
1 teaspoon Shaoxing rice wine or dry sherry
1 teaspoon sugar
1 tablespoon *Chicken Stock (see p.56)* or water
1 tablespoon sesame oil

FOR THE MARINADE

1 tablespoon Shaoxing rice wine or dry
  sherry
1 tablespoon light soy sauce
2 teaspoons sesame oil
1 teaspoon cornstarch

Cut the pork into thin slices 2 inches (5 cm) long. Put the slices into a small bowl and mix them well with the Marinade ingredients. Leave to marinate for about 20 minutes.

Heat a wok or large frying pan until it is hot. Add half the oil and, when it is very hot and almost smoking, lift the pork out of the marinade with a slotted spoon, put it in the wok and quickly stir-fry for about 2-3 minutes. Drain well.

Wipe the wok clean, reheat it and add the rest of the oil. Then quickly add the garlic, green onions and chili bean sauce. A few seconds later add the rest of the ingredients. Bring the mixture to a boil and then return the pork to the wok or pan. Stir-fry the entire mixture for another 5 minutes. Turn it onto a warm platter and serve at once.

SZECHUAN-STYLE PORK

Szechuan is among my favorite food regions of China. I love the lusty flavors of the spices and diversity of its cuisine. Many of the best dishes are the home-cooked ones. These utilize simple ingredients to make a delicious meal.

Here pork is stir-fried with Szechuan preserved vegetables for a robust, tasty dish that is quite easy to prepare. In the wok, it literally takes minutes. The key to success in this recipe is not to overcook the pork. You can buy the preserved vegetables in Chinese grocers or delicatessens.

SERVES 4

1 lb (450 g) lean, boneless pork

2 oz (50 g) beanthread (transparent) noodles

1½ tablespoons peanut oil

2 tablespoons coarsely chopped garlic

2 teaspoons finely chopped fresh gingerroot

4 tablespoons rinsed and coarsely chopped
  Szechuan preserved vegetables

1 tablespoon light soy sauce

1 tablespoon Shaoxing rice wine or dry
  sherry

1 teaspoon sugar

⅔ cup *Chicken Stock (see p.56)* or water

FOR THE MARINADE

1 tablespoon Shaoxing rice wine or dry
  sherry

1 tablespoon light soy sauce

2 teaspoons sesame oil

2 teaspoons cornstarch

Cut the pork into thin slices 2 inches (5 cm) long. Put the sliced pork into a bowl and mix in the Marinade ingredients. Let the mixture sit for 10-15 minutes so that the pork absorbs the flavors of the marinade.

Soak the noodles in a large bowl of warm water for 15 minutes. When soft, drain and discard the water. Cut into 3 inch (7.5 cm) lengths using scissors or a knife.

Heat a wok or frying pan to a very high heat. Add the oil and, when it is very hot and slightly smoking, add the pork slices and stir-fry them until they are brown. Add the garlic, gingerroot and Szechuan vegetables. Add the beanthread noodles, soy sauce, Shaoxing rice wine or dry sherry, sugar and stock and continue to stir-fry until the pork is cooked and slightly firm. This should take about 5 minutes. Remove and arrange the pork, noodles and vegetables on a warm serving platter. Pour any juices remaining in the wok over the pork and serve at once.

GINGER TOMATO BEEF

I remember eating this delightful and refreshing dish during a visit to Malaysia. The ginger plant of tropical Southeast Asia, with its yellowish-green flowers and strongly aromatic rhizome, is a basic seasoning throughout Asia. The lively and zesty flavor pairs well with tomatoes, they in turn balancing the robust beef. This dish can be served with pasta or rice.

SERVES 4

1 lb (450 g) lean beef steak

1 tablespoon light soy sauce

2 teaspoons Shaoxing rice wine or dry sherry

1 teaspoon sesame oil

2 teaspoons cornstarch

1 lb (450 g) fresh or canned tomatoes

3 tablespoons peanut oil

8 oz (225 g) onions, coarsely chopped

1 tablespoon finely chopped fresh gingerroot

2 tablespoons coarsely chopped garlic

1 teaspoon salt

½ teaspoon freshly ground black pepper

1 teaspoon sugar

½ teaspoon chili flakes

FOR THE GARNISH

Handful of sprigs of fresh cilantro

Cut the beef into thick ¼ inch (5 mm) x 2 inch (5 cm) slices and put them into a bowl. Add the light soy sauce, Shaoxing rice wine or dry sherry, sesame oil and cornstarch and mix well.

If you are using fresh tomatoes, peel, seed and cut them into 1 inch (2.5 cm) cubes. If you are using canned tomatoes, chop them into small chunks.

Heat a wok or large frying pan over a high heat until it is hot. Add the oil and, when it is very hot and slightly smoking, add the beef and stir-fry for 2 minutes to brown. Remove the beef with a slotted spoon and drain in a colander. Drain off all but about 1 tablespoon of the oil.

Reheat the wok, add the onions, gingerroot and garlic and stir-fry for 2 minutes. Then add the tomatoes, salt, pepper, sugar and chili flakes. Turn the heat to low, cover and simmer for 15 minutes. Return the beef to the wok and heat through. Garnish with the cilantro and serve at once.

SPICY ORANGE LAMB

Although Chinese ordinarily do not like lamb, they have not tasted lamb in the West, where it is delicate and more subtle than the stronger-tasting one from China.

Here I have combined the lamb with orange for a lovely contrast to the rich meat. The tartness of the fresh orange peel works well to balance the robust taste of the lamb. It is an easy dish to make and the spicy flavors add to its appeal. Serve it with plain rice and vegetables for a wholesome meal.

SERVES 4

1 lb (450 g) lean boneless lamb chops

3 tablespoons peanut oil

1½ teaspoons finely chopped fresh
  gingerroot

2 tablespoons thinly sliced garlic

1 tablespoon grated orange zest

1 teaspoon roasted Szechuan peppercorns,
  finely ground (optional)

2 tablespoons orange juice

1 tablespoon dark soy sauce

2 teaspoons chili bean sauce

½ teaspoon salt

½ teaspoon freshly ground black pepper

1 teaspoon sugar

2 teaspoons sesame oil

FOR THE MARINADE

1 tablespoon light soy sauce

2 teaspoons Shaoxing rice wine or dry sherry

1 teaspoon sesame oil

2 teaspoons cornstarch

Cut the lamb into thin slices 2 inches (5 cm) long, cutting against the grain. Put the lamb into a bowl together with all the Marinade ingredients. Mix well and then let the mixture marinate for about 20 minutes.

Heat a wok or large frying pan over a high heat until it is very hot. Add the oil and, when it is very hot and slightly smoking, remove the lamb from the marinade with a slotted spoon. Add it to the pan and stir-fry it for 2 minutes until it browns. Remove it and leave to drain in a colander or sieve. Pour off all but about 2 teaspoons of the oil.

Reheat the wok or pan over a high heat and then add the gingerroot, garlic, orange zest and peppercorns, if using. Stir-fry for 20 seconds. Then return the lamb to the pan, add the rest of the ingredients and stir-fry for 4 minutes, mixing well. Serve the dish at once.

STIR-FRIED VIETNAMESE-STYLE LEMON GRASS BEEF

Beef goes especially well with lemon grass in this Vietnamese-inspired recipe. The delicate citrus flavor is a complement to the hearty beef. The garnish of roasted peanuts adds texture and crunch to this unusually aromatic dish, which you can serve with rice and another vegetable dish to create a complete meal.

SERVES 4

1 lb (450 g) lean beef steak

3 tablespoons peanut oil

4 oz (100 g) onions, thinly sliced

2 fresh red or green chilies, seeded and coarsely chopped

3 tablespoons coarsely chopped garlic

1 tablespoon Shaoxing rice wine or dry sherry

2 teaspoons sugar

FOR THE MARINADE

2 teaspoons Thai fish sauce

2 teaspoons Shaoxing rice wine or dry sherry

2 teaspoons sesame oil

$\frac{1}{2}$ teaspoon salt

$\frac{1}{4}$ teaspoon freshly ground black pepper

2 teaspoons cornstarch

2 stalks fresh lemon grass

FOR THE GARNISH

$\frac{1}{4}$ cup roasted peanuts, coarsely chopped

Handful of sprigs of fresh cilantro

Put the beef in the freezer for 20 minutes. This will allow the meat to harden slightly for easier cutting. Then cut it into thin slices 1½ inches (4 cm) long. Put the beef slices into a bowl and add the fish sauce, Shaoxing rice wine or dry sherry, sesame oil, salt, pepper and cornstarch. Peel the lemon grass stalk to reveal the tender, whitish center and crush it with the flat of a knife. Then cut it into 3 inch (7.5 cm) pieces. Add this to the meat mixture. Mix well and let the slices steep in the marinade for 30 minutes.

Heat a wok or large frying pan over a high heat until it is very hot. Add the oil and, when it is very hot and slightly smoking, add the beef with the marinade and stir-fry for about 2 minutes. Remove the meat and drain it in a colander.

Pour off all but 1½ tablespoons of the oil and reheat it over a high heat. When it is very hot, add the onions, chilies and garlic and stir-fry for 1 minute. Then add the Shaoxing rice wine or dry sherry and sugar. Continue to stir-fry for 3 minutes. Quickly return the meat to the wok and continue to stir-fry for 2 minutes or until the beef is heated through. Turn the mixture onto a warm platter, garnish with the chopped peanuts and cilantro and serve at once.

SAVORY PORK TOMATO SAUCE

This is a tasty sauce that is delicious over rice, noodles or pasta. It is a variation of the bean sauce used with noodles. Tomatoes, a relatively recent arrival to the Asian food scene, have become very popular and are used in every way possible. No wonder, they are such a wonderful food.

This sauce can be made in advance, even frozen. It is easily reheated, which makes it ideal for entertaining as well as for a quick family dinner.

SERVES 4

1½ tablespoons peanut oil

3 tablespoons coarsely chopped garlic

1 tablespoon finely chopped fresh gingerroot

3 tablespoons finely chopped green onions

2 small onions, thinly sliced

2 red or green chilies, seeded and finely chopped

1 lb (450 g) ground pork

2 teaspoons salt

½ teaspoon freshly ground black pepper

1 tablespoon sugar

1 lb (450 g) fresh tomatoes, cored and quartered

1¼ cups *Chicken Stock (see p.56)* **or water**

2½ tablespoons Thai fish sauce

2 tablespoons light soy sauce

FOR THE GARNISH

Handful of sprigs of fresh cilantro

Heat a wok or large frying pan over a high heat until it is hot. Add the oil and, when it is very hot and slightly smoking, add the garlic, gingerroot, green onions, onions and chilies and stir-fry for 2 minutes.

Add the pork, stir well to break up all the pieces and continue to stir-fry for about 5 minutes or more until the pork loses its pink color. Then add the salt, pepper, sugar and tomatoes.

Finally add the stock or water, fish sauce and soy sauce. Bring the mixture to the boil, turn the heat down to low and simmer for 15 minutes. Transfer the sauce to a warm platter, garnish with the cilantro and serve at once.

THAI-STYLE MEATBALLS

*W*alking through the streets of Bangkok, one is pleasantly overwhelmed by the exotic fragrances and mouth-watering aromas characteristic of Thai cooking. They emanate from the many small restaurants and street-stall kitchens that line the thoroughfares.

Street vendors sell an assortment of fish cakes, snacks and meatballs, and I first tasted this dish at such a stall. What makes the meatballs so good are the spices blending so nicely into the succulent beef and pork. The egg whites give the meatballs a delicate, light texture.

The meatballs are very easy to prepare and they are excellent party snacks with drinks.

SERVES 4

1 cup ground beef

1 cup ground pork

2 egg whites

2 tablespoons very cold water

1 teaspoon salt

½ teaspoons freshly ground black pepper

2 tablespoons finely chopped garlic

3 tablespoons finely chopped fresh cilantro

3 tablespoons finely chopped green onions

2 teaspoons Thai fish sauce

2 teaspoons sugar

All-purpose flour, for dusting

2 cups peanut oil

Mix the beef and pork in a food processor for a few seconds. Slowly add the egg whites and cold water and mix them for a few more seconds until they are fully incorporated into the meat. Then add the rest of the ingredients except the flour and oil and mix for about a minute until the meat mixture has become a light paste.

Using your hands, form the mixture into 1½ inch (4 cm) balls—about the size of a golf ball. (This recipe makes about 10 balls.) Dust them evenly with the flour, shaking off any excess. The meatballs will be quite fragile and soft.

Heat a wok or large frying pan over a high heat until it is hot. Add the oil and, when it is very hot and slightly smoking, gently drop in as many meatballs as will fit easily in one layer. Carefully fry them for about 4 minutes until the meatballs are crispy and browned. Adjust the heat as necessary. Take the meatballs out with a slotted spoon and drain on paper towels. (You may have to do this in several batches.) Serve them at once.

SZECHUAN-STYLE PORK WITH PEANUTS

This is a pork version of a classic Szechuan Chinese dish that is usually made with chicken. It is quick and easy to make and is quite savory — as is to be expected from any Szechuan recipe. The pork is quite robust enough to stand up to the various seasonings, while the peanuts add a wonderful textural quality to the dish. Serve it with plain rice and another vegetable dish for a complete meal.

SERVES 4

1 lb (450 g) boneless pork chops
1½ tablespoons peanut oil
1 dried red chili, split lengthwise
¼ cup raw peanuts, shelled *(see p.20)*

FOR THE MARINADE

1 tablespoon light soy sauce
2 teaspoons Shaoxing rice wine or dry sherry
1 teaspoon sesame oil
2 teaspoons cornstarch

FOR THE SAUCE

2 tablespoons *Chicken Stock (see p.56)* or water
2 tablespoons Shaoxing rice wine or dry sherry
1 tablespoon dark soy sauce
2 teaspoons sugar
1 tablespoon coarsely chopped garlic
1½ tablespoons finely chopped green onions
2 teaspoons finely chopped fresh gingerroot
1 tablespoon Chinese black rice vinegar or cider vinegar
1 teaspoon salt
1 teaspoon sesame oil

Cut the pork into 1 inch (2.5 cm) cubes. Combine the pork with the Marinade ingredients.

Heat a wok or large frying pan over a high heat. Add the oil and, when it is hot, add the chili and stir-fry for a few seconds. (You may remove it when it turns black or leave it in; leaving it in will make the flavor stronger.) Add the peanuts and stir-fry them for 1 minute. Remove the peanuts from the wok and reserve.

Lift the pork from the marinade with a slotted spoon, add to the wok and stir-fry for 3 minutes or until the pork is lightly browned. Remove the pork and drain in a colander.

Wipe the wok clean and put all the sauce ingredients, except the sesame oil, into the wok. Bring the sauce to a boil and then turn the heat down. Return the pork to the wok and cook for about 2 minutes in the sauce, mixing well all the time. Finally, return the peanuts and add the sesame oil, give the mixture a good stir and serve immediately.

STIR-FRIED BEEF CURRY

Although curry, as such, is not a Chinese seasoning, it has nevertheless made its way into Chinese cuisine in a rather mild form. The hint of exotic spices adds a special, very subtle flavor to any Chinese dish. Curry works extremely well when beef is matched with vegetables.

This is a substantial dish that easily makes a filling meal for two or three. It may also be served as part of a multicourse Chinese-style menu.

The best type of curry paste or powder to use is the Madras variety. It is favored by most Chinese cooks.

SERVES 2-4

1 lb (450 g) lean beef steak

3 tablespoons peanut oil

8 oz (225 g) onions, sliced

2 tablespoons coarsely chopped garlic

FOR THE MARINADE

1 tablespoon light soy sauce

2 teaspoons sesame oil

1 tablespoon Shaoxing rice wine or dry sherry

2 teaspoons cornstarch

FOR THE CURRY SAUCE

1 tablespoon Shaoxing rice wine or dry sherry

1 tablespoon Madras curry paste or powder

1 tablespoon dark soy sauce

1 teaspoon light soy sauce

1 teaspoon sugar

2 tablespoons *Chicken Stock (see p.56)* or water

FOR THE GARNISH

1½ tablespoons finely chopped green onions

Cut the beef into thin slices 2 inches (5 cm) long and ¼ inch (5 mm) thick and put them into a bowl. Add the Marinade ingredients and let the mixture marinate for 20 minutes.

Heat a wok or large frying pan until it is very hot. Add the oil and, when it is very hot and slightly smoking, add the beef slices and stir-fry for 3 minutes or until they are lightly browned. Remove them and drain them well in a colander set inside a bowl.

Wipe the wok or pan clean and reheat it over a high heat until it is hot. Add 1 tablespoon of the drained oil, then add the onions and garlic and stir-fry for 1 minute. Add all the curry sauce ingredients and bring the mixture to a simmer and cook for 3 minutes. Return the drained beef slices to the wok or pan and toss them thoroughly with the sauce. Turn the mixture onto a warm serving platter, garnish with the green onions and serve at once.

VIETNAMESE-STYLE BEEF STEW

■■■■

This recipe is a Vietnamese version of beef stew that is similar in some ways to the Chinese one. However, the seasonings are slightly different, with the use of aromatic lemon grass.

Be sure to use an inexpensive cut of beef such as brisket or shin. This is a perfect dish for a cold winter's night. Plain steamed rice is an ideal accompaniment to this hearty and very tasty dish. The stew can also be made and allowed to cool, then reheated later, garnished and served.

SERVES 4-6

4 stalks fresh lemon grass

3 lb (1.4 kg) stewing beef, such as brisket or shank

4 green onions

2 tablespoons peanut oil

1 small onion, coarsely chopped

6 slices fresh gingerroot

6 garlic cloves, lightly crushed

1 tablespoon crushed red chili

1 lb (450 g) carrots

FOR THE BRAISING SAUCE

3¾ cups *Chicken Stock (see p. 56)*

¼ cup rock sugar or plain sugar

3 tablespoons light soy sauce

2 tablespoons dark soy sauce

3 tablespoons Shaoxing rice wine or dry sherry

4 whole star anise

2 teaspoons five-spice powder

2 tablespoons tomato paste

2 teaspoons salt

1 teaspoon freshly ground black pepper

FOR THE GARNISH

6 tablespoons coarsely chopped fresh basil

Peel the lemon grass stalks to reveal the tender, whitish center and crush with the flat of a knife. Then cut it into 3 inch (7.5 cm) pieces. Cut the meat into 2 inch (5 cm) cubes. Slice the green onions at a slight diagonal into 2 inch (5 cm) segments.

Heat a wok or large frying pan until it is hot. Add the oil and, when it is very hot and slightly smoking, add the beef. Pan-fry until it is brown. This should take about 10 minutes. Pour off all but 1 tablespoon of the oil from the pan. Add the green onions, chopped onion, gingerroot, garlic and chili and stir-fry with the beef for about 5 minutes.

Transfer this mixture to a large casserole or pan. Add the braising sauce ingredients. Bring the liquid to the boil, skim off any fat from the surface and turn the heat as low as possible. Cover and braise for 1½ hours.

Meanwhile, peel the carrots and cut them at a slight diagonal into 2 inch (5 cm) chunks. Add these to the meat and continue to cook the mixture for another 30 minutes or until the beef is quite tender. Remove the vegetables with a slotted spoon and set aside. Then turn the heat up to high and rapidly reduce the liquid for about 15 minutes. The sauce should thicken slightly. Return the vegetables to the pan and cook for 2 minutes or until they are warmed through. Ladle the stew into a large warm dish. Garnish with the chopped fresh basil and serve immediately.

CALF'S LIVER WITH SPICY BLACK BEAN SAUCE

*T*he sturdy flavor and distinct taste of liver almost demands something as spicy as Chinese black bean sauce. This delightful recipe is an delicious alternative to the usual liver with onions. The dish is easy to make. Liver should never be overcooked; it should remain moist, soft in texture and slightly pink in color. Thus, the stir-frying time is quite short, which means you can quickly make this dish the center attraction of a nutritious menu.

SERVES 4

1 lb (450 g) fresh calf's liver
Cornstarch, for dusting

FOR THE MARINADE

1 tablespoon Shaoxing rice wine or dry
   sherry
2 teaspoons sesame oil
2 teaspoons salt
½ teaspoon freshly ground black pepper

FOR THE SAUCE

4 tablespoons peanut oil
1½ tablespoons coarsely chopped black
   beans
1 tablespoon finely chopped garlic
2 teaspoons finely chopped fresh gingerroot
3 tablespoons finely chopped green onions
1 tablespoon chopped shallots
1 tablespoon light soy sauce
2 teaspoons dark soy sauce
1 tablespoon chili bean sauce
1 teaspoon sugar
1 tablespoon *Chicken Stock (see p.56)* or water
1 tablespoon sesame oil

Cut the calf's liver into thin slices 3 inches (7.5 cm) long. Mix together the Marinade ingredients in a bowl, add the liver slices and coat them thoroughly with the marinade. Cover the bowl tightly with plastic wrap and leave to marinate in the refrigerator for at least 20 minutes. Remove the liver slices from the marinade and dust with cornstarch, shaking off any excess.

Heat a wok or large frying pan over a high heat until it is hot. Add 3 tablespoons of the oil and, when it is very hot and slightly smoking, add the liver and stir-fry for about 2-3 minutes. Drain well in a colander.

Reheat the wok, adding 1 tablespoon of oil, then add the black beans, garlic, gingerroot, green onions and shallots. A few seconds later add the rest of the ingredients. When the sauce comes to the boil, return the liver to the wok or pan and toss it well, coating it with the sauce. Stir-fry for 30 seconds, turn it onto a warm platter and serve at once.

SPICY PORK WITH FRAGRANT BASIL

This is a mouth-watering Thai-inspired dish. The ground pork is quickly stir-fried and tossed with so much fragrant basil that the seasoning almost plays the role of a green vegetable. Thai cookery, it seems, can never use too much basil. And here it is used to such good effect, helping to produce a marvelously aromatic dish that goes extremely well with plain rice. It is easy to make and is therefore ideal for a quick but exotic family meal.

SERVES 4

1½ tablespoons peanut oil

3 tablespoons coarsely chopped garlic

3 tablespoons seeded and finely chopped
   red chili

4 cups ground pork

2 tablespoons finely chopped fresh cilantro

2 tablespoons Thai fish sauce

1 tablespoon oyster sauce

2 teaspoons sugar

⅔ cup Chicken Stock (see p. 56)

A large handful of fresh basil leaves

Heat a wok or large frying pan over a high heat until it is hot. Add the oil and, when it is very hot and slightly smoking, add the garlic and chili and stir-fry for 30 seconds. Then add the pork and continue to stir-fry for 3 minutes. Then add the cilantro, fish sauce, oyster sauce, sugar and stock. Continue to stir-fry for 3 minutes. Then add the basil and stir-fry for another minute. Turn onto a warm platter and serve at once.

THAI-STYLE CHILI BEEF

Imitation being the sincerest form of flattery, this recipe is an admitted replica of one of the culinary creations of my good friend, Chalie Amatylakul. He is among the foremost authorities on Thai cookery and has taught me very much about the essentials of this great cuisine.

With the exception of the fresh chilies, it is quite similar to many stir-fried Chinese dishes. It is delightful, aromatic and quick to make. Serve it with rice, as a main course, or with another vegetable dish.

SERVES 4

1 lb (450 g) lean beef steak

1 teaspoon salt

½ teaspoon freshly ground black pepper

1 teaspoon sesame oil

1 oz (25 g) dried shiitake mushrooms

1½ tablespoons peanut oil

8 oz (225 g) onions, shredded

2 tablespoons coarsely chopped garlic

4 red chilies, seeded and finely shredded

1 tablespoon Shaoxing rice wine or dry sherry

1 tablespoon oyster sauce

1 tablespoon light soy sauce

1 teaspoon sugar

3 tablespoons *Chicken Stock (see p.56)* or water

FOR THE GARNISH

1½ tablespoons finely shredded green onions

Cut the beef into thin slices 2 inches (5 cm) long and ¼ inch (5 mm) thick, then finely shred them. In a bowl, combine the beef with the salt, pepper and sesame oil.

Soak the mushrooms in warm water for 20 minutes. Then drain them and squeeze out the excess liquid. Remove and discard the stems and finely shred the caps into thin strips.

Heat a wok or large frying pan until it is very hot. Add the oil and, when it is very hot and slightly smoking, add the onions and garlic and stir-fry for 3 minutes. Then add the beef and chilies and continue to stir-fry for 2 minutes. Finally, add the Shaoxing rice wine or dry sherry, oyster sauce, soy sauce, sugar and stock or water. Add the mushrooms and continue to stir-fry the mixture for 2 minutes until the beef is thoroughly mixed through. Turn the mixture onto a serving platter, garnish it with the green onions, and serve at once.

STIR-FRIED CHILI PORK WITH CASHEWS

*P*ork, the preferred Chinese "red meat," is delicious when combined with the taste and texture of nuts — in this case, cashews. A touch of chili bean sauce is added for zest and you have a quick, savory dish that can grace the center of a family table. Serve this with plain rice and another vegetable dish for a wholesome and satisfying meal.

SERVES 4

1 lb (450 g) lean boneless pork chops

1½ tablespoons peanut or peanut oil

1 teaspoon salt

½ teaspoon freshly ground black pepper

½ cup cashew nuts

1 tablespoon Shaoxing rice wine or dry sherry

1 tablespoon light soy sauce

1 tablespoon chili bean sauce

2 teaspoons sugar

FOR THE MARINADE

1 tablespoon Shaoxing rice wine or dry sherry

2 teaspoons light soy sauce

2 teaspoons sesame oil

1 teaspoon cornstarch

FOR THE GARNISH

1 tablespoon finely chopped green onions

Cut the pork into thin slices 2 inches (5 cm) long. Put the sliced pork into a bowl and mix in the Marinade ingredients. Let the mixture sit for 10-15 minutes so that the pork absorbs the flavors of the marinade.

Heat a wok or frying pan over a very high heat. Add the oil and, when it is very hot and slightly smoking, add the pork slices, salt and pepper and stir-fry for 2 minutes. Remove them with a slotted spoon. Add the cashew nuts and stir-fry them for 1 minute. Then add the rest of the ingredients. Return the pork to the wok or pan and stir-fry the mixture for another 2 minutes. Garnish with the green onions and serve at once.

POULTRY

Like meats, poultry is very easy to cook in the wok. The hot wok seals in the juicy flavors of the chicken, then allows it to unite with an array of seasonings and aromatics. Garlic, chili bean sauce, lemon grass and ginger are some of the many flavors used to turn prosaic poultry into a special treat. Many of these recipes are inspired not only by my Chinese heritage but also by my travels to Southeast Asia.

The wok, widely used in that part of Asia, is clearly a key piece of equipment in the kitchen. You will find many of these tasty recipes easy to make and, from Peter Ng's Sesame-Ginger Chicken to Indonesian-style Coconut Chicken, the wok transforms the lowly chicken into wonderful savory dishes.

PETER NG'S SESAME-GINGER CHICKEN

*P*eter Ng is a lover of good food and an excellent cook. Of Chinese descent, he was born in *Malaysia and now lives in Adelaide, Australia. His cultural inheritance is obvious in his cooking, which combines Malaysian flavors with Chinese techniques.*

Peter recalls that this recipe was prepared by his mother as a special treat for his sister when she was pregnant. Ginger is highly regarded by the Chinese who believe its "warming" (or yang) properties are beneficial to both mother and child. Be that as it may, gingerroot, chicken thighs and selected spices make a happy marriage as they cook in the wok. The dish is the centerpiece of a marvelous meal when combined with rice and vegetables.

SERVES 4

1 lb (450 g) boneless, skinless chicken thighs

1 tablespoon peanut oil

2 teaspoons sesame oil

3 tablespoons finely shredded fresh gingerroot

2 tablespoons dark soy sauce

2 teaspoons sugar

1 teaspoon salt

½ teaspoon freshly ground black pepper

⅔ cup *Chicken Stock (see p. 56)* or water

2 tablespoons Shaoxing rice wine or dry sherry

FOR THE MARINADE

2 teaspoons light soy sauce

1 teaspoon dark soy sauce

1 tablespoon Shaoxing rice wine or dry sherry

½ teaspoon salt

½ teaspoon freshly ground black pepper

1 teaspoon sesame oil

2 teaspoons cornstarch

FOR THE GARNISH

3 tablespoons finely shredded green onions

Cut the chicken into 2 inch (5 cm) chunks. Mix the soy sauces, Shaoxing rice wine or dry sherry, salt, pepper and sesame oil and pour it over the chicken. Then mix in the cornstarch until all the chicken pieces are thoroughly coated. Leave the chicken to marinate for about 30 minutes. Drain the chicken and discard the marinade.

Heat a wok or large frying pan over a high heat until it is hot. Add the peanut and sesame oils and, when they are very hot and slightly smoking, add the gingerroot and pan-fry for about 1 minute until it is crispy. Then add the chicken and stir-fry for 5 minutes or until the chicken begins to brown. Add the soy sauce, sugar, salt, pepper and stock or water and continue to stir-fry for 1 minute. Reduce the heat, cover the wok or pan and simmer for 8 minutes. Remove the cover and boil over a high heat to reduce the sauce. When only a few tablespoons of the sauce remains, add the Shaoxing rice wine or dry sherry and continue to stir-fry for about 2 minutes until the chicken is cooked. Garnish with the green onions and serve.

GINGER-FLAVORED PROVENÇAL CHICKEN

The Provençal style of French cookery is justly famous and is among my very favorite cuisines. Its bright, clean, aromatic character is reminiscent of the Cantonese cooking of my childhood. Earthy spices, garlic and herbs are given wings in imaginative combinations that delight the eye as well as the palate.

I often create "East-West" dishes and even entire menus by blending my Chinese cuisine with representative Western foods and styles. Both cultures share a commitment to good food, simply made, but a delight to see and to eat. Here I use chicken thighs, as the Chinese prefer to do, and I combine spices and seasonings from the two cuisines.

Unless they are in season and vine-ripened, you are better off using canned tomatoes. The dish reheats well, so it can be prepared in advance. It can also be increased, without any decline in quality, to accommodate a larger group of people.

SERVES 4

1¾ lb (750 g) boneless, skinless chicken thighs

3 tablespoons olive oil

6 garlic cloves, crushed

2 tablespoons finely chopped fresh gingerroot

1 onion, coarsely chopped

1 teaspoon salt

½ teaspoon freshly ground black pepper

1¾ lb (750 g) canned tomatoes, with liquid

½ cup pitted black Nice olives

1¼ cups *Chicken Stock (see p.56)*

20 basil leaves

2 teaspoons sugar

2 teaspoons salt

½ teaspoon finely ground black pepper

FOR THE MARINADE

1 tablespoon light soy sauce

2 teaspoons dark soy sauce

1 tablespoon Shaoxing rice wine or dry sherry

1 teaspoon salt

½ teaspoon freshly ground black pepper

Cut the chicken into 2 inch (5 cm) pieces. In a large bowl, combine the chicken with the soy sauces, Shaoxing rice wine or dry sherry, salt and pepper and mix well. Leave to marinate in the refrigerator for 30 minutes. Drain the chicken and discard any excess marinade.

Heat a wok or large frying pan over a high heat until it is hot. Add the oil and, when it is very hot, add the chicken and brown on both sides. Turn the heat down to medium and continue to brown for 5 minutes until it is golden brown. Remove the chicken from the wok and drain in a colander. Pour off all but 2 tablespoons of the oil and fat.

Reheat the wok, add the garlic, gingerroot, onion, salt and pepper and stir-fry for 1 minute. Reduce the heat and continue to cook for 3 minutes or until the onion is soft and transparent. Then add the tomatoes, olives and stock. Bring the mixture to a simmer, return the chicken to the wok, reduce the heat, cover and simmer for 15 minutes or until the chicken is cooked. Add the basil leaves, sugar, salt and pepper and cook for another 2 minutes. Turn on to a warm platter and serve at once.

SOOTHING CHICKEN PORRIDGE

This is a common "comfort food" throughout Asia: nutritious, soothing, satisfying, simple to make and always available. People eat it for breakfast, lunch or dinner, and as a snack. What makes this dish so special are the seasonings and the garnishes, which elevate the porridge to the level of a special treat. Of course, you can determine what those flavors are according to your own whims and preferences. That is what makes it a comfort. Here I use Southeast Asian touches because I like them and because they add up to a light but very satisfying dish at any time of the day.

The porridge and chicken can be made in advance. In this case, reheat them slowly and simply add some more water if the porridge is too thick.

You can buy the Tiensien preserved vegetables in Asian grocery shops and some delicatessens.

SERVES 4

3 lb (1.5 kg) chicken

9½ cups water

2 teaspoons salt

½ teaspoon freshly ground white pepper

⅔ cup short-grain or long-grain rice, unwashed

2 tablespoons peanut oil

3 tablespoons thinly sliced garlic

3 tablespoons thinly sliced shallots

4 eggs

2 red chilies

2 tablespoons finely shredded fresh gingerroot

2 tablespoons light soy sauce

2 teaspoons salt

1 teaspoon freshly ground white pepper

3 tablespoons finely chopped Tiensien preserved vegetables

3 tablespoons finely chopped green onions

Sprigs of fresh cilantro

Put the chicken and water together in a large pan and bring to the boil. Lower the heat and simmer uncovered for 20 minutes, skimming occasionally. Add the salt and pepper, cover and simmer for another 15 minutes. Remove the chicken and let it cool thoroughly.

Bring the liquid back to the boil and add the rice. Let the mixture come back to the boil and give it several good stirs. Turn the heat down to medium and cover the pan. Let the mixture simmer for about 1 hour, stirring occasionally. The rice grains should break down into a smooth porridge.

Heat a wok or large frying pan over a high heat until it is hot. Add the oil and, when it is very hot and slightly smoking, reduce the heat, add the garlic and shallots and stir-fry them for 1 minute or until they are brown. Remove them from the wok and drain thoroughly on paper towels.

In a small pan, boil the eggs for 10 minutes. Drain and refresh with cold running water. Crack them lightly and peel them. Continue to run them under cold running water until they are cool enough to handle easily. Cut the cooked eggs into quarters and put them in a bowl. Seed and finely slice the chilies and put them into a small dish. Place the gingerroot in a small dish. Do the same with the soy sauce, salt and pepper.

Rinse the preserved vegetables under cold running water, squeeze them dry and chop them. Put them into a small dish. Do the same with the green onions and fresh cilantro.

When the chicken is cool enough to handle, remove the meat with your hands and pull it apart into shreds with a fork. Put the chicken in a bowl.

Now uncover the rice and simmer for another 5 minutes. Ladle the porridge into individual bowls, adding some of the chicken, egg and each of the garnishes to each serving. Serve at once.

QUICK AND HEALTHY STEAMED CHICKEN

Steaming is not only a healthy way to cook food, it also brings out the subtle flavors. By keeping food moist and cooking it slowly in warm vapors, good chicken comes out even better. Chinese cooks tend to steam the entire chicken, but, when I am in a hurry, I simply steam chicken breasts. The result is a quick but healthy meal that takes little time to prepare. The juices from the steamed chicken taste delicious over rice.

SERVES 4

1 lb (450 g) skinless, boneless chicken breasts

1 teaspoon coarse sea salt or plain salt

1 tablespoon light soy sauce

1 tablespoon Shaoxing rice wine or dry sherry

½ teaspoon freshly ground white pepper

1 egg white

2 teaspoons cornstarch

1 teaspoon sesame oil

1½ tablespoons finely shredded fresh gingerroot

FOR THE GARNISH

3 tablespoons finely shredded green onions

1 tablespoon peanut oil

2 teaspoons sesame oil

Combine the chicken with the salt, soy sauce, Shaoxing rice wine or dry sherry, pepper, egg white, cornstarch and sesame oil. Leave to marinate for at least 20 minutes.

Next set up a steamer or put a rack into a wok or deep pan and fill it with 2 inches (5 cm) of water. Bring the water to the boil over a high heat. Put the chicken in one layer on a heat-proof plate and scatter the gingerroot evenly over the top. Put the plate of chicken into the steamer or onto the rack. Cover the pan tightly and gently steam the chicken until it is just white and firm. It will take about 8-10 minutes to cook, depending on the thickness of the chicken.

Remove the plate of cooked chicken and sprinkle on the green onions. Heat the two oils together in a small pan. When they are hot, pour the oil mixture over the top of the chicken. Serve at once.

THAI-STYLE CHICKEN

I greatly enjoy the Thai way with chicken. The combinations of exotic lemon grass, garlic and fresh chilies always have my mouth watering. The Thais also use a type of wok and they stir-fry many of their dishes. In this particular Thai-inspired dish, I have taken some elements of Thai flavorings and have created my own tasty chicken dish. It works brilliantly with rice.

SERVES 4

1 lb (450 g) skinless, boneless chicken thighs or 2 lb (900 g) chicken thighs with bone in

1 stalk fresh lemon grass

1 tablespoon peanut oil

1 onion, thinly sliced

2 tablespoons coarsely chopped garlic

2 teaspoons salt

2 teaspoons finely chopped lime zest

3 fresh red or green chilies, seeded and finely shredded

2 teaspoons sugar

Large handful of fresh basil leaves

FOR THE MARINADE

2 teaspoons light soy sauce

2 teaspoons Shaoxing rice wine or dry sherry

1 teaspoon sesame oil

2 teaspoons cornstarch

If you are using unboned thighs, remove the skin and bones from the chicken thighs or have your butcher do it for you. Cut the chicken into 1 inch (2.5 cm) chunks and combine it in a bowl with the soy sauce, Shaoxing rice wine or dry sherry, sesame oil and cornstarch. Leave to marinate for 20 minutes.

Peel the lemon grass stalk to reveal the tender, whitish center and cut into 2 inch (5 cm) pieces. Smash them with the flat of a knife or cleaver.

Heat a wok or large frying pan until it is very hot. Add the oil, then the chicken and stir-fry for 5 minutes until the chicken is brown. Remove the chicken and drain off the oil. Return the drained chicken to the wok and add the rest of the ingredients, except the basil leaves. Continue to cook for another 8-10 minutes, stirring from time to time, until the chicken is cooked. Add the basil leaves and give the mixture a good stir. Pour onto a warm platter and serve at once.

BRAISED CHICKEN WITH FRESH WATER CHESTNUTS

Chicken is best when its mild flavor and soft texture are combined with other distinctive tastes and contrasting textures. Sweet, fresh, crispy water chestnuts are thus an admirable partner in any chicken dish.

The clarity of the flavors here, with plain rice, make it a perfect dish for a cool fall evening. With vegetables, it makes a very satisfying complete meal: nutritious and tasty, but not heavy. Because it reheats so well, it can be prepared in advance and stored in the refrigerator.

I do not recommend the use of canned water chestnuts as they are so watery and soft. If fresh water chestnuts are unavailable, substitute firm, fresh, peeled Asian pear apples or firm, crispy apples. Added at the last moment of cooking, they retain their sweet crunchiness.

SERVES 4

1 lb (450 g) boneless, skinless chicken thighs or 2 lb (900 g) chicken thighs with bone in

2 tablespoons peanut oil

3 garlic cloves, thinly sliced

1½ tablespoons finely shredded fresh gingerroot

8 oz (225 g) fresh water chestnuts, peeled and sliced

3 tablespoons *Chicken Stock (see p.56)* or water

2 tablespoons oyster sauce

1 tablespoon Shaoxing rice wine or dry sherry

1 teaspoon dark soy sauce

1 teaspoon light soy sauce

1 teaspoon sugar

FOR THE MARINADE

2 teaspoons light soy sauce

2 teaspoons Shaoxing rice wine or dry sherry

1 teaspoon sesame oil

2 teaspoons cornstarch

If you are using unboned thighs, remove the skin and bones from the chicken thighs or have your butcher do it for you. Cut the chicken into 1 inch (2.5 cm) chunks and combine it in a bowl with the light soy sauce, Shaoxing rice wine or dry sherry, sesame oil and cornstarch. Leave to marinate for at least 30 minutes in the refrigerator.

Heat a wok or large frying pan over a high heat until it is hot. Add the oil and, when it is very hot and slightly smoking, add the chicken and stir-fry for 5 minutes. Remove and drain the chicken. Now drain off all but 2 teaspoons of the oil from the wok.

Reheat the wok, add the garlic and ginger-root and stir-fry for 30 seconds. Then add the drained chicken to the wok with the water chestnuts and the remaining ingredients. Reduce the heat to low, cover and cook for 10 minutes, stirring from time to time, until the chicken is cooked. Give the mixture a good stir, pour onto a warm platter and serve at once.

FRAGRANT ROAST EGGPLANT WITH CHICKEN

I often spend at least two weeks of my summer holiday with my good friends the Pébeyres, who have a country home outside Souillac in southwest France. One of the great pleasures is plucking fresh produce from their gardens to create Asian-inspired dishes. They frequently have fresh eggplants, so one evening I combined them with chicken in a spicy sauce with mint that also happened to be handy. The result was a popular and tasty dish that I have subsequently often cooked for other friends.

To cut down the fat, I first roast the eggplants in the oven, instead of frying them in the traditional Chinese way. This way, they don't absorb any oil. This step can be done hours in advance and the rest is a quick and easy stir-fry.

SERVES 4

1 lb (450 g) Chinese (see p. 16) or ordinary
  eggplants
1 lb (450 g) skinless, boneless chicken thighs
  or 2 lb (900 g) chicken thighs with bone in
1½ tablespoons peanut oil
2 tablespoons thinly sliced garlic
1 tablespoon finely chopped fresh gingerroot
3 tablespoons finely chopped green onions
1 tablespoon chili bean sauce
1 tablespoon hoisin sauce
2 teaspoons oyster sauce
2 teaspoons Shaoxing rice wine or dry sherry
1 teaspoon light soy sauce
1 teaspoon dark soy sauce
1 teaspoon sugar
Small handful of fresh mint leaves

FOR THE MARINADE

2 teaspoons light soy sauce
2 teaspoons Shaoxing rice wine or dry sherry
1 teaspoon sesame oil
2 teaspoons cornstarch

Preheat the oven to 400°F/200°C.

If you are using Chinese eggplants, roast them for 20 minutes and if you are using the large eggplants, roast them for about 30-40 minutes or until they are soft and cooked through. Leave them to cool. Peel them and if using larger eggplants cut them into chunks, then put them in a colander and let them drain for at least 30 minutes. This procedure can be done hours in advance.

If you are using unboned thighs, remove the skin and bones from the chicken thighs or have your butcher do it for you. Cut the chicken into 1 inch (2.5 cm) chunks and combine them in a bowl with the light soy sauce, Shaoxing rice wine or dry sherry, sesame oil and cornstarch.

Heat a wok or large frying pan until it is very hot, add the oil, then the chicken and stir-fry for 5 minutes. Remove the chicken from the wok and drain off all but 2 teaspoons of the oil or fat. Return the drained chicken to the wok with the garlic, gingerroot and green onions and stir-fry for 5 minutes. Then add the eggplants and all the remaining ingredients, except the mint leaves. Continue to cook for another 3 minutes, stirring from time to time, until the chicken is cooked. Add the mint leaves and give the mixture a good stir. Pour onto a warm platter and serve at once.

BRAISED GARLIC CHICKEN

The wok is a perfect cooking utensil for any type of cookery, not just Chinese or Asian. Its versatility is what makes it so universally popular. This recipe was inspired by a friend's mother from the south of France. Madame Taurines often braised veal with whole garlic. I have substituted chicken and added my own Chinese touches, which work just as well. Braised in this way, the whole garlic becomes mild and sweet. Most of the resulting sauce cooks off, leaving a tender, aromatic chicken dish, and the bonus is that it is quick to make. Serve this dish with potatoes or plain rice and another vegetable dish.

SERVES 4

2 lb (900 g) chicken thighs with bone in

2 teaspoons salt

1 teaspoon freshly ground black pepper

2 tablespoons all-purpose flour

3 tablespoons peanut oil

15 whole garlic cloves, unpeeled

2 tablespoons Shaoxing rice wine or dry sherry

1 tablespoon light soy sauce

3 tablespoons *Chicken Stock (see p. 56)* or water

FOR THE GARNISH

2 tablespoons finely snipped fresh chives

Blot the chicken thighs dry with a paper towel. Sprinkle them evenly with the salt and pepper, then sprinkle with the flour, shaking off any excess.

Heat a wok or large frying pan over a high heat until it is hot. Add the oil and, when it is very hot and slightly smoking, turn the heat to low. Add the chicken skin-side down and slowly brown on both sides for about 10 minutes. Drain off all the excess fat, add the garlic and stir-fry for 2 minutes. Then add the Shaoxing rice wine or dry sherry, soy sauce and stock or water. Turn the heat to as low as possible, cover and braise for 20 minutes until the chicken is tender.

When the chicken and garlic are cooked, remove them from the wok with a slotted spoon and place them on a warm platter. Sprinkle with the chives and serve at once.

LETTUCE-WRAPPED CHICKEN

This is my version of a popular Hong Kong dish that uses squab or young pigeon, which is expensive and not always as easily available as chicken.

A simple, savory dish that goes well with the refreshing crunch of the lettuce and the fried bean-thread (transparent) noodles, it is a fun dish to eat and makes a wonderful starter for any meal. Each guest puts a helping of each ingredient into a hollow lettuce leaf (rather like stuffing a crêpe) and eats the filled leaf with his or her fingers.

SERVES 4-6

1 lb (450 g) skinless, boneless chicken thighs, coarsely ground
8 oz (225 g) red or green bell pepper (about 1 large or 2 small)
½ oz (15 g) dried shiitake mushrooms
6 oz (175 g) fresh or canned (drained weight) water chestnuts
8 oz (225 g) iceberg lettuce
1¼ cups plus 1 tablespoon peanut oil
2 oz (50 g) beanthread (transparent) noodles
1 tablespoon finely chopped garlic
1 tablespoon finely chopped shallots
3 tablespoons finely chopped green onions
2 teaspoons dark soy sauce
2 teaspoons Shaoxing rice wine or dry sherry
3 tablespoons oyster sauce
½ teaspoon salt
½ teaspoon freshly ground black pepper

FOR THE MARINADE

1 tablespoon Shaoxing rice wine or dry sherry
1 tablespoon light soy sauce
2 teaspoons sesame oil
2 teaspoons cornstarch

TO SERVE

4 tablespoons hoisin sauce

The chicken can be cut by hand or pulsed in a food processor. Put the ground chicken into a bowl with the Shaoxing rice wine or dry sherry, soy sauce, sesame oil and cornstarch, mix well and leave to marinate for about 20 minutes.

Meanwhile cut the bell pepper into small dice. Soak the dried mushrooms in warm water for 20 minutes, drain them and squeeze out any excess liquid. Trim off the stems and coarsely chop the caps. If you are using fresh water chestnuts, peel and coarsely chop them. If you are using canned ones, rinse them in cold water and coarsely chop them. Separate and wash the lettuce leaves, wiping off any excess water, and set them aside.

In a large wok or deep-fat fryer, heat the 1¼ cups of oil until it is slightly smoking. Deep-fry the noodles until they are crisp and puffed up. Drain them on paper towels. (Drain off and reserve the oil, letting it cool; it can be saved for future use.)

Reheat the wok until it is very hot, then add 1 tablespoon of the oil in which you fried the noodles. When the oil begins to smoke, add the chicken and stir-fry for about 5 minutes. Remove the chicken and drain.

Wipe the wok or pan clean. Reheat the wok or pan over a high heat and, when it is hot, add the 1 tablespoon of fresh oil. When it is smoking slightly, add the garlic, shallots and green onions and stir-fry for 10 seconds. Then add the bell peppers and stir-fry for another minute.

Now add the mushrooms, water chestnuts, dark soy sauce, Shaoxing rice wine or dry sherry, oyster sauce, salt and pepper. Stir-fry the mixture for 3 minutes and then return the chicken to the mixture and continue to stir-fry for 1 minute, mixing well. Turn onto a warm platter. Arrange the lettuce and noodles on separate platters, put the hoisin sauce into a small bowl, and serve at once.

HONEYED CHICKEN WINGS

often think that chicken wings are a neglected and unglamorous food. Yet I find them one of the most delectable parts of the chicken. They are extremely versatile and quite economical. The Chinese especially love eating them because of their special taste. In this easy-to-make recipe, they are simply braised in a honey-soy mixture. Cooked in a large quantity, they can make an unusual party dish. Served at room temperature, they make wonderful picnic food.

SERVES 4

2 tablespoons peanut oil

1¾ lb (750 g) chicken wings

3 garlic cloves, crushed

1 inch (2.5 cm) thick piece fresh gingerroot, unpeeled and crushed

¼ cup dark soy sauce

2 tablespoons light soy sauce

2 tablespoons Shaoxing rice wine or dry sherry

2 tablespoons honey

Heat a wok or large frying pan over a high heat until it is hot. Add the oil and, when it is very hot and slightly smoking, add the chicken wings and stir-fry for 5 minutes or until they are brown. Remove them from the wok with a slotted spoon and drain on paper towels.

Drain off all the oil and fat and wipe the wok clean. Add the garlic, gingerroot, soy sauces, Shaoxing rice wine or dry sherry and honey and bring the mixture to a simmer. Return the chicken to this mixture. Reduce the heat to very low, cover and simmer for 30-35 minutes or until the chicken is cooked. Serve at once.

SPICY CHICKEN WITH MINT

The wok is ideal for making quick but tasty dishes. Here is a lovely, spicy chicken dish with fresh mint as a counterbalance. If you grow your own mint, it is likely to be even more delicate and subtle than the shop-bought variety. Mint is probably the most widely used of all the aromatic herbs and the one most readily accessible. A touch of curry is used with the chili bean sauce to give this dish a real kick. The chicken is "velveted" to preserve its juiciness and flavor. You can use the traditional oil method or, for a less fattening version, substitute water instead. The bell peppers provide the dish with a crunchy texture that makes a wonderful complement to the soft, tender chicken. Serve with plain steamed rice and a salad for a quick, delicious meal.

SERVES 4

1 lb (450 g) skinless, boneless chicken breasts

8 oz (225 g) red or green bell peppers

1¼ cups peanut oil or water

1 tablespoon peanut oil

1 tablespoon thinly sliced garlic

⅔ cup *Chicken Stock (see p. 56)*

1½ tablespoons Madras curry paste

2 teaspoons chili bean sauce

2 teaspoons sugar

1½ tablespoons Shaoxing rice wine or dry sherry

1 tablespoon light soy sauce

1 teaspoon cornstarch blended with 1 tablespoon water

8 fresh mint leaves

FOR THE MARINADE

1 egg white

1 teaspoon salt

2 teaspoons cornstarch

Cut the chicken breasts into 1 inch (2.5 cm) cubes. Combine them with the Marinade ingredients in a small bowl. Put the mixture into the refrigerator for 20 minutes.

Wash and seed the bell peppers and cut them into 1 inch (2.5 cm) cubes.

Heat a wok or frying pan over a high heat until it is hot, then add the 1¼ cups of oil. When the oil is very hot, remove the wok from the heat and immediately add the chicken pieces, stirring vigorously to keep them from sticking. When the chicken pieces turn white (about 2 minutes), quickly drain the chicken.

If you choose to use 1¼ cups of water instead of oil, bring the water to the boil in a pan. Remove the pan from the heat and immediately add the chicken pieces, stirring vigorously to keep them from sticking. When the chicken pieces turn white (about 2 minutes), quickly drain the chicken.

Wipe the wok or pan clean and reheat until it is very hot. Then add the 1 tablespoon of oil. When it is very hot, add the peppers and garlic and stir-fry for 2 minutes. Then add the rest of the ingredients, except the cornstarch mixture and mint leaves, and cook for another 2 minutes. Add the cornstarch mixture and cook for 20 seconds, stirring, then add the drained chicken to the wok and stir-fry for another 2 minutes, coating the chicken thoroughly with the sauce. Finally add the mint leaves and stir to mix well for 1 minute. Turn onto a warm platter and serve at once.

INDONESIAN-STYLE COCONUT CHICKEN

One of the great pleasures of visiting Indonesia is eating its rich and exotic foods. As in Chinese cuisine, the wok is widely used, but Indonesians also use spices and combinations distinctly un-Chinese. Like many nations in Southeast Asia, Indonesia has Chinese influences, but their unique culture makes their food different from that of China.

Here is a delicious recipe that I have adapted from my many visits to Jakarta. This dish reheats well and, served with rice, can easily make a hearty meal.

SERVES 4

2 lb (900 g) chicken thighs with bone in

2 teaspoons salt

1 teaspoon freshly ground black pepper

2 tablespoons all-purpose flour

3 tablespoons peanut oil

6 oz (175 g) onions, thinly sliced

5 garlic cloves, crushed

1 tablespoon finely chopped fresh gingerroot

1 teaspoon ground cumin

2 teaspoons ground coriander

2 tablespoons grated lemon zest

1 tablespoon light soy sauce

3 tablespoons water

2 teaspoons salt

1 (14 fl oz) (400 ml) can coconut milk

Blot the chicken dry with paper towels. Sprinkle evenly with the salt and pepper, then sprinkle with the flour, shaking off any excess.

Heat a wok or large frying pan over a high heat until it is hot. Add the oil and, when it is very hot and slightly smoking, turn the heat to low. Add the chicken skin-side–down and slowly brown on both sides. Remove the chicken and drain on paper towels.

Drain off all but 1 tablespoon of the oil and fat. Then add the onions, garlic and gingerroot and stir-fry for 3 minutes. Then add the cumin, coriander, lemon zest, soy sauce, water, salt and coconut milk. Return the chicken to the sauce, turn the heat to as low as possible, cover and braise for 20 minutes until the chicken is cooked. Transfer to a warm platter and serve at once.

BURMESE-STYLE CHICKEN

Although I have never been to Burma, I have visited a number of Burmese restaurants that have opened in California. The food seems to be a cross between Chinese-Vietnamese and Thai. It is an aromatic and fragrant style of cooking that uses spices to coax flavors from foods.

Here I have adapted a favorite Burmese chicken dish I have enjoyed. It is a dry-braised dish that is slowly cooked in spices and its own juices. It is again easy to make and delicious to eat. Serve it with plain rice and another vegetable dish for a wholesome meal.

SERVES 4

2 lb (900 g) chicken thighs with bone in

2 teaspoons salt

1 teaspoon freshly ground black pepper

2 stalks fresh lemon grass

3 tablespoons peanut oil

1 small onion, thinly sliced

6 garlic cloves, crushed

1 tablespoon finely chopped fresh gingerroot

1 teaspoon ground turmeric

1 teaspoon chili powder

1 tablespoon light soy sauce

3 tablespoons water

Blot the chicken dry with paper towels. Sprinkle evenly with the salt and pepper.

Peel the lemon grass to reveal the tender, whitish center, crush the stalk and cut into 3 inch (7.5 cm) pieces.

Heat a wok or large frying pan over a high heat until it is hot. Add the oil and, when it is very hot and slightly smoking, turn the heat to low. Add the chicken skin-side–down and slowly brown on both sides. Remove the chicken and drain on paper towels.

Drain off all but 1 tablespoon of the oil and fat. Then add the onions, garlic, gingerroot and lemon grass and stir-fry for 3 minutes. Then add the turmeric, chili powder, soy sauce and water. Return the chicken to the wok and stir-fry to coat with this mixture. Turn the heat to as low as possible, cover and braise for 20 minutes until the chicken is cooked. Transfer to a warm platter and serve at once.

BALINESE-STYLE CHICKEN

B*ali is not only known for its exotic culture but also for its earthy foods. I remember on my first visit many years ago how impressed I was at the diversity of Balinese cooking. Many of their dishes are simmered or roasted. Here is one of my favorites. It is simple to make and reheats easily. Serve it with plain rice and vegetables for a complete meal.*

SERVES 4

2 lb (900 g) chicken thighs with bone in

2 teaspoons salt

1 teaspoon freshly ground black pepper

2 tablespoons all-purpose flour

3 tablespoons peanut oil

8 oz (225 g) onions, coarsely chopped

5 garlic cloves, crushed

1 tablespoon finely chopped fresh gingerroot

3 fresh red or green chilies, seeded and
  chopped

2 teaspoons sugar

1 tablespoon lemon juice

2 tablespoons orange juice

1 tablespoon dark soy sauce

1 (14 fl oz) (400 ml) can coconut milk

Blot the chicken dry with paper towels. Sprinkle evenly with the salt and pepper. Then sprinkle with the flour, shaking off any excess.

Heat a wok or large frying pan over a high heat until it is hot. Add the oil and, when it is very hot and slightly smoking, turn the heat to low. Add the chicken skin-side–down and slowly brown on both sides. Remove the chicken and drain on paper towels.

Drain off all but 1 tablespoon of the oil and fat. Then add the onions, garlic, gingerroot and chilies and stir-fry for 3 minutes. Then add the sugar, lemon juice, orange juice, soy sauce and coconut milk. Return the chicken to the sauce, turn the heat as low as possible, cover and braise for 20 minutes until the chicken is cooked. Transfer to a warm platter and serve at once.

DELECTABLE BROCCOLI CHICKEN

*C*hicken and broccoli are a wonderful combination. In this Vietnamese-inspired recipe, the chicken is first marinated, then fried. Then it is paired with crunchy green broccoli. In Vietnam, Chinese broccoli, which is slightly more woody and bitter, would be used. But here I use the variety found in the West, which is sweeter with a distinctive, mild flavor. Chicken thighs are used because of their robust taste which holds up well to the frying. Serve this dish with rice and another vegetable dish for a wholesome meal.

SERVES 4

1 lb (450 g) fresh broccoli
1 lb (450 g) boneless, skinless chicken thighs
1¼ cups plus 1 tablespoon peanut oil
3 tablespoons coarsely chopped garlic
1 small onion, quartered
2 tablespoons Shaoxing rice wine or dry sherry
3 tablespoons water or *Chicken Stock (see p. 56)*
8 oz (225 g) tomatoes, quartered
3 tablespoons oyster sauce
2 tablespoons Thai fish sauce
1 teaspoon sugar
1 teaspoon salt
½ teaspoon freshly ground black pepper
2 teaspoons sesame oil

FOR THE MARINADE

½ teaspoon freshly ground black pepper
1 tablespoon Thai fish sauce
1 teaspoon light soy sauce
Cornstarch, for dusting

Separate the broccoli heads into small florets and peel and slice the stems. Blanch the broccoli pieces in a large pan of boiling salted water for several minutes, then immerse them in cold water. Drain thoroughly.

Cut the chicken into 1 inch (2.5 cm) pieces and combine them with the pepper, fish sauce and light soy sauce. Mix well and leave to marinate for 30 minutes. Dust the chicken pieces with cornstarch, shaking off any excess.

Heat a wok or large frying pan over a high heat until it is hot. Add the 1¼ cups of oil and, when it is very hot and slightly smoking, deep-fry the chicken pieces for 8 minutes or until they are golden brown. Remove them with a slotted spoon and drain on paper towels. You may have to do this in two or more batches.

Drain off all the oil. Reheat the wok and add the 1 tablespoon of oil. When it is hot, add the garlic and onion and stir-fry for 1 minute. Then add the blanched broccoli and continue to stir-fry for 1 minute. Add the Shaoxing rice wine or dry sherry and water or stock and continue to stir-fry at a moderate to a high heat for 4 minutes until the broccoli is thoroughly heated through. Add the tomatoes, oyster sauce, fish sauce, sugar, salt, pepper and sesame oil and continue to stir-fry for 30 seconds, then add the drained chicken and stir-fry for 2 minutes or until the chicken is thoroughly heated through. Transfer to a warm platter and serve at once.

VIETNAMESE-STYLE LEMON GRASS CHICKEN

Lemon grass is a tropical grass (Cymbopogon citratus) *native to southern India and Sri Lanka, yielding an aromatic oil used as flavoring and in perfumery and medicine. It appears often in Vietnamese dishes, giving them a wonderful citrus aroma.*

I especially like its use with chicken, and here is a Vietnamese-inspired recipe that is redolent with lemon grass. It is a tasty dish that is relatively easy to make. Instead of using a whole chicken, I use chicken thighs, which I feel are tastier and easier to handle.

SERVES 4

1 lb (450 g) boneless, skinless chicken thighs
   or 2 lb (900 g) chicken thighs with bone in
1 tablespoon peanut oil
6 oz (175 g) onions, thinly sliced
6 garlic cloves, crushed
1 tablespoon finely chopped fresh gingerroot
2 red or green chilies, seeded and coarsely
   chopped
2 teaspoon sugar
1 cup coarsely chopped roasted peanuts
1 tablespoon Thai fish sauce

FOR THE MARINADE

5 stalks fresh lemon grass
1 teaspoon salt
½ teaspoon freshly ground black pepper
3 tablespoons finely chopped green onions

Blot the chicken dry with paper towels. If you are using unboned thighs, remove the skin and bones from the chicken thighs or have your butcher do it for you. Cut the chicken into 1 inch (2.5 cm) pieces.

Peel the lemon grass to reveal the tender, whitish center, crush the stalk and cut it into 3 inch (7.5 cm) pieces.

In a large bowl, combine the chicken with the lemon grass, salt, pepper and green onions and leave to marinate at room temperature for 45 minutes.

Heat a wok or large frying pan over a high heat until it is hot. Add the oil and, when it is very hot and slightly smoking, turn the heat to low. Add the chicken together with the marinade ingredients and stir-fry for 5 minutes. Then add the onions, garlic, gingerroot and chilies and continue to stir-fry for 10 minutes. Add the sugar and peanuts and continue to stir-fry for 2 minutes. Finally, add the fish sauce and continue to stir-fry for 2 minutes, mixing all the ingredients well. Transfer the contents of the wok to a warm platter and serve at once.

PINEAPPLE CHICKEN

This might be called "nouvelle Hong Kong" or "Southeast Asia meets Hong Kong." It is an exotic and unlikely combination. I have eaten this dish several times in Hong Kong and found it delicious every time. The acidic sweetness and texture of the pineapple works extremely well with the delicate taste of the chicken. The pineapple is cooked very quickly, just enough to warm it through.

SERVES 4

1 lb (450 g) boneless, skinless chicken breasts, cut into 1 inch (2.5 cm) pieces

2½ cups peanut oil or water

2 teaspoons peanut oil

1 tablespoon finely chopped fresh gingerroot

1 tablespoon thinly sliced garlic

1½ tablespoons Shaoxing rice wine or dry sherry

1 teaspoon salt

1 teaspoon sesame oil

12 oz (350 g) small pineapple, peeled and cut into 1 inch (2.5 cm) cubes

FOR THE MARINADE

1 egg white

1 teaspoon sesame oil

2 teaspoons cornstarch

1 teaspoon salt

½ teaspoon freshly ground white pepper

FOR THE GARNISH

1 tablespoon finely chopped fresh cilantro

Combine the chicken with the egg white, sesame oil, cornstarch, salt and pepper in a bowl. Mix well and chill for about 20 minutes.

Heat a wok until it is very hot and then add the oil. When the oil is very hot, remove the wok from the heat and immediately add the chicken pieces, stirring vigorously to keep them from sticking. When the chicken pieces turn white (after about 2 minutes), quickly drain the chicken.

If you choose to use water instead of oil, bring it to a boil in a pan. Remove the pan from the heat and immediately add the chicken pieces, stirring vigorously to keep them from sticking. When the chicken pieces turn white (about 2 minutes), quickly drain the chicken.

Add the 2 teaspoons of oil to the wok and reheat. Add the gingerroot and garlic and stir-fry for 30 seconds. Then add the Shaoxing rice wine or dry sherry, salt, sesame oil and pineapple cubes. Gently stir-fry for 2 minutes or until the pineapple is heated through. Add the drained chicken and stir gently to mix well. Turn onto a warm platter, garnish with the cilantro and serve at once.

VIETNAMESE-STYLE CHICKEN CURRY

*L*ike other cuisines of Southeast Asia, Vietnamese cooking is highly perfumed with herbs such as lemon grass and purple basil. Hot chilies and aromatic gingerroot are also some of the essentials shared. Curry powder, as well as rich coconut milk, is also used. However, the light influence of China is also evident, Vietnamese curry dishes are slightly lighter and more delicate than Indian dishes.

In this fragrant dish, the chicken is marinated in a curry paste, then stir-fried with vegetables. It is delicious and goes perfectly with plain rice.

SERVES 4

1 lb (450 g) boneless, skinless chicken thighs

2 tablespoons peanut oil

2 onions, cut into eighths

1¼ cups *Chicken Stock (see p. 56)*

1 (14 fl oz) (400 ml) can coconut milk

4 fresh tomatoes, cut into quarters

FOR THE MARINADE

2 stalks fresh lemon grass

4 whole garlic cloves

2 red or green chilies, seeded and chopped

2 teaspoons sugar

1 tablespoon Madras curry paste

2 tablespoons Madras curry powder

1 teaspoon salt

½ teaspoon freshly ground black pepper

3 tablespoons Thai fish sauce

1 tablespoon water

FOR THE GARNISH

Handful of sprigs of fresh cilantro

Cut the chicken into about 2 inch (5 cm) chunks.

Peel the lemon grass stalk to reveal the tender, whitish center and crush it with the flat of a knife. Then cut it into small chunks. In a food processor, combine the garlic, chilies, sugar, curry paste, curry powder, salt, pepper, fish sauce and water and blend to a paste. Mix this with the lemon grass and chicken pieces, and stir until all the pieces are thoroughly coated. Leave the chicken to marinate for about 1 hour at room temperature.

Heat a wok or large frying pan over a high heat until it is hot. Add the oil and, when it is very hot and slightly smoking, turn the heat to moderate, add the chicken and stir-fry for 5 minutes or until the chicken begins to brown. Add the onions and stir-fry for 3 minutes. Add the stock and coconut milk. Bring the mixture to a simmer, reduce the heat and simmer uncovered for 10 minutes. Then add the tomatoes, stir well and continue to cook for another 2 minutes. Transfer the contents to a bowl. Garnish with cilantro and serve.

LEMON GRASS CHICKEN WITH CHILI

*T*he use of lemon grass with chili can transform any ordinary chicken into a special treat. The aromatic oils from the lemon grass when used as a marinade and later cooked, give the dish a wonderful citrus scent as well as a subtle taste. Here it is paired with chili powder or flakes for an explosive combination you are sure to enjoy. This dish reheats well and goes with plain rice.

SERVES 4

1 lb (450 g) boneless, skinless chicken thighs

1 tablespoon peanut oil

2 teaspoons Thai fish sauce

1 teaspoon sugar

1 teaspoon dried chili powder or flakes

FOR THE MARINADE

2 stalks fresh lemon grass

2 tablespoons coarsely chopped garlic

½ teaspoon freshly ground black pepper

2 tablespoons Thai fish sauce

2 teaspoons sugar

Cut the chicken into 1 inch (2.5 cm) pieces.

Peel the lemon grass stalk to reveal the tender, whitish center and crush it with the flat of a knife. Then cut it into 3 inch (7.5 cm) pieces.

In a large bowl, combine the chicken with the lemon grass, garlic, pepper, fish sauce and sugar. Leave it to marinate at room temperature for 40 minutes.

Heat a wok or large frying pan over a high heat until it is hot. Add the oil and, when it is very hot and slightly smoking, add the chicken pieces and the marinade ingredients and stir-fry for 5 minutes or until the chicken is golden brown. Remove the chicken from the wok with a slotted spoon and drain.

Drain off all the oil and fat and reheat the wok, without wiping. When it is hot, return the chicken to the wok, add the fish sauce, sugar and chili powder or flakes. Continue to stir-fry for 3 minutes. Serve at once.

THAI-STYLE GINGER CHICKEN

This Thai-inspired recipe is an extremely close relative of a Chinese recipe. Contrary to what most people think, not all Thai dishes have chilies and are spicy. Many of the Thais who have Chinese ancestry come from southern China and their cooking reflects their roots. That is, subtle cooking with nuances, rather than the strong, assertive flavors of chilies that characterize much of Thai cooking. This dish is delicious with plain rice.

SERVES 4

1 lb (450 g) boneless, skinless chicken thighs

½ oz (12 g) Chinese dried wood ears

1 tablespoon peanut oil

1 small onion, cut into 8 wedges

2 tablespoons coarsely chopped garlic

4 tablespoons finely shredded fresh
  gingerroot

1 tablespoon yellow bean sauce

2 teaspoons sugar

1 teaspoon salt

2 tablespoons Shaoxing rice wine or dry
  sherry

FOR THE MARINADE

2 teaspoons light soy sauce

1 teaspoon dark soy sauce

1 tablespoon Shaoxing rice wine or dry
  sherry

½ teaspoon salt

½ teaspoon freshly ground black pepper

1 teaspoon sesame oil

2 teaspoons cornstarch

FOR THE GARNISH

3 tablespoons finely shredded green onions

Cut the chicken into 2 inch (5 cm) chunks. Mix the soy sauces, Shaoxing rice wine or dry sherry, salt, pepper and sesame oil and pour it over the chicken. Then mix in the cornstarch until all the chicken pieces are thoroughly coated. Leave the chicken to marinate for about 30 minutes, then drain the chicken and discard the marinade.

Soak the dried wood ears for about 20 minutes until soft. Rinse the wood ears in cold water, cut off any hard bits and finely shred them.

Heat a wok or large frying pan over a high heat until it is hot. Add the oil and, when it is very hot and slightly smoking, add the chicken and stir-fry for 5 minutes or until the chicken begins to brown. Remove the chicken and drain. Pour off all but 1 tablespoon of oil from the wok. Add the onion, garlic, gingerroot and wood ears and stir-fry for 1 minute. Then add the bean sauce, sugar and salt and continue to stir-fry for 30 seconds. Return the chicken to the wok and continue to stir-fry for 4 minutes. Finally, add the Shaoxing rice wine or dry sherry and continue to stir-fry for 2 minutes or until the chicken is cooked. Garnish with green onions and serve.

BRAISED DUCK WITH CHESTNUTS

*C*hestnuts have been discovered in tombs dating back to the earliest part of China's recorded history, and are still used fresh and dried in China, as well as in Japan. In China, they are mainly used with braised dishes. Dried chestnuts can be found already peeled in Chinese grocers or supermarkets. They are delicious and actually easier to use than the fresh ones. Soak them overnight, then simmer them for an hour before using them.

This classic duck recipe reheats very well. It makes a wonderful, hearty meal especially in cool weather. Serve it with rice and another vegetable dish.

SERVES 4-6

6 oz (175 g) dried or fresh chestnuts
3½-4 lb (1.6-1.8 kg) duck, fresh or frozen
   (preferably a white Pekin duck)
5 cups peanut oil

FOR THE SAUCE

7½ cups *Chicken Stock (see p.56)* or water
2½ cups dark soy sauce
1¼ cups light soy sauce
1¾ cups Shaoxing rice wine or
   equal quantities dry sherry and *Chicken*
   Stock (see p.56)
½ cup rock sugar
5 whole star anise
3 pieces Chinese cinnamon bark or cinnamon
   sticks
6 green onions
3 slices fresh gingerroot
5 garlic cloves, crushed

FOR THE GARNISH

A few sprigs of fresh cilantro

If you are using dried chestnuts, soak them in warm water overnight. Cook the soaked chestnuts in hot water for 1 hour. If you are using fresh chestnuts, peel them.

Cut the duck in half lengthwise. Dry the halves thoroughly with paper towels. Heat the oil in a wok or large frying pan until it is almost smoking, then deep-fry the 2 halves of the duck, skin-side–down. Turn the heat to medium and continue to fry slowly until the skin is browned. This should take about 15-20 minutes. Do not turn the pieces over but baste the duck as it fries. Drain the lightly browned duck on paper towels.

Combine all the sauce ingredients together in a large pan and bring the mixture to a boil. Add the duck halves and chestnuts and turn the heat down to a simmer. Cover the pan and slowly braise the duck for 1 hour or until it is tender.

Skim off the large amount of surface fat which will be left when the duck is cooked. This procedure will prevent the duck from becoming greasy. Now remove the duck pieces with a slotted spoon. Let them cool and then chop them into smaller pieces. Arrange on a warm platter, garnish with the fresh cilantro and serve at once.

Alternatively, you can let the duck cool thoroughly and serve it at room temperature. Once the sauce has cooled, remove any lingering surface fat. Now the sauce can be frozen and re-used to braise duck or chicken.

AROMATIC FRIED CHICKEN

One of the best fried chicken I have ever eaten was in a Vietnamese restaurant. The chicken had been marinated in an exotic mixture of fish sauce, lime juice, garlic, chili and sugar. It was then simply tossed in flour and slowly fried. It was absolutely delicious and, with simple steamed rice as a accompaniment, made a memorable meal. A salad or vegetable dish would also complement it nicely.

SERVES 4

2 lb (900 g) chicken thighs with bone in

3 tablespoons peanut oil

FOR THE MARINADE

2 teaspoons salt

1 teaspoon freshly ground black pepper

6 garlic cloves, peeled

5 tablespoons Thai fish sauce

5 tablespoons white Shaoxing rice wine vinegar or cider vinegar

2 fresh red or green chilies, seeded and chopped

1 tablespoon sugar

2 tablespoons lime juice

3 tablespoons chopped shallots

1 tablespoon light soy sauce

1 tablespoon Shoaxing rice wine or dry sherry

All-purpose flour, for dusting

Blot the chicken dry with paper towels.

In a blender, mix the salt, pepper, garlic, fish sauce, vinegar, chilies, sugar, lime juice, shallots, soy sauce and Shaoxing rice wine or dry sherry. Rub this mixture evenly over the thighs and leave to marinate for 1 hour at room temperature. Drain off any excess marinade.

Dust the chicken with flour and shake off any excess. Heat a wok or large frying pan over a high heat until it is hot. Add the oil and, when it is very hot and slightly smoking, turn the heat to low. Add the chicken skin-side-down and slowly brown over a moderately low heat for 10 minutes on each side or until the chicken is cooked. Remove the chicken from the wok, drain on paper towels, then transfer to a warm platter and serve at once.

STRANGE-TASTE STIR-FRIED EGGS

The term "strange-taste" is one I have often wondered about. It is of Szechuan origin and is regularly applied to fragrant Szechuan fish recipes. Given the rather warm climate and lack of refrigeration in the area, I wonder if something other than the cook's imaginative use of seasonings may have generated the strange taste!

Be that as it may, the food is delicious and I am willing to accept the traditional explanation that it is popularly known as "strange-taste" because it incorporates so many flavors, being hot, spicy, sour, sweet and salty all at the same time. Here the ingredients are used to enliven pork and combined with eggs to make a simple but delicious dish that goes superbly with rice.

SERVES 3-4

2 cups ground pork

2 teaspoons light soy sauce

2 teaspoons Shaoxing rice wine or dry sherry

2 teaspoons sesame oil

1 teaspoon cornstarch

6 eggs, beaten

½ teaspoon salt

2 tablespoons peanut oil

FOR THE SAUCE

2 teaspoons dark soy sauce

2 teaspoons Chinese black rice vinegar or cider vinegar

2 teaspoons chili bean sauce

2 teaspoons sesame oil

2 teaspoons sugar

1 tablespoon Shaoxing rice wine or dry sherry

1 teaspoon roasted Szechuan peppercorns (see p.24)

1½ tablespoons finely chopped green onions

FOR THE GARNISH

1 tablespoon finely chopped green onion tops

Combine the pork with the light soy sauce, Shaoxing rice wine or dry sherry, 1 teaspoon of sesame oil and the cornstarch in a small bowl. In another small bowl, combine the eggs with the salt and remaining sesame oil.

Heat a wok until it is very hot and then add 1 tablespoon of the peanut oil. When the oil is very hot and slightly smoking, add the pork and stir-fry for 1 minute. Add the sauce ingredients and cook with the pork for 3 minutes. Remove the pork and sauce and set it aside.

Wipe the wok clean and reheat it and, when it is hot, add the remaining peanut oil. Immediately, add the eggs and stir-fry until they are barely set. Then return the pork and sauce to the eggs and mix well. Continue to stir-fry for 2 minutes. Transfer to a warm platter and serve at once, sprinkling the green onion tops over to garnish.

CANTONESE-STYLE CHICKEN WINGS WITH OYSTERS

A thrifty, economical dish my mother use to make which I still love today is this one of chicken wings simmered in a rich oyster sauce. It is extremely easy to make and reheats quite well. In fact, the chicken wings are also tasty served cold and terrific for picnics.

SERVES 4

1½ lb (675 g) chicken wings
3¾ cups peanut oil

FOR THE MARINADE

1 tablespoon light soy sauce
1 tablespoon Shaoxing rice wine or dry sherry
2 teaspoons sesame oil
½ teaspoon salt
¼ teaspoon freshly ground black pepper
2 teaspoons cornstarch

FOR THE SAUCE

1 tablespoon peanut oil
3 garlic cloves, crushed
1 inch (2.5 cm) thick piece fresh gingerroot, unpeeled and crushed
3 tablespoons oyster sauce
1 tablespoon light soy sauce
2 tablespoons Shaoxing rice wine or dry sherry
2½ cups *Chicken Stock (see p.56)* or *Vegetable Stock (see p.60)*

In a large bowl, combine the wings with the marinade ingredients and mix well. Leave to sit in the marinade for at least 30 minutes.

Heat a wok or large frying pan over a high heat until it is hot. Add the oil and, when it is very hot and slightly smoking, add the chicken wings and fry them for 5 minutes or until they are golden brown. Remove them from the wok with a slotted spoon and drain on paper towels. You may have to do this in several batches.

Drain off all the oil and fat and wipe the wok clean, then make the sauce. Reheat the wok until it is very hot, then add 1 tablespoon of oil. Add the garlic and gingerroot and stir-fry for 30 seconds. Then add the oyster sauce, soy sauce, Shaoxing rice wine or dry sherry and stock and bring the mixture to a simmer.

Return the chicken to the wok. Reduce the heat to very low, cover and simmer for 30-35 minutes or until the chicken is very tender. Remove the wings with a slotted spoon to a warm platter. Turn up the heat and boil to reduce the sauce until it is slightly thick. Pour this over the chicken and serve at once.

VEGETABLES

Perhaps no other food is more associated with the wok than vegetables. In fact, stir-fried vegetables are almost synonymous with the wok.

The idea of stir-frying vegetables is what generated the initial popularity of the wok in the West more than 20 years ago. In those early days of over-cooked, boiled, soggy, bland vegetables, the idea of stir-fried vegetables full of color, flavor and crunchiness came as a revelation. The wok took home kitchens by storm and many adults and children discovered how wonderful fresh vegetables could taste for the first time.

Today, stir-frying vegetables in the wok is almost as normal as sautéing a piece of steak. This chapter utilizes the wok in every way possible to cook vegetables. Though it is not all strictly vegetarian, there are many wok recipes here to satisfy the vegetarian.

Most of the vegetable recipes are meant to accompany other dishes, but you will find a few main-course vegetable dishes, like the Savory Stuffed Tomatoes *or* Rainbow Vegetables with Curry.

These vegetable recipes are, in the main, simple and extremely easy to make in the wok.

EAST-WEST FRIES

The wok is perfect for making potato fries, or chips as they are known in other parts of the world. Its round, concave shape makes it ideal for deep-frying without wasting any oil.

The secret to making good fries lies in the cooking technique. First, chill the cut potatoes for several hours. This allows the natural starch to set so that when the fries hit the hot oil, they do not act like sponges and become greasy. They must then be dried thoroughly so they are without a trace of moisture. Then use the double-frying technique. The first quick-fry cooks them, then, after letting the fries drain and allowing the oil in the wok to regain the frying point, put the fries in for the second quick-fry. They cook to a crisp and golden perfection.

I then toss the fries in a tasty mix of salt, cayenne, five-spice powder and crushed Szechuan peppercorns. These fries are marvelous with grilled foods and as a snack they are unbeatable. They are a perfect vegetarian dish.

SERVES 4

1¾ lb (750 g) potatoes
3¾ cups peanut oil

FOR THE SEASONING MIXTURE

2 teaspoons salt
½ teaspoon cayenne pepper
½ teaspoon five-spice powder
½ teaspoon whole Szechuan peppercorns,
   roasted (see p. 24) and finely ground
½ teaspoon freshly ground black pepper

Peel and cut the potatoes into strips about 3 inches x ½ inch (7.5 cm x 5 mm). Put the strips into a large bowl, cover with cold water and chill for 2 hours or overnight.

Combine the ingredients for the seasoning mixture in a small bowl and set aside. Drain the potatoes in a colander, then spin them dry in a salad spinner or pat them dry with paper towels. The potatoes should be as dry as possible for the best results.

Heat a wok or large frying pan over a high heat until it is hot. Add the oil and, when it is very hot and slightly smoking, fry half of the potatoes for 8 minutes. Remove the potatoes with a slotted spoon and drain in a colander; then fry the second batch.

When you are ready to serve them, reheat the oil until it is very hot. Fry half of the potatoes until they are crispy and golden brown. Remove and drain well on paper towels. Reheat the oil until it is very hot, fry the other half and drain. Transfer the potatoes to a warm platter, toss with the seasoning mix and serve at once.

QUICK AND EASY NOODLE AND BEAN SPROUT SALAD

Northern Chinese love to have small side dishes accompanying their more elaborate meals. Such dishes serve as refreshing interludes between the main courses. They are easily prepared in advance and most often served at room temperature.

But many of these side dishes are excellent when served as components of simpler meals. Here is a basic bean sprout salad that I first enjoyed a few years ago at a friend's home in Beijing. It is a wonderful dish to serve with grilled meats on a warm summer evening.

SERVES 4

1 oz (25 g) beanthread (transparent) noodles

1 lb (450 g) fresh bean sprouts

3 tablespoons white rice vinegar

1 teaspoon salt

1 teaspoon sugar

2 teaspoons sesame oil

1 green onion, finely shredded on the
 diagonal

Soak the noodles in a large bowl of warm water for 15 minutes. When soft, drain and discard the water. Cut them into 3 inch (7.5 cm) lengths using scissors or a knife. Pick over the bean sprouts, discarding any brown ones. Blanch them for 1 minute in a wok filled with boiling water. Drain well and place in a bowl.

In a small bowl, combine the vinegar, salt, sugar and sesame oil. Toss the bean sprouts with this mixture while they are still warm. Mix in the beanthread noodles and green onion. Chill for at least 30 minutes before serving.

SIMPLE BEIJING-STYLE MARINATED CUCUMBER SALAD

My good friend, Lillian Robyn, is originally from Beijing. Now married to an American and living in the United States, she still cooks in the Beijing style. A meal in her home is always a special treat for me. I have often enjoyed this refreshing salad at her home. It can be prepared hours ahead and is thus perfect for multicourse meals or simply by itself with hot rice.

SERVES 4

1¾ lb (750 g) cucumbers

2 teaspoons salt

1 tablespoon chili bean sauce

1 teaspoon light soy sauce

1 teaspoon sugar

½ teaspoon chili oil

2 teaspoons sesame oil

Cut the unpeeled cucumbers into 1 inch (2.5 cm) slices, sprinkle with salt and put them into a colander to drain for 20 minutes. Squeeze the cucumber slices in a linen dish towel to remove any moisture. Blot them dry with paper towels.

In a small bowl, mix the chili bean sauce, soy sauce, sugar, chili oil and sesame oil. Toss the cucumber slices in this sauce and let them sit in the refrigerator overnight. Drain off any excess moisture before serving.

RAINBOW VEGETABLES WITH CURRY

M ild curry dishes with vegetables are popular in Hong Kong. The particular spices in curry add an exotic taste that is quite a change from the usual garlic and/or ginger seasonings most commonly used in Chinese cookery. This assortment of differently colored vegetables (hence the name) is usually served at banquets. But there is no need to wait for a special occasion to enjoy such a vegetarian taste treat.

SERVES 4

8 oz (225 g) Chinese or Napa cabbage

8 oz (225 g) Chinese greens, such as Chinese flowering cabbage or bok choy

8 oz (225 g) carrots

8 oz (225 g) asparagus

FOR THE SAUCE

1 tablespoon peanut oil

2 tablespoons finely chopped shallots

1½ tablespoons Madras curry paste

1¼ cups canned coconut milk

2 teaspoons sugar

2 teaspoons salt

1 tablespoon Shaoxing rice wine or dry sherry

2 teaspoons sesame oil

Cut the cabbage into 1½ inch (4 cm) strips. Then cut the Chinese greens into 1½ inch (4 cm) pieces. Peel and cut the carrots into 1½ inch (4 cm) x ½ inch (5 mm) segments. Cut the asparagus into 1½ inch (4 cm) pieces.

In a large pan of boiling salted water, blanch the leaves for about 5 minutes. Remove them with a slotted spoon and drain thoroughly. Then blanch the Chinese greens for 3 minutes in the same water. Remove and drain. Now blanch the carrots for 5 minutes and the asparagus for 3 minutes. Remove and drain thoroughly. Arrange the blanched vegetables on a warm serving platter.

Heat a wok or large frying pan over a high heat until it is hot. Add the oil and, when it is very hot and slightly smoking, add the shallots and stir-fry for 1 minute. Then add the curry paste and coconut milk. Bring the mixture to a boil and add the sugar, salt and Shaoxing rice wine or dry sherry. Stir to mix well. Finally, add the sesame oil. Pour the sauce over the platter of vegetables and serve at once.

STIR-FRIED LETTUCE WITH SAVORY BACON

Stir-fried lettuce always sounds a bit strange to Western ears, but once you realize that there are few things that cannot be cooked in the wok, you understand everything. The intense heat of the wok stir-frying technique means quick cooking. This preserves the nutritional content as well as the taste and texture of almost any vegetable. Indeed, as in this recipe, contact with the wok imparts a gentle smoky flavor to the food. Thus, we turn inexpensive and prosaic iceberg lettuce into a surprisingly tasty dish. The savory bacon gives the lettuce an added flavor, but omit the bacon and you have a fine vegetarian dish.

SERVES 4 AS A SIDE DISH

6 oz (175 g) bacon
1¾ lb (750 g) iceberg lettuce
2 tablespoons peanut oil
1 teaspoon light soy sauce
1 teaspoon dark soy sauce
½ teaspoon sugar
½ teaspoon salt
½ teaspoon freshly ground black pepper
2 teaspoons Shaoxing rice wine or dry sherry
2 teaspoons sesame oil

Cut the bacon into thin shreds widthwise. Heat a wok or large frying pan over a high heat until it is hot. Turn the heat to low, add the bacon and cook until it is brown and crispy. Remove with a slotted spoon and drain well on paper towels.

Separate the lettuce leaves and tear all the large leaves in half.

Heat a wok or large frying pan over a high heat until it is hot. Add the oil and, when it is very hot and slightly smoking, add the lettuce leaves and stir-fry for 1 minute. Then add the rest of the ingredients except the sesame oil and continue to stir-fry for 1 minute. Finally, stir in the sesame oil. Remove the lettuce leaves with a slotted spoon with some of the sauce and arrange on a warm serving dish. Garnish with the bacon and serve at once.

BROCCOLI IN FRAGRANT WINE SAUCE

Broccoli is a vegetable of sturdy character. It has a rich color and a distinctive taste and texture that allows it to be paired with strong seasonings and flavors — for example, the ginger and Shaoxing rice wine of this dish. The recipe is of Shanghai origin. The justly famous yellow Shaoxing wine is produced in that region of China and quite understandably it has attained a prominent place in Shanghai cuisine. This is a quick, easy and fragrant wok dish that can serve as a perfect side dish or as a main vegetarian treat.

SERVES 4

450 g (1 lb) fresh broccoli

1½ tablespoons peanut oil

2 tablespoons finely shredded fresh
   gingerroot

1 teaspoon salt

½ teaspoon sugar

½ teaspoon freshly ground black pepper

5 tablespoons Shaoxing rice wine or dry
   sherry

2 teaspoons sesame oil

Separate the broccoli heads into small florets, then peel and slice the stems. Blanch the broccoli pieces in a large pan of boiling salted water for 3 minutes and then immerse them in cold water. Drain thoroughly.

Heat a wok or large frying pan over a high heat until it is hot. Add the oil and, when it is very hot and slightly smoking, add the ginger shreds, salt, sugar and pepper and stir-fry for a few seconds. Add the blanched broccoli. Add the Shaoxing rice wine or dry sherry and continue to stir-fry over a moderate to a high heat for 4 minutes until the broccoli is thoroughly heated through. Add the sesame oil and to stir-fry for another 30 seconds. Transfer to a warm plate and serve at once.

BRAISED CHINESE RADISH WITH CHILI

*C*hinese white radish, sometimes called mooli, deserves a greater role in cookery than it usually receives. Its central virtue is its ability to absorb the flavors of other ingredients. This results in a very satisfying and tasty vegetable dish that stands on its own and is also an excellent companion to other dishes. It is easy to make — again, the wok does its magic — and reheats nicely. If you use water instead of stock, the result is an ideal vegetarian dish.

SERVES 2-4

1¾ lb (750 g) Chinese white radish (mooli)

1 tablespoon peanut oil

2 dried red chilies

3 tablespoons finely chopped green onions

1 teaspoon salt

1 tablespoon yellow bean paste

1 teaspoon chili bean sauce

2 teaspoons sugar

2 teaspoons dark soy sauce

⅔ cup Shaoxing rice wine or dry sherry

⅔ cup water or *Chicken Stock (see p.56)*

2 teaspoons sesame oil

Peel the radish and cut it at a slight diagonal into 1 inch (2.5 cm) thick slices.

Heat a wok or large frying pan over a high heat until it is hot. Add the oil and, when it is very hot and slightly smoking, add the chilies and stir-fry for 30 seconds. Add the green onions and radish and continue to stir-fry for 1 minute. Then add the rest of the ingredients, except the sesame oil. Bring the mixture to a boil, lower the heat, cover and simmer for 30 minutes or until the radish is soft and tender.

Add the sesame oil, turn the heat up to high and rapidly reduce the liquid until most of it has evaporated. Transfer to a warm platter and serve at once.

HONG KONG-STYLE BROCCOLI AND BABY CORN

Creative innovation is a virtue in Hong Kong cuisine and chefs there are quick to adopt non-traditional vegetables into their repertoire. In this case, we find broccoli, flown in fresh daily from California, and baby corn, flown in from Thailand. Put them together with traditional Chinese seasonings and flavorings and you have a colorful and nutritious blending of East and West, and so easy to prepare in your wok and serve as a side dish. If you use the dark soy sauce instead of the oyster sauce, it would make this dish a perfect one for vegetarians.

SERVES 4

1 lb (450 g) fresh broccoli

8 oz (225 g) fresh baby corn

2 oz (50 g) dried shiitake mushrooms

1½ tablespoons peanut oil

1 teaspoon salt

½ teaspoon freshly ground black pepper

1 teaspoon sugar

1 tablespoon Shaoxing rice wine or dry sherry

1 tablespoon light soy sauce

3 tablespoons oyster sauce or dark soy sauce

2 teaspoons sesame oil

Separate the broccoli heads into small florets, then peel and slice the stems. Blanch the broccoli pieces and baby corn in a large pan of boiling salted water for 3 minutes and then immerse them in cold water. Drain thoroughly.

Soak the mushrooms in warm water for 20 minutes. Drain them and squeeze out the excess liquid. Remove and discard the stems and finely shred the caps into thin strips.

Heat a wok or large frying pan over a high heat until it is hot. Add the oil and, when it is very hot and slightly smoking, add the broccoli, corn and mushrooms and stir-fry for 3 minutes. Add the salt, pepper, sugar, Shaoxing rice wine or dry sherry, soy sauce and oyster sauce or dark soy sauce and continue to stir-fry at a moderate to a high heat for 2 minutes until the vegetables are thoroughly heated through. Add the sesame oil and continue to stir-fry for 30 seconds. Transfer to a warm platter and serve at once.

BRAISED SHIITAKE MUSHROOM TOFU CASSEROLE

I first tasted this vegetarian dish while visiting a Daoist temple in China. The rich and flavorful mushrooms impart their smoky tang to the deep-fried tofu, while the various spices and sauces add delightful dimensions. It is a typically vegetarian way to experience simple but memorable pleasures — and so easy to prepare. The "wok master" in the temple handled his wok in a way that was poetry in action, but we can all prepare this dish. If you use water instead of stock, the dish is quite suitable for vegetarians.

SERVES 4

2 oz (50 g) dried shiitake mushrooms

4 oz (100 g) button mushrooms

8 oz (225 g) firm fresh tofu

2 cups peanut oil

3 tablespoons finely chopped green onions

1 tablespoon coarsely chopped garlic

1 tablespoon light soy sauce

2 teaspoons dark soy sauce

1 tablespoon Shaoxing rice wine or dry sherry

2 teaspoons sugar

1 teaspoon chili bean sauce

½ teaspoon freshly ground black pepper

¼ cup *Chicken Stock (see p.56)* or water

Soak the mushrooms in warm water for 20 minutes. Drain them and squeeze out the excess liquid. Remove and discard the stems and finely shred the caps into thin strips.

Wash and slice the button mushrooms.

Cut the tofu into 1 inch (2.5 cm) cubes. Drain on paper towels for 10 minutes.

Heat a wok or large frying pan over a high heat until it is hot. Add the oil and, when it is very hot and slightly smoking, deep-fry the tofu cubes in batches. Drain each batch on paper towels. Drain off all but 1½ tablespoons of the oil. When the tofu is cool enough, slice each cube in half.

Reheat the wok or large frying pan with the reserved oil over a high heat until it is hot. When it is very hot and slightly smoking, add the green onions and garlic and stir-fry for 30 seconds. Add all the mushrooms and stir-fry for 2 minutes, mixing them well. Then add the soy sauces, Shaoxing rice wine or dry sherry, sugar, chili bean sauce, pepper and stock or water. Turn the heat down and cook for 5 minutes, stirring continuously, until the fresh mushrooms are thoroughly cooked. Add the tofu and continue to cook for 2 minutes. Turn the heat back to high and continue to cook until most of the liquid has been evaporated. Transfer to a warm platter and serve at once.

BRAISED CHINESE OR NAPA CABBAGE WITH BEAN SPROUTS Ⓥ

Chinese cuisine is justifiably famous for its vegetable cookery and for its vegetarian sub-cuisines. In its long history, Chinese cuisine has always given vegetables pride of place. This means, of course, that vegetables are treated with care and discernment. Only the most appropriate cooking techniques are employed and only the most congenial flavorings are added. Here is a traditional and very economical recipe using Chinese or Napa cabbage and nutritious crunchy bean sprouts. Delicious, and it is so easily prepared and cooked.

SERVES 4

1¾ lb (750 g) Chinese or Napa cabbage

8 oz (225 g) fresh bean sprouts

1½ tablespoons peanut oil

2 tablespoons finely shredded fresh
   gingerroot

2 tablespoons dark soy sauce

1 tablespoon light soy sauce

2 teaspoons sugar

½ teaspoon salt

½ teaspoon freshly ground black pepper

⅔ cup *Vegetable Stock (see p.60)*

2 teaspoons sesame oil

Cut the cabbage into 2 inch (5 cm) wide strips. Trim and discard any brown ends from the bean sprouts.

Heat a wok or large frying pan over a high heat until it is hot. Add the oil and, when it is very hot and slightly smoking, add the gingerroot and stir-fry for 10 seconds. Add the cabbage and stir-fry for 30 seconds. Add the soy sauces, sugar, salt and pepper and continue to stir-fry for 1 minute. Add the stock and cook for 10 minutes. Finally, add the bean sprouts and stir-fry for 2 minutes. Stir in the sesame oil, transfer to a warm platter and serve at once.

EASY SNOW PEAS AND SWEET WATER CHESTNUTS

*S*now peas is the apt French name for these delicious, small, crisp, sweet early peas which can indeed be completely consumed as they are, right out of the garden. I recommend only that you trim their ends and delicate strings. Paired with the sweet crunchiness of the fresh water chestnuts, and with the shiitake mushrooms adding a contrasting texture and distinct flavor, the snow peas make a refreshing change to ordinary peas, carrots, onions and whatever. With your wok, it takes but minutes to cook and, as a side dish, it nicely complements any meat or chicken.

SERVES 4

8 oz (225 g) fresh or canned (drained weight) water chestnuts

2 oz (50 g) dried shiitake mushrooms

1 tablespoon peanut oil

3 tablespoons finely chopped green onions

8 oz (225 g) snow peas, trimmed

1 tablespoon light soy sauce

1 tablespoon Shaoxing rice wine or dry sherry

2 tablespoons dark soy sauce

1 teaspoon salt

½ teaspoon freshly ground black pepper

1 teaspoon sugar

3 tablespoons water

2 teaspoons sesame oil

If you are using fresh water chestnuts, peel them. If you are using canned water chestnuts, drain them well and rinse in cold water. Thinly slice the water chestnuts. Soak the mushrooms in warm water for 20 minutes. Drain them and squeeze out the excess liquid. Remove and discard the stems and finely shred the caps into thin strips.

Heat a wok or large frying pan over a high heat until it is hot. Add the oil and, when it is very hot and slightly smoking, add the green onions and stir-fry for 10 seconds. Add the snow peas, mushrooms and fresh water chestnuts if you are using them and stir-fry for 1 minute. Make sure you coat them thoroughly with the oil. Add the rest of the ingredients, except the sesame oil, and continue to stir-fry for another 3 minutes. If you are using canned water chestnuts, add these now and cook for a final 2 minutes or until the vegetables are cooked. Stir in the sesame oil, transfer to a warm platter and serve at once.

STIR-FRIED CELERY IN TWO-BEAN SAUCE

*C*elery *is a much-neglected vegetable in my opinion. It is used in stocks, chopped and added to salads or simply used as a filler. I love its distinctive taste and flavor and often use it as a main vegetable by itself, simply stir-fried. It should be still be crunchy, which is part of its attraction. This is an easy dish to make and is a wonderful accompaniment to any meal.*

SERVES 4

1¾ lb (750 g) celery (about 1 head)

1 tablespoon peanut oil

1 teaspoon sesame oil

2 tablespoons thinly sliced garlic

3 tablespoons Shaoxing rice wine or dry sherry

2 teaspoons yellow bean sauce

2 teaspoons chili bean sauce

3 tablespoons water

Remove the stalks of the celery and rinse thoroughly under cold running water. String the tough outer stalks of celery with a paring knife. Chop the celery stalks and leaves across into 1 inch (2.5 cm) pieces.

Heat a wok or large frying pan over a high heat until it is hot. Add the oils, and when they are very hot and slightly smoking, add the garlic and celery and stir-fry for 2 minutes. Then add the Shaoxing rice wine or dry sherry, bean sauces and water and continue to stir-fry for 5 minutes or until the celery is thoroughly cooked. Transfer to a warm dish and serve at once.

SPINACH WITH FRIED GARLIC

*T*his *recipe, inspired by one of the best Chinese restaurants in London, Fung Shing, is a delicious but simple method for cooking spinach. The garlic is slowly fried, removed and then the spinach is cooked in the same oil. The garlic is then added just as a crispy aromatic garnish. It is very simple to prepare and may be served hot or cold.*

SERVES 4

1¾ lb (750 g) fresh spinach

1½ tablespoons peanut oil

1 teaspoon salt

2 tablespoons thinly sliced garlic

1 teaspoon sugar

Wash the spinach thoroughly. Remove all the stems, leaving just the leaves.

Heat a wok or large frying pan over a high heat until it is hot. Add the oil and reduce the heat to moderate. Add the salt and garlic and slowly stir-fry for 2 minutes or until the garlic is golden brown and crisp. Remove the garlic with a slotted spoon and drain on paper towels. Then add the spinach. Stir-fry for about 2 minutes to coat the spinach leaves thoroughly with the oil and salt. When the spinach warm plate and pour off any excess liquid. Sprinkle with the fried garlic. Serve either hot or cold.

STIR-FRIED ZUCCHINI WITH FRESH CHILI

Zucchini are economical and abundantly available. A quick stir in the wok and this easy side vegetable dish can be prepared in minutes, or it can be a delicious vegetarian treat. Here I add fresh chilies to give them a lift. These vegetables can be watery depending on size; I recommend the smaller ones.

SERVES 4

1¾ lb (750 g) zucchini
1 tablespoon peanut oil
2 tablespoons thinly sliced garlic
1 tablespoon finely chopped fresh gingerroot
2 tablespoons finely chopped green onions
4 fresh red or green chilies, seeded and finely
   shredded
1 teaspoon salt
½ teaspoon freshly ground black pepper
2 teaspoons sugar
3 tablespoons water
2 teaspoons sesame oil

Diagonally slice the zucchini into ¼ inch (5 mm) rounds.

Heat a wok or large frying pan over a high heat until it is hot. Add the oil and, when it is very hot and slightly smoking, add the garlic, gingerroot, green onions and chilies and stir-fry for about 30 seconds. Then add the zucchini, salt, pepper and sugar and stir for another 30 seconds until they are well coated with the spices and flavorings. Add the water and continue to stir-fry over a high heat for 5 minutes until most of the water has evaporated and the zucchini are cooked. At this point, add the sesame oil, transfer to a warm dish and serve immediately.

RICH EGGPLANT WITH TOMATO AND BASIL

This savory treat combines two of my favorite vegetables, eggplants and tomatoes. The smaller, long, thin Chinese eggplants are preferable to the thicker European variety because of their slightly sweeter and milder taste. However, you may use the European type. Leave the skins of the eggplants on as they enhance the texture of the dish.

Normally, such a dish is oven-baked but because many Chinese homes lack modern stoves, the wok is used instead. It is, in practice, the perfect utensil for preparing this Italian-inspired dish. It can be served hot or at room temperature, and is delicious as a vegetarian plate or as a wonderful accompaniment to grilled meats.

SERVES 4

1 lb (450 g) Chinese (see p. 16) or ordinary eggplants

8 oz (225 g) fresh or canned tomatoes

5 tablespoons extra-virgin olive oil

5 garlic cloves, peeled and crushed

2 teaspoons salt

½ teaspoon freshly ground black pepper

2 teaspoons sugar

3 tablespoons finely chopped fresh basil leaves

1 tablespoon lemon juice

Trim the eggplants and cut them on the diagonal into 2 inch x ½ inch (5 cm x 12 mm) slices.

If you are using fresh tomatoes, plunge them into a large pan of boiling water for a few seconds, removing them with a slotted spoon. Then peel, seed and cut them into 1 inch (2.5 cm) chunks. If you are using canned tomatoes, chop them into small chunks.

Heat a wok or large frying pan over a high heat until it is hot. Add the oil and, when it is moderately hot, add the garlic and stir-fry for 30 seconds. Then add the eggplant slices, salt and pepper and continue to stir-fry for 2 minutes.

Add the tomatoes and sugar to the eggplant and continue to cook for 5 minutes. Turn the heat to low, cover and cook slowly for 15 minutes until the eggplant is quite tender. Stir in the basil leaves and lemon juice and give the mixture several good stirs. Transfer to a warm platter and serve at once or leave to cool and serve at room temperature.

STIR-FRIED SPICY BROCCOLI

think we need to look again at ways in which to cook this nutritious and delectable vegetable. All too often it is simply boiled to death, which is so unappealing. Stir-frying it with spices transforms it into a special treat. Served warm or at room temperature, it makes a lovely side dish or part of a vegetarian feast.

SERVES 4

1 lb (450 g) fresh broccoli

1½ tablespoons peanut oil

2 tablespoons garlic, coarsely chopped

1 teaspoon salt

½ teaspoon freshly ground black pepper

2 tablespoons Shaoxing rice wine or dry sherry

1 tablespoon chili bean sauce

1 teaspoon sugar

4-5 tablespoons water

2 teaspoons sesame oil

Separate the broccoli heads into small florets and peel and slice the stems. Blanch the broccoli pieces in a large pan of boiling salted water for several minutes, then immerse them in cold water. Drain thoroughly.

Heat a wok or large frying pan over a high heat until it is hot. Add the oil and, when it is very hot and slightly smoking, add the garlic, salt, pepper, Shaoxing rice wine or dry sherry, chili bean sauce and sugar. Stir-fry for a few seconds and then add the blanched broccoli. Add a few tablespoons of water. Stir-fry over a moderate to a high heat for 4 minutes until the broccoli is thoroughly heated through. Add the sesame oil and continue to stir-fry for 30 seconds. The broccoli is now ready to serve.

SESAME TOFU

ofu is not only nutritious but can be delicious if it is cooked properly. The Japanese are skilled at turning this seemingly bland food into a tasty dish. This Japanese-inspired recipe is simple to make and fun to eat. The tofu is fried and then served with a dipping sauce. It makes a terrific vegetarian dish.

SERVES 4

1 lb (450 g) soft tofu

5 tablespoons all-purpose flour

2 eggs, beaten

5 tablespoons roasted sesame seeds

6 tablespoons peanut oil

Drain the tofu thoroughly, then place it on paper towels and continue to drain for 15 minutes.

Gently cut the tofu into 1 inch (2.5 cm) pieces. Sprinkle the tofu evenly with the flour, then dip it in the beaten egg and sprinkle with the sesame seeds.

Heat the oil in a wok until it is moderately hot, then gently add the tofu and allow it to

4 tablespoons Japanese mirin rice wine
4 tablespoons Japanese rice vinegar
¼ cup light soy sauce
½ teaspoon freshly ground black pepper
2 teaspoons sugar

brown slowly without burning. Turn over and cook the other side. Drain well on paper towels. You may have to do this in several batches.

Mix the sauce ingredients together. When the tofu is cooked, arrange on a warm platter with the sauce and serve at once.

CRISPY TOFU WITH TOMATOES

ofu is a protein-rich food coagulated from an extract of soybeans and when it is not properly prepared, it can be quite bland and boring. However, it is simple to turn this food into something special and delicious. This is an easy dish to make, especially when tomatoes are in season. If you use water instead of the chicken stock, you can turn this into a delectable vegetarian dish.

SERVES 2-4

1 lb (450 g) firm fresh tofu
1 lb (450 g) fresh or canned tomatoes
2 cups peanut oil
2 tablespoons coarsely chopped garlic
3 tablespoons thinly sliced shallots
1 tablespoon light soy sauce
1 teaspoon salt
½ teaspoon freshly ground black pepper
2 teaspoons sugar
⅔ cup *Chicken Stock (see p.56)* or water

FOR THE GARNISH

Handful of sprigs of fresh cilantro

Drain the tofu thoroughly, then set it on paper towels and continue to drain for 15 minutes. Gently cut the tofu into 1 inch (2.5 cm) pieces.

If you are using fresh tomatoes, plunge them in boiling water for 10 seconds, drain them, peel, seed and cut them into 1 inch (2.5 cm) cubes. If you are using canned tomatoes, chop them into small chunks.

Heat the oil in a wok until it is hot and deep-fry the tofu in batches. When each batch is lightly browned, remove and drain well on paper towels.

Drain off all but 1 tablespoon of the oil, reheat and when it is hot, add the garlic and shallots and stir-fry for 30 seconds. Then add the tomatoes, soy sauce, salt, pepper and sugar and stir-fry for 1 minute. Now add the stock or water, reduce the heat and simmer for 5 minutes. Return the tofu to the wok and heat through. Transfer to a warm platter, garnish with cilantro and serve at once.

SAVORY STUFFED TOMATOES

When visiting family friends in the south of France, I always look forward to eating stuffed tomatoes. Mme Taurines seasons her dish with abundant garlic and Provençal herbs. It is so aromatic that you can smell it down the street. It is served with plain rice and a simple salad. A bonus is that it can be made in advance and reheated with no noticeable deterioration in the quality of the dish. Here is my East-West version of her delectable dish.

SERVES 4-6

6 large tomatoes

1 oz (25 g) dried shiitake mushrooms

2 tablespoons peanut oil

3 tablespoons coarsely chopped garlic

3 tablespoons finely chopped shallots

3 tablespoons finely chopped green onions

2 teaspoons finely chopped fresh gingerroot

3 cups ground pork

2 teaspoons salt

½ teaspoon freshly ground black pepper

1 teaspoon sugar

1 tablespoon light soy sauce

1 tablespoon Shaoxing rice wine or dry
  sherry

1 teaspoon sesame oil

1 egg white, beaten

⅔ cup *Chicken Stock (see p. 56)* or water

3 tablespoons oyster sauce

2 teaspoons sugar

Cut a small slice off the top of each tomato, with the dimple in the center. Using a spoon, gently scoop out the pulp of the tomato. Strain the pulp and reserve the liquid, which will be used to moisten the filling. Blot the insides of the tomatoes with paper towels.

Soak the mushrooms in warm water for 20 minutes. Then drain them and squeeze out the excess liquid. Remove and discard the stems and finely chop the caps.

Heat a wok or large frying pan over a high heat until it is hot. Add 1 tablespoon of the oil, and, when it is very hot and slightly smoking, add the garlic, shallots, green onions and gingerroot and stir-fry for 1 minute. Remove and leave the mixture to cool thoroughly. In a large bowl, combine the pork with the mushrooms, salt, pepper, sugar, soy sauce, Shaoxing rice wine or dry sherry, sesame oil and egg white. Mix well and add the stir-fried garlic mixture. Stuff the mixture into the tomatoes.

Wipe the wok or pan clean and reheat over a high heat. When it is hot, add the remaining 1 tablespoon of oil and turn the heat down to moderate. Brown the tomatoes, filling side down. This should take about 5 minutes. Then gently turn the tomatoes and cook for another 3 minutes. Add the stock or water, oyster sauce, sugar and the reserved tomato juice from the pulp. Bring the mixture to a simmer, turn the heat to low, cover and cook for 15-20 minutes or until the stuffing in the tomatoes is cooked thoroughly. Gently transfer to a warm platter and serve at once.

SWEET AND SOUR ONIONS

*T*he wok is ideal for preparing this delicious vegetable recipe. These sweet and sour onions are a simple food that can proudly complement any main course. The onions are stir-fried in the wok, then left to cool in the sauce. The result is a delicious relish for any meats or fish. Or it can be served as part of a tasty vegetarian meal. Try to get the red onions which are sometimes a bit sweeter.

SERVES 4-6

1 lb (450 g) red or yellow onions
1 tablespoon peanut oil
2 tablespoons coarsely chopped garlic
½ teaspoon salt
1 tablespoon dark soy sauce
2 tablespoons black or red rice vinegar
2 tablespoons sugar

Cut the onions into 1 inch (2.5 cm) thick slices.

Heat a wok or large frying pan over a high heat until it is hot. Add the oil and, when it is very hot and slightly smoking, add the garlic and stir-fry for 20 seconds, then add the salt and onions. Continue to stir-fry for 1 minute. Now add the soy sauce, vinegar and sugar and continue to cook for 3 minutes, until it is well mixed. Turn the mixture onto a platter, let it cool and then chill for at least 1 hour so that it is well chilled before serving.

SIMPLE STIR-FRIED MUSHROOMS

*T*he wok is perfect for making quick and easy dishes that are also very tasty and satisfying. Here is one of my favorites, always reliable fare when I am in a hurry but want an enjoyable treat. It is quick, easy and economical. Stir-frying them in the wok leaves the mushrooms slightly firm with a wonderful texture: nothing mushy about them. I like to leave them whole which makes their preparation even easier.

SERVES 2-4

1 tablespoon peanut oil
1 lb (450 g) fresh button mushrooms
1 teaspoon salt
2 teaspoons Shaoxing rice wine or dry sherry
2 teaspoons light soy sauce
1 teaspoon sugar
⅔ cup water
2 teaspoons sesame oil

Heat a wok or large frying pan over a high heat until it is hot. Add the oil and, when it is very hot and slightly smoking, add the mushrooms and salt and stir-fry them for 1 minute. Then add the Shaoxing rice wine or dry sherry, soy sauce, sugar and water and continue stir-frying for 5 minutes or until the mushroom liquid has been reabsorbed by the mushrooms or evaporates. Finally, add the sesame oil, give the mushrooms a few stirs and serve at once.

RED-COOKED SMOKY BRAISED MUSHROOMS

All mushrooms are not equal in taste or texture. Chinese dried or shiitake mushrooms have a rich, smoky flavor and they most readily absorb all the seasonings and flavors of the juices in which they have been braised.

Here is a luscious vegetarian dish which is easy to make and unlocks the special taste and deep aromas of these mushrooms. The sugar in this recipe adds a nice dimension and gives the mushrooms a wonderful sheen. This dish is easy to make and reheats well, which makes it ideal for multicourse entertaining. It also pairs well with other vegetable dishes. Chinese dried or shiitake mushrooms can be bought at Chinese grocers and some supermarkets but if you can't get them, this recipe is almost as delicious made entirely with fresh ones.

SERVES 2-4

2 oz (50 g) Chinese dried or shiitake
   mushrooms

Boiling water

1 tablespoon peanut oil

1½ tablespoons Shaoxing rice wine or dry
   sherry

2 tablespoons dark soy sauce

1 tablespoon rock sugar or ordinary sugar

Pick through the mushrooms and choose the largest and best-looking ones. Soak the mushrooms in just enough boiling water to cover them for 30 minutes and then drain them well through a fine sieve. Keep the mushroom soaking liquid. Let it settle and pour off most of the liquid, leaving any sand at the bottom. Save 1¼ cups of the liquid and set it aside. Squeeze out any excess liquid from the mushrooms through the sieve and add to the rest of the mushroom liquid. Remove the tough stems and leave the caps whole.

Heat a wok or large frying pan over a high heat until it is hot. Add the oil and, when it is very hot and slightly smoking, add the mushrooms and stir-fry for 15 seconds. Now add the Shaoxing rice wine or dry sherry, soy sauce, sugar and reserved mushroom soaking liquid. Reduce the heat to a simmer and cook for 10 minutes until most of the liquid has been reduced. Serve at once or leave it to cool and reheat when ready to serve.

STEAMED EGGPLANTS WITH RED PEPPERCORNS

Chinese cooks rarely steam vegetables, preferring either to blanch them quickly in hot, lightly salted water or to stir-fry them quickly in the wok. However, eggplants do lend themselves to steaming. They are rarely baked, as most Chinese homes lack ovens, but steaming them whole and then covering them with a tasty sauce is not only easy but also a very nutritious way of enjoying eggplants. Steaming brings out the subtle taste and texture of the eggplants, which have enough robustness to stand up to an assertive sauce. Try to get the Chinese variety if you can; you will find them slightly sweeter. This is a most enjoyable vegetarian recipe.

SERVES 4

1 lb (450 g) Chinese (see p. 16) or ordinary
  eggplants

1½ tablespoons peanut oil

3 tablespoons coarsely chopped garlic

1½ tablespoons finely chopped fresh
  gingerroot

3 tablespoons finely chopped green onions,
  white part only

2 tablespoons light soy sauce

1 tablespoon sugar

1 tablespoon Chinese black vinegar or cider
  vinegar

2 teaspoons Szechuan peppercorns (see
  p. 24), roasted and ground

1 tablespoon sesame oil

FOR THE GARNISH

2 tablespoons chopped green green onion
  tops

If you are using the Chinese eggplants, leave them whole. If you are using the ordinary large variety, trim and cut them in half and score them on the skin side by cutting diagonal crosswise indentations.

Next, set up a steamer or put a rack into a wok or deep pan and fill it with 2 inches (5 cm) of water. Bring the water to the boil over a high heat. Put the eggplants on to a heatproof plate and carefully lower it into the steamer or onto the rack. Turn the heat to low and cover the wok or pan tightly. Steam gently for 30-40 minutes or until the eggplants are very soft to the touch. Remove from the wok and keep in a warm place. Clean out the wok and wipe it dry.

Heat a wok or large frying pan over a high heat until it is hot. Add the oil and, when it is very hot and slightly smoking, add the garlic and stir-fry for 30 seconds, then add the gingerroot and green onions and continue to stir-fry for 1 minute. Add the rest of the ingredients. Turn the heat down and cook, uncovered, for 2 minutes and pour the sauce over the eggplants. Garnish with the chopped green onion tops and serve at once.

STIR-FRIED CARROTS AND PARSNIPS

The wok adapts itself to the needs of all vegetables: soft, hard, dry, leafy, moist, sliced or diced. Carrots and parsnips have a natural sweetness that the wok preserves and that makes them enjoyable by themselves and wonderful company for meat or poultry.

SERVES 4

1 lb (450 g) carrots
1 lb (450 g) parsnips
1½ tablespoons peanut oil
2 garlic cloves, crushed
2 teaspoons finely chopped fresh gingerroot
1 teaspoon salt
½ teaspoon freshly ground black pepper
1 tablespoon light soy sauce
1 tablespoon sugar
⅔ cup water

FOR THE GARNISH

2 tablespoons finely chopped fresh cilantro

Peel and roll-cut the carrots and parsnips by cutting a diagonal slice at one end, then rolling it halfway before making the next diagonal slice.

Heat a wok or large frying pan over a high heat until it is hot. Add the oil and, when it is very hot and slightly smoking, add the garlic and ginger and stir-fry for 10 seconds. Add the carrots and parsnips and stir-fry for 1 minute. Then add the salt, pepper, soy sauce, sugar and water. Cover and cook over a high heat for 8 minutes or until all the vegetables are tender. There should be very little sauce left. Turn onto a warm platter, garnish with the cilantro and serve at once.

ZESTY ONION AND PEAS

Green peas can be extraordinarily full of taste when picked fresh from the garden. However, with today's busy lifestyle, frozen small peas can be a great alternative. With modern freezing techniques and the wok, you can easily whip up a lovely vegetarian side dish for your table in a matter of minutes. Just don't overcook this or any other vegetable.

SERVES 2-4

8 oz (225 g) red onions, peeled
1 tablespoon peanut oil
1¼ cups frozen petits pois (peas)
1 teaspoon salt
½ teaspoon freshly ground black pepper
3 tablespoons water
2 teaspoons sesame oil

Cut the onions in half, then into 1 inch (2.5 cm) slices.

Heat a wok or large frying pan over a high heat until it is hot. Add the oil and, when it is very hot and slightly smoking, add the onions and stir-fry for 2 minutes until they become slightly soft. Then add the peas, salt, pepper and water and continue to stir-fry for 2 minutes. Finally stir in the sesame oil and give the mixture several good turns. Transfer to a serving dish and serve at once.

Stir-fried Carrots and Parsnips

COCONUT VEGETABLE STEW

This is an adaptation of a popular Thai standard. I learned it from my good friend, Chalie Amatyakul, who founded the Thai Cooking School at The Oriental in Bangkok. It is a simple dish that can easily be done in the wok. There is a secret, however: do not add all the vegetables at once. As in the technique of stir-frying, with stewing, different vegetables require different cooking times. When the cooking times are carefully observed, the whole dish comes out perfectly done.

SERVES 4

2 (14 fl oz) (400 ml) cans coconut milk

2 teaspoons salt

½ teaspoon freshly ground black pepper

1 tablespoon Thai fish sauce

4 oz (100 g) fresh baby corn

6 oz (175 g) Chinese Napa cabbage, shredded

6 oz (175 g) string or runner beans, trimmed

4 oz (100 g) bamboo shoots, shredded

6 oz (175 g) spinach leaves, washed

Bring the coconut milk to a simmer in the wok. Add the salt, pepper and fish sauce. Add the corn and cabbage, cover and simmer for 3 minutes. Then add the beans, cover and simmer for another 3 minutes. Finally, add the bamboo shoots and spinach leaves and cook for another 2 minutes, uncovered. Transfer to a warm dish and serve immediately.

MUSHROOM TOFU

This is a superb vegetarian dish that is simple to make and delicious to eat. Shiitake mushrooms, with their intriguing smoky flavors, are braised with tofu, which readily absorbs the seasonings and the essence of the mushrooms. An unusual and very nutritious treat. This dish also reheats well which makes it ideal for entertaining.

SERVES 4

4 oz (100 g) dried shiitake mushrooms

2½ cups boiling water

1 lb (450 g) firm fresh tofu

1½ tablespoons peanut oil

3 tablespoons finely shredded green onions

1½ tablespoons finely shredded fresh
   gingerroot

1½ tablespoons Shaoxing rice wine or dry
   sherry

Soak the mushrooms in the boiling water for 30 minutes, then drain well through a fine sieve. Keep the mushroom soaking liquid. Let it settle and pour off most of the liquid, leaving any sand at the bottom. Squeeze out any excess liquid from the mushrooms through the sieve and add to the reserved mushroom liquid. Remove the tough stems and finely shred the caps. Cut the tofu into 1 inch (2.5 cm) cubes.

Heat a wok or large frying pan over a high heat until it is hot. Add the oil and, when it is

2 tablespoons dark soy sauce

1 teaspoon salt

½ teaspoon freshly ground black pepper

1 teaspoon sugar

1 tablespoon sesame oil

very hot and slightly smoking, add the green onions and gingerroot and stir-fry for 15 seconds. Add the Shaoxing rice wine or dry sherry, soy sauce, salt, pepper and sugar. Then add the mushroom caps, tofu cubes and the reserved mushroom soaking liquid. Reduce the heat to a simmer, cover and cook for 15 minutes. Add more liquid if needed.

Return the heat to high and continue to cook until most of the liquid has been reduced. Add the sesame oil and turn the mixture gently several times to mix well. Transfer to a serving dish and serve at once or leave it to cool and reheat when ready to serve.

THAI-STYLE CAULIFLOWER

T*his is a Thai-inspired way to cook cauliflower. The flavors are assertive, which is fine as the cauliflower is a sturdy vegetable. This dish is tasty enough to serve as a main course by itself.*

SERVES 4

1¾ lb (750 g) cauliflower

1 tablespoon peanut oil

4 garlic cloves, crushed

2 tablespoons seeded and finely shredded fresh red chili

3 tablespoons finely shredded green onions

2 tablespoons finely chopped fresh cilantro

1 tablespoon light soy sauce

1 teaspoon dark soy sauce

1 teaspoon salt

1 teaspoon sugar

½ teaspoon turmeric

2 cups water

2 teaspoons sesame oil

Cut the cauliflower into small florets.

Heat a wok or large frying pan over a high heat until it is hot. Add the oil and, when it is very hot and slightly smoking, add the garlic, chili and green onions. Stir-fry for about 20 seconds to flavor the oil. Quickly add the cauliflower florets and stir-fry them for 1 minute. Next add the fresh cilantro, soy sauces, salt, sugar, turmeric and water. Turn the heat down, cover and simmer for 10 minutes or until the cauliflower is tender. Stir in the sesame oil and turn onto a warm serving platter and serve at once.

HEALTHY TOFU WITH BROCCOLI

*Although tofu is a very nutritious food, on its own it is naturally quite bland in taste.
But, most emphatically, it does not have to remain bland. Here it is paired with some assertive
spices and robustly flavored broccoli for a colorful vegetable dish that is anything but bland. It may
serve as a main course or an alternative vegetable side dish.*

SERVES 4

1 lb (450 g) fresh broccoli

1 lb (450 g) firm fresh tofu

1¼ cups peanut oil

1 teaspoon salt

½ teaspoon freshly ground black pepper

2 tablespoons coarsely chopped garlic

3 tablespoons thinly sliced shallots

1 tablespoon Shaoxing rice wine or dry
  sherry

1 tablespoon light soy sauce

2 tablespoons dark soy sauce

2 teaspoons sugar

3 tablespoons water

1 tablespoon sesame oil

Separate the broccoli heads into small florets;
then peel and slice the stems. Blanch the broccoli pieces in a large pan of boiling salted water
for 3 minutes and then immerse them in cold
water. Drain thoroughly. Drain the tofu thoroughly, then set it on paper towels and continue to drain for 15 minutes. Gently cut the
tofu into 1 inch (2.5 cm) pieces.

Heat the oil in a wok until it is hot and deep-fry the tofu in two batches. When each batch is
lightly browned, remove and drain it well on
paper towels.

Drain off all but 1 tablespoon of the oil from
the wok. Reheat the wok and, when it is hot,
add the salt, pepper, garlic and shallots and stir-fry for 30 seconds. Then add the broccoli,
Shaoxing rice wine or dry sherry, soy sauces,
and sugar and stir-fry for 1 minute. Now add
the water, cover, reduce the heat and simmer
for 5 minutes. Return the tofu to the wok and
heat through. Add the sesame oil, transfer to a
warm serving dish and serve at once.

bistro and hung
...ci's Delight." I had
...ich recipe books
...ones.
...t the restaurant,
...y as I had left them.
...nstead of four, the
..., and the early morn-
...ere was no bread. I
...ling of being needed,
...coat. I would solve the
...e the calls to find
...sense of smug self sat-
...t they were without me? See how I
...? I was enjoying my warm little
...ce right up until I opened the freez-
...nearly bare. Where was the food? I
...e house and questioned the waiters.
...got on the phone with Brian, another
...nt, who told me that the owner had
...e last delivery bill so they refused to
...got paid. As I was trying to wrap my
...enormous problem, the tardy hostess

...hie, what fabulous delight do you have
...welve top?" The hostess asked.
...e me. Do you not see that I am on the
...with a serious problem?" I glared at her.
...rry! Geeez." she said. "What bug bit your

...e to go, Brian. See if you can find the boss
...one and call me back. Thanks. " I hung up
...h Sandra.
...u don't seem to understand. We have less
...the stock we usually have and I was trying to
...with Tim and... Did you say twelve top?" My
...g open in shock.
...es, fancy party or something. One of the
...uld be here soon. She wanted to go over the
...s the word "details" hung in the air between
...IT door swung in and a tall slender woman
...in. Both Sandra and I stared at her like a
...eadlights.
..."Excuse me. I am looking for the head chef. I am
...y Strickland and I have reserved the private
...r an important luncheon and I simply must speak
...head chef to arrange the aperitifs." She stood in her
...nt suit and waited for us to bow or curtsy or reply
...hething. I have never been in charge completely.
...woman looked like she might collapse if she did not
...the queen of Siam, and soon. So I stepped forward.
..."I am Sophie. How can I help you?" I reached
...hand out to shake hers. She looked at it like it was a

dead fish before grinning a tight-lipped grin in my
general direction.

"Yes, well, Sophie. I am looking for your
head chef in order to arrange my soiree." She looked
around expectantly for the chefs of Europe to appear
out of the walk in. So, I lied.

"I am the head chef," I said, which could
have been translated to: I am your only prayer, so be
nice. I bowed from the waist and put my dead fish
forward again. She looked me up and down, wrin-
kled her nose and shook my finger tips. I looked at
her tanned hand and tried not to stare at the most
enormous diamond I had ever seen. It looked like it
would pull her hand to the floor.

"Yes, well, nice to meet you. Anyway, I am
having eleven of my most dear friends meet me here
for lunch and I wanted to make sure all would be
spectacular." Her southern drawl hung in the air as
she glanced around the kitchen and rested her expec-
tant gaze on me. Sandra slowly sashayed out and left
me alone to deal with Ms. Kimberly.

"Well, we pride ourselves on the quality of
our product here." I tried to sound as official as possible while I was shrinking inside, considering what
few things I actually had to cook. " Are any of your
friends vegetarians?" I thought it was a simple
straightforward question but it led her to tilt her
head back and laugh like a jackal.

"That's a good one, honey. I guess I like you.
You do not seem to understand, sugar. I am Kimberly
Strickland of Strickland Cattle. We think of vegetarians the way you might think of anarchists or demons
or something." She lifted the hand not weighted
down by jewels and tried to wipe the mascara she
believed must be running down her face after such a
funny joke.

"Well, we would like some vegetables on
the side, but beef or chicken would be fine. I'm not
much of a fish eater. When I was in Florence I had
the most delicious filet mignon in the most scrump-
tious delicate mushroom cream sauce. I don't sup-

behind the olives. ...
walk-in.

We had basic veggies: carrots, potatoes,
onions. I moved into the meat freezer. We
had a few chickens, no filet mignon in sight.
I dug to the back of the shelf and touched
something larger than a chicken. I pulled
out a large piece of bottom round. What
could I do to a cheap cut of meat that would
make it fancy enough for my new friend
Kimmy?

As I stood there in the freezer, with the
cold air of the vent running its frigid fingers
through my hair, I saw my grandmother. I
smelled the garlic sweetness of her kitchen and I
had a powerful food memory. We had gone to
South Carolina to visit her. It was a month before
she died. All her sons and their fabulous cooking
ability and she would not let them in her kitchen.
But I, being the only grandchild in residence, was
allowed the formidable privilege of helping her
cook dinner. I had been on vegetable duty: cutting up carrots and onions, cubing potatoes, peel-
ing all those cloves of garlic. Then she took all the
roots I had sliced and diced and filled them
around the giant bottom round. She smiled and
laughed as she told me that this was an ancient
family recipe from before the war and I must
never tell my father the truth behind the round.
She dumped onion soup mix and cream of mushroom soup on top of it and baked it in a covered
pan at 350° for three hours while we made fruit
Jello and then played hearts. All of her sons loved
it and we all raved as grandma took in the praise
and winked at me. I smiled as I thought of grandma. I missed her almost as much as I missed my
father. I stepped back out of the freezer. Would I?
Could I? If I served free drinks, if I sliced it thin
and added some asparagus on the side, would
they guess they were eating about as low brow as
you can go?

Sandra returned to the kitchen and
looked for something to pick on.

"So, how'd it go? What's the big plan for
the ladies?" I glanced around to make sure
nobody else was in the kitchen.

"It's going to be great. No Jello mold
though. So, do me a favor. Run to the store and
buy a Betty Crocker® lemon cake mix. OK?"

I know grandma and Betty would have
been proud if they could have seen me that day.
When Kimmy and her sauced friends came in
begging for the recipes, all I replied was:
"Ancient family secrets from before the war."

...dating back as far as 100 AD were built by the Mogollon (see Western New Mexico University Museum above). Stop in at the ranger station at the trail head to pick up information on good day hikes in the area. Note: the hot springs you will find here are nice, but not as impressive as those found in the Jemez mountains. Camping available. Call the park's Visitor's Center 1-505-536-9461

Faywood Hot Springs.
This privately-owned hot springs, southeast of Silver City on the way to City of Rocks State Park, offers private and public man-made pools and tubs holding natural mineral waters that have brought weary travelers here for centuries. Half of the public space is designated clothing optional. Private pools rent by the hour ($20 for two people, $60 for a group of 7-15 people). Camping available, including a big carpeted tepee. 505-536-9663

City of Rocks State Park. Thirty-three million year old ash deposits hardened to stone and were sculpted through the millennia to produce this astounding natural wonder — an expanse of giant rocks whose smooth forms remind one of a topiary garden. Definitely worth a few hours of exploring. Stop for a drink of cool delicious water from the well. Lots of camping available. 505-536-2800. Follow Hwy 180 East, then south toward Deming. Turn left onto Hwy 61 and it's a few miles up on the left.

The hike along the main trail in **Whitewater Canyon** is one of the most exciting and most accessible hikes in New Mexico. Steel scaffolding now traces the path of a pipe (dubbed "the catwalk" by engineers who maintained it) that once channeled water to a generator for an ore mining settlement in the late 1800's. The scaffold permits passage along the sheer canyon walls, reaching up to 180 feet in height. River water rushes and cascades below. There are several opportunities to step off the trail for a swim or to relax in the shade. Trails extend into the hills beyond the main canyon walk. Found east of the town of Glenwood, about an hour north from Silver City along Hwy 180.

Call the visitor center (1-800-548-9378) or listed numbers for more information on these and other **upcoming events** in and around Silver City. September 4 – *Silver City Arts Fair* (Call 1-505-388-5725) Labor Day Weekend *Hillsboro Apple Festival*.
October 4-6 *Gem and Mineral Show* .

GETTING THERE:
Silver City is located 240 miles from Albuquerque, the quickest root being south on I-25, then west on Hwy. 152 five or so miles south of Truth or Consequences. After passing through the town of Hillsboro and climbing into the mountains of the Gila, the road gets windy, and its slow going, but the view are exceptional. Be sure to stop just west of the town of Hillsboro, at the **Sweetwood Barbeque** barn. Owner Sam Rutledge roasts her famous barbeque over wood cut from the orchard out back. She has shipped her expertly cooked meats as far as Russia and Pakistan. Call 895-3317. *For more information on Silver City try www.silvercity.org.*

Humor man. Let's call him Dave. He said he'd tell me everything he knew. We arranged to meet for an interview right after his haircut. Hours went by. He never showed. I called his phone number that same day: "Dave doesn't live here anym— He went on tour." Still think I'm p

Then what about this: A m into a CD store run by a good friend mine. He says he drives an ice cream and he wants to find some other musi might be appropriate which he could r mend to his boss, because he's getting s of hearing the same three songs again an again. He says it's "driving him crazy" (m friend swears that he used those exact words). They have a long conversation about it, coming up with a list of possible alternatives. They discuss the larger implications — how this could have a wide-ranging effect on the world of ice cream vendors, how neighborhoods across America might one day rejoice to hear a sprightly Nino Rota melody or a happily spinning mbira tune from Zimbabwe, instead of the same three rancid airs. He leaves, pledging to return soon. But guess what? HE NEVER CAME BACK.

But fear not, fellow citizens, for all is not darkness. In my neighborhood I've witnessed a sign that goodness and innocence still exist in our world: friendly humans pushing brightly painted ice cream carts on wheels, decorated with festive colored ribbons; on the push bar hang several small brass bells that jingle delightfully as they roam the streets. The bells are high enough in pitch to cut through the ambient noise and be heard at a distance, yet they insinuate themselves gently into my awareness — just enough of a nudge to make my brain joyfully register "Ice cream!" without any trace of hostility or dread. It actually makes me smile, makes me feel like I live in another time and country where life is sweet and simple. It gives me hope. And I'm happy to report that I've even seen some kids venture out to buy popsicles from the guy. I might just go buy one myself. I hope he's got those blue ones...

Steve Peters writes regularly for la cocinita *about the intersection of music and food. Send him your alternative ice cream truck repertoire suggestions c/o this publication.*

make a fuss abo good chun on a sign that read "Da Vin groaned, put away my Fre and pulled out the Italian

When I arrived a things were about as craz There were two waiters i hostess was not there ye ing baker had quit, so th smiled, taking in the fee and pulled on my chef problems. I would mal another waiter. I felt a isfaction. See how ine always saved the day buzz of self importan er to find the shelves ran to the front of th They had no idea. chef at the restaura forgotten to pay th deliver until they brain around this waltzed in.
"So, Sop planned for the "Excus phone dealing "Sorr butt?" "I ha man's cell ph and turned o "Yo than half of get in touch mouth hum ladies sho details." us, the O marched deer in Kimber room f to the silk p or so This mee

my

la cocinita • late su

THAI-STYLE SWEET AND SOUR VEGETABLES

This is a straightforward vegetarian dish, quick and easy to make. It takes but a few minutes of cooking time in the wok. The sweet and sour flavoring gives depth and zest to this colorful mixture of vegetables. Serve this as a side dish or a main vegetarian course.

SERVES 4

1 lb (450 g) firm fresh tofu

4 green onions

8 oz (225 g) cucumber

10 oz (275 g) pineapple

1¾ cups peanut oil

3 garlic cloves, crushed

1 medium onion, sliced

1 green bell pepper, seeded and sliced

3 tablespoons light soy sauce

2 teaspoons salt

2 teaspoons sugar

2 teaspoons Chinese white rice vinegar or cider vinegar

1 teaspoon chili bean sauce

2 tablespoons water

Cut the tofu into 1 inch (2.5 cm) cubes. Trim the green onions and cut them into 1 inch (2.5 cm) segments.

Peel the cucumber, slice it in half lengthwise and, using a teaspoon, remove the seeds. Then cut the cucumber into 1 inch (2.5 cm) pieces. Peel, core and cut the pineapple into 1 inch (2.5 cm) pieces.

Heat the oil in a deep-fat fryer or large wok until it almost smokes, then deep-fry the tofu cubes in two batches. When each batch of tofu cubes is lightly browned, remove and drain well on paper towels.

Drain most of the oil from the wok, leaving 1 tablespoon. Reheat the wok until it is hot, add the garlic and stir-fry for 30 seconds. Then add the onion and bell pepper and continue to stir-fry for 2 minutes. Add the tofu and cucumber and stir-fry for another 4 minutes. Finally add the pineapple, soy sauce, salt, sugar, vinegar, chili bean sauce and water and stir-fry for 2 minutes more. Transfer to a warm dish and serve at once.

FRIED SWEET POTATO STICKS

The wok is perfect for making these sweet potato sticks. Its round, concave shape makes it ideal for deep-frying without wasting any oil. Sweet potatoes are easier to handle than white potatoes and they can be used in more and different ways. Their distinctive taste and texture make them ideal to eat as snacks or as an accompaniment to any main course.

SERVES 4

1¼ lb (750 g) sweet pototoes
3¾ peanut oil
1 tablespoon salt
½ teaspoon freshly ground black pepper
1 teaspoon sugar

Peel and cut the sweet potatoes into strips about 3 inch x ¼ inch (7.5 cm x 5 mm). Put the sweet potatoes into a large bowl and cover with cold water. Chill for 2 hours or overnight.

Drain the sweet potatoes in a colander, then spin them dry in a salad spinner or pat them dry with paper towels, making sure they are as dry as possible.

Heat a wok or large frying pan over a high heat until it is hot. Add the oil and, when it is very hot and slightly smoking, fry half the sweet potatoes for 8 minutes. Remove the sweet potatoes with a slotted spoon and drain in a colander; then fry the second batch.

When you are ready to serve them, reheat the oil until it is very hot again. Fry half the potatoes until they are crispy and golden brown. Remove and drain well on paper towels. Reheat the oil until it is very hot, fry the other half and drain. Transfer the potatoes to a warm platter, toss with the salt, pepper and sugar and serve at once.

RICE, NOODLES AND PASTA

Probably the question I am most frequently asked about the wok is how to use it to make fried rice. This is a question that seems to intrigue many cooks. I am not surprised because properly stir-fried rice will result in a smoky and delicious flavor that is quite addictive.

Using the wok to stir-fry rice or noodles, or even to make pasta or porridge, again shows the versatility of the wok. It has so many uses in rice and pasta cookery — such as to brown noodles or to stir-fry a large amount of pasta — that it is unbeatable. In fact, once you discover how easy it is to stir-fry a large batch of noodles, you will never think of using your frying pan again!

EGG FRIED RICE

The Chinese hate to waste anything. To throw away food is unconscionable. This is a lesson my mother taught me very well and, to this day, even in the affluent and, I must say, wasteful United States, I cannot bring myself simply to discard leftover food.

Fortunately, the wok is most useful when it comes to making the best of leftovers. The trick is to create tasty, nutritious meals by means of the wok stir-fry technique. Here I take bits of leftover cucumber and corn and blend them with spicy embellishments. You will enjoy a tasty treat and feel virtuous as well. Remember that your cooked rice should be very cold before you put it into the wok. If you want a vegan version, simply leave out the eggs.

SERVES 2-4

1¼ cups long-grain white rice

2 eggs, beaten

2 teaspoons sesame oil

½ teaspoon salt

2 tablespoons peanut oil

8 oz (225 g) onions, coarsely chopped

2 teaspoons salt

½ teaspoon freshly ground black pepper

6 oz (175 g) cucumber, peeled, seeded and diced

⅔ cup fresh or frozen corn kernels

1 teaspoon chili oil

Cook the rice according to the *Steamed Rice* recipe *(see p.210)* at least 2 hours in advance or the night before. Leave it to cool thoroughly and then put it in the refrigerator.

Combine the eggs with the sesame oil and salt.

Heat a wok or large frying pan over a high heat until it is hot. Add the oil and, when it is very hot and slightly smoking, add the onions, salt and pepper and stir-fry for 2 minutes. Then add the beaten eggs and stir-fry for 1 minute. Add the rice and continue to stir-fry for 3 minutes. Finally, add the cucumber, corn and chili oil and stir-fry for another 5 minutes. Turn onto a warm platter and serve hot or cold as a rice salad.

SPICY MALAY-STYLE LAKSA

This is another well-traveled dish. Laksa means a one-dish meal of rice noodles, with either seafood or chicken. Although it originated in far-off Malaysia, I first encountered it in London thanks to my friend Jenny Lo. Being of Chinese-Malaysian descent herself, she is fortunate in that the fine Malaysian restaurant, the Singapore Garden, is located near her home.

The authentic version of the recipe calls for some rather exotic and difficult-to-find ingredients. Moreover, it demands a great deal of preparation time. I have therefore modified it to make it more accessible for home cooking. I believe I have retained the spirit of the dish in the process. It certainly looks and tastes as good as the original! Once the chicken has been prepared, the wok infuses smoky flavors to the aromatic ingredients, which makes it all rather easy to cook and enjoy.

SERVES 4

3 lb (1.4 kg) whole chicken

9½ cups water

2 teaspoons salt

½ teaspoon freshly ground white pepper

1 lb (450 g) raw prawns

2 fresh red chilies

2 tablespoons peanut oil

2 tablespoons finely chopped garlic

2 tablespoons finely chopped fresh
   gingerroot

4 oz (100 g) shallots or onions, thinly sliced

1 teaspoon ground coriander

½ teaspoon turmeric

8 oz (225 g) rice noodles, rice vermicelli or
   rice sticks

1 (14 fl oz) (400 ml) can coconut milk

2 teaspoons Madras curry paste

1½ tablespoons salt

½ teaspoon freshly ground black pepper

1 teaspoon sugar

FOR THE GARNISH

3 tablespoons thinly sliced green onions

7 oz (200 g) bean sprouts, blanched

Sprigs of fresh cilantro

Put the chicken and water together in a large pan and bring it to a boil. Lower the heat and simmer uncovered for 20 minutes, skimming all the time. Add the salt and pepper, cover and simmer for another 25 minutes. Remove the chicken and leave it to cool thoroughly. Reserve the liquid.

Peel the prawns and remove the fine digestive cord. Wash the prawns and pat them dry with paper towels. Cut the chilies in half and finely shred them, removing the seeds.

Heat a wok or frying pan over a high heat until it is hot. Add the oil and, when it is very hot and slightly smoking, reduce the heat, add the garlic, gingerroot, chilies and shallots or onions and stir-fry for 2 minutes. Add the coriander, turmeric and the liquid from the chicken. Turn the heat to low, cover and simmer for 20 minutes.

When the chicken is cool enough to handle, remove the meat with your hands and pull it apart into shreds with a fork. Set aside. Soak the rice noodles, vermicelli or sticks in a bowl of warm water for 25 minutes. Drain them in a colander or sieve.

Add the coconut milk, prawns and rice noodles, vermicelli or sticks to the simmering liquid. Season with curry paste, salt, pepper and sugar and continue to cook for 2 minutes. Add the chicken and cook for 2 minutes. Ladle the mixture into a large soup tureen and serve with the garnishes on the side.

HAINANESE CHICKEN RICE

Hainan is a large island off the south China coast. It is not noted for its cuisine, but this chicken rice dish is famous as a most popular and satisfying "comfort food." The best versions of it are to be found in Singapore and Malaysia and it is a standard item in street food stalls, restaurants, hotel room services and home kitchens there. I always enjoy this dish when I visit that part of the world.

Note, though, that this is not the original recipe. In Hainan the whole chicken is traditionally used, including the head and feet. The version here uses a normal Western chicken and is still delectable, but do use the best and freshest chicken available. It may be served at room temperature and, as it reheats nicely, it can be prepared in advance.

SERVES 4

2¼ - 3¼ lb (1-1.5 kg) free-range or corn-fed chicken
1 tablespoon salt
7½ cups or more *Chicken Stock (see p.56)*
6 slices fresh gingerroot
6 green onions
½ teaspoon freshly ground black pepper
1 tablespoon peanut oil
2 tablespoons finely chopped garlic
1 teaspoon salt
1¼ cups long-grain white rice

FOR THE GARNISH

1 lb (450 g) cucumber (about 1)
8 oz (225 g) tomatoes
2 green onions

FOR THE GINGER AND GREEN ONION SAUCE

4 tablespoons finely chopped green onions, white part only
2 teaspoons finely chopped fresh gingerroot
1 teaspoon salt
2 tablespoons peanut oil

Rub the chicken evenly with salt. Place it in a large pan and cover with the stock. Add more stock if necessary to cover and bring to a boil. Add the gingerroot, green onions and pepper. Cover tightly, reduce the heat and simmer gently for 30 minutes. Turn off the heat and leave covered tightly for 1 hour. Remove the chicken from the pan and let it cool. Skim off any surface fat from the stock. Measure 3¾ cups of stock and set it aside. (This will be used to cook the rice.)

Heat a wok or large frying pan over a high heat until it is hot. Add the oil and, when it is very hot and slightly smoking, add the garlic and salt and stir-fry for 1 minute. Then add the rice and continue to stir-fry for 2 minutes. Now add the reserved stock to the rice, bring the mixture to a boil and continue boiling until most of the liquid has evaporated. Turn the heat to very low and cover tightly. Let the rice cook undisturbed for 15 minutes. Remove the wok from the heat and let the rice rest for 5 minutes before serving it.

Now prepare the garnishes. Peel the cucumber, slice it in half lengthwise and, using a teaspoon, remove the seeds. Then slice the cucumber. Thinly slice the tomatoes. Slice the green onions on the diagonal. Arrange the slices on a platter and set aside.

To make the ginger and green onion sauce, mix the green onions, gingerroot and salt

FOR THE CHILI-SESAME SAUCE

2 fresh red chilies, seeded and finely chopped

2 teaspoons sesame oil

1 teaspoon sugar

½ teaspoon salt

together in an ovenproof bowl. Heat the wok until it is very hot, add the oil and, when it is very hot and slightly smoking, pour it on the ginger-green onion mixture and mix well.

To make the chili-sesame sauce, add the red chilies to the sesame oil, sugar and salt and mix well in a small bowl.

Transfer the chicken to a chopping board, cut it into bite-sized pieces and arrange it on a warm platter. Reheat the remaining stock and serve it in a soup tureen. Serve the rice in bowls with the garnishes and the sauces.

GUO BU LI'S BEEF NOODLE SOUP

Versatility is what the wok is all about, and here it is used to make a soup that is hearty, savory and satisfying, using braised beef and beanthread noodles. I discovered the dish at a modest Chinese restaurant in Berkeley, California.

SERVES 4

2¼ lb (1 kg) beef brisket (with some fat and tendon), cut into 1½ inch (4 cm) cubes

3 tablespoons Shaoxing rice wine or dry sherry

2 tablespoons dark soy sauce

1 tablespoon light soy sauce

3 whole star anise

½ teaspoon freshly ground black pepper

Salt to taste

7½ cups *Chicken Stock (see p.56)*

4 oz (100 g) beanthread (transparent) noodles

1 lb (450 g) spinach

FOR THE GARNISH

5 tablespoons chopped green onions

Bring a large pan of salted water to a boil. Put the meat in the water and blanch for 10 minutes. Skim the surface constantly; this removes all the scum and impurities. Drain the meat and discard the water.

Add the beef to a wok, then add the Shaoxing rice wine or dry sherry, soy sauces, star anise, pepper, salt and stock. Bring the mixture to a simmer, reduce the heat, cover and simmer slowly over a low heat for 2 hours or until the meat is tender.

While the meat is cooking, soak the noodles in a large bowl of warm water for 15 minutes. When soft, drain and discard the water. Wash the spinach thoroughly. Remove all the stems, leaving just the leaves.

When the meat is cooked, skim off any surface fat, add the noodles and simmer for another 10 minutes. Then add the spinach leaves and cook for another 2 minutes. Ladle the soup into a large tureen or individual bowls, garnish with green onions and serve immediately.

PIQUANT HOKKIEN-STYLE PRAWN AND NOODLE SOUP

I n Malaysia there are many Chinese. Understandably, therefore, Malaysian cuisine has many Chinese characteristics. This dish is Malaysian, but "Hokkien" refers to that region of southern China from whence many Chinese migrated centuries ago, bringing with them, of course, their regional style of cooking. By all accounts, the Malaysian influence greatly improved the Hokkien approach to food.

In China, Hokkien is not regarded as a gourmet's paradise. However, this dish is certainly a fine blending of Malay and Chinese influences. I first enjoyed it as a specialty offering at one of the many street food stalls one finds in every city throughout Asia. The wok, together with a fierce and fiery heat, is the implement of choice in such places. These food stalls and the open-air food markets are marvelous spectacles to behold. Most impressive are the stir-fried dishes, the quick fried noodles, and the simple soups one can see being made and enjoy, produced as if on assembly line. I have simplified this recipe, adapting it to rely upon what ingredients can be readily found locally. Even with this modification, it remains a delicious treat.

SERVES 4-6

8 oz (225 g) fresh Chinese egg noodles

1 tablespoon sesame oil

8 oz (225 g) rice noodles, rice vermicelli or rice sticks

1 lb (450 g) raw prawns

4 tablespoons peanut oil

6 oz (175 g) shallots, thinly sliced

5 tablespoons coarsely chopped garlic

1 tablespoon chili bean sauce

1 tablespoon Madras curry paste

7½ cups Chicken Stock (see p. 56)

2 teaspoons salt

FOR THE GARNISH

8 oz (225 g) bean sprouts, blanched

3 tablespoons green onions, thinly cut on the diagonal

Cook the egg noodles for 3-5 minutes in a pan of boiling water. Drain and plunge them into cold water. Drain thoroughly and toss them in the sesame oil. (Tightly covered with plastic wrap, they can be kept in this state for up to 2 hours in the refrigerator.) Soak the rice noodles, vermicelli or sticks in a bowl of warm water for 25 minutes. Drain them in a colander or sieve. Peel the prawns and discard the shells. Using a small sharp knife, remove the fine digestive cord. Wash the prawns and pat them dry with paper towels.

Heat a wok or large frying pan over a high heat until it is hot. Add 3 tablespoons of the oil and, when it is very hot and slightly smoking, turn the heat to low, add the shallots and fry until they are lightly brown and crispy. Remove them with a slotted spoon and drain well on paper towels. Reheat the wok and add the remaining oil. When it is hot, add the garlic and stir-fry for 1 minute. Add the chili bean sauce and curry paste and stir-fry for 2 minutes. Pour this into a bowl and set aside.

Bring the stock to a simmer in a large pan, add the salt, then add the prawns and cook gently over low heat for 2 minutes. Now add the garlic-chili-curry mixture and continue to simmer for 1 minute. Add the egg and rice noodles, vermicelli or sticks and cook for another 3 minutes. Turn the contents of the wok into a large soup tureen, garnish with the bean sprouts, green onions and fried shallots and serve at once.

FRIED RICE WITH CHINESE SAUSAGE

The wok offers the best means of transforming leftover rice into something a bit special. In this recipe, the Chinese sausages and dried smoky mushrooms combine with the rice to make an elegant and substantial one-dish meal.

If you have no leftover rice, simply prepare some from scratch using chicken stock instead of plain water. This will enrich the flavor of the rice. The dried Chinese sausages with their aromatic slightly sweet taste will enhance the flavor of any dish. They may be found at Chinese grocers and are well worth the search. They freeze successfully if well wrapped.

SERVES 4

1¼ cups long-grain white rice

2 oz (50 g) dried shiitake mushrooms

8 oz (225 g) Chinese sausages

2 eggs, beaten

1 teaspoon sesame oil

1 teaspoon salt

½ teaspoon freshly ground black pepper

2 tablespoons peanut oil

3 tablespoons finely chopped green onions

2 teaspoons sesame oil

Cook the rice according to the *Steamed Rice* recipe *(see p.210)* using stock instead of water at least 2 hours in advance or the night before. Let it cool thoroughly and then put it in the refrigerator.

Soak the mushrooms in warm water for 20 minutes. Then drain them and squeeze out the excess liquid. Remove and discard the stems, then finely shred the caps into thin strips. Cut the sausages into small dice. In a bowl, combine the eggs with the sesame oil, salt and pepper.

Heat a wok or large frying pan over a high heat until it is hot. Add the oil and, when it is very hot and slightly smoking, add the sausage and stir-fry for 2 minutes. Then add the mushrooms and eggs and continue to stir-fry for 2 minutes. Add the rice, mix well and continue to stir-fry for another 5 minutes until the rice is heated through and well mixed. Add the green onions and sesame oil and stir-fry for 2 minutes more. Transfer to a warm platter and serve at once.

QUICK PRAWN FRIED RICE

Here we have an example of how the wok is ideal for preparing quick, nutritious, tasty meals. This popular Cantonese prawn and rice dish takes but a few minutes to put on the table once the major ingredients have been assembled.

SERVES 4

1¼ cups long-grain white rice

8 oz (225 g) raw prawns

⅔ cup fresh or frozen peas

2 tablespoons peanut oil

1 tablespoon finely chopped garlic

2 teaspoons salt

½ teaspoon freshly ground black pepper

3 tablespoons finely chopped green onions, white part only

FOR THE GARNISH

2 tablespoons finely chopped green onions

Cook the rice according to the *Steamed Rice* recipe *(see p.210)* at least 2 hours in advance or the night before. Let it cool thoroughly and then put it in the refrigerator.

Peel the prawns and, if you are using large uncooked ones, cut them to remove the fine digestive cord. Wash them and pat them dry with paper towels. Blanch the prawns in a pan of boiling water for 2 minutes. Remove with a slotted spoon and discard the water. When the prawns are cool enough to handle, cut them into 1 inch (2.5 cm) pieces.

Blanch the peas in a pan of boiling water for about 5 minutes if they are fresh; if they are frozen, simply defrost them. Drain them in a colander.

Heat a wok or large frying pan over a high heat until it is hot. Add the oil and, when it is very hot and slightly smoking, add the garlic and stir-fry for 30 seconds. Add the cooked rice and stir-fry for 3 minutes. Then add the peas, salt and pepper. Continue to stir-fry the mixture for 5 minutes over a high heat. Then add the green onions and prawns and continue to stir-fry for 2 minutes. Turn the mixture onto a warm platter and garnish with the green onions. Serve at once, or let it cool and serve as a cold rice salad.

REFRESHING CUCUMBER WITH NOODLES

Cucumbers are too often ignored or taken for granted. But they have their virtues and this recipe displays them nicely. Prepared this way, the cucumbers retain their distinctive taste and a bit of their crunchiness. This noodle dish takes minutes to cook in the wok and is a sparkling alternative to potatoes or rice. It is a perfect vegetarian dish.

SERVES 4

8 oz (225 g) fresh or dried thin egg noodles

2 teaspoons sesame oil

1¾ lb (750 g) cucumbers (about 1½)

2 teaspoons salt

2 tablespoons peanut oil

1½ tablespoons finely chopped garlic

3 tablespoons finely chopped green onions

2 teaspoons chili bean sauce

1 teaspoon salt

½ teaspoon freshly ground black pepper

2 teaspoons sugar

2 teaspoons sesame oil

If you are using fresh noodles, blanch them first by boiling them for 3-5 minutes in a pot of boiling water. If you are using dried noodles, cook them in boiling water for 4-5 minutes. Plunge the noodles in cold water, drain them thoroughly, toss them in sesame oil and put them aside until you are ready to use them. They can be kept in this state, if tightly covered with plastic wrap, for up to 2 hours in the refrigerator.

Peel the cucumbers, slice them in half lengthwise and, using a teaspoon, remove the seeds. Then cut the cucumber halves into 3 inch x ⅛ inch (7.5 cm x 3 mm) shreds. Sprinkle them with the salt and mix well. Put the mixture in a colander and let it sit for 20 minutes to drain. This rids the cucumber of any excess liquid. When the cucumber shreds have drained, rinse them in water and then squeeze any excess moisture from them in a linen dish towel. Set aside.

Heat a wok or large frying pan over a high heat until it is hot. Add the oil and, when it is very hot and slightly smoking, add the garlic, green onions and cucumbers and stir-fry for about 30 seconds. Then add the noodles, chili bean sauce, salt, pepper and sugar and stir for another 30 seconds until they are well coated with the spices and flavorings. Continue to stir-fry over a high heat for 3-4 minutes until most of the water has evaporated and the cucumbers are cooked. At this point, add the sesame oil, transfer to a warm platter and serve immediately.

STIR-FRIED PASTA WITH ORANGE AND CURRY

One of the quickest and easiest ways to prepare Italian pasta is in the wok. I love using whatever leftovers I have in the refrigerator and quickly stir-frying cooked pasta with some curry paste. With a bit of imagination, the wok turns a simple pasta dish into an ambrosial delight.

This recipe makes a fine starter for a multicourse meal or can easily be a main course with salad. In warm weather, serve it at room temperature.

SERVES 4

1 lb (450 g) dried Italian pasta, such as fusilli
  or farfalle
3 tablespoons olive oil
3 tablespoons coarsely chopped garlic
1 tablespoon finely chopped fresh gingerroot
1 small onion, chopped
2 tablespoons finely chopped orange zest
6 bacon slices, rinded and chopped
8 oz (225 g) red bell pepper, cut into ½ inch
  (1 cm) dice
8 oz (225 g) yellow bell pepper, cut into
  ½ inch (1 cm) dice
2 teaspoons sugar
1¼ cups *Chicken Stock (see p.56)*
1(14 oz) (400 g) can chopped tomatoes
3 tablespoons Madras curry paste
2 tablespoons tomato paste
1 teaspoon salt
½ teaspoon freshly ground black pepper

FOR THE GARNISH

Handful of fresh basil, chopped
Handful of fresh chives, snipped

Cook the pasta in a large pan of salted water, according to the directions on the package. Drain well and set aside.

Heat a wok or large frying pan over a high heat until it is hot. Add the olive oil and, when it is very hot and slightly smoking, add the garlic, gingerroot, onion and orange zest and stir-fry for 2 minutes. Then add the bacon and continue to stir-fry for 3-4 minutes or until the bacon is browned. Next add the peppers, sugar, stock, tomatoes, curry paste, tomato paste, salt and pepper. Turn the heat down, cover and simmer for 30 minutes.

Add the drained pasta and mix well in the wok. Turn the mixture out onto a large warm platter, garnish abundantly with plenty of basil and chives and serve at once.

THAI-STYLE NOODLES WITH CHICKEN

During my frequent visits to Bangkok, I always savour this modest noodle dish. It is a typical Thai creation and a very popular item at the city's street stalls, where it is cooked in a wok while the customer waits. The aromas rising from the hot wok as the noodles are being prepared make it impossible to pass by without sampling the dish. I suspect in origin it is a south Chinese recipe, but distinctive spices and flavorings make it an authentic Thai treat. It is equally good cold or at room temperature and it may be served during warm months as part of a simple grill.

SERVES 4

8 oz (225 g) flat rice noodles, rice vermicelli
  or rice sticks
1 lb (450 g) boneless, skinless chicken breasts
1 egg white
½ teaspoon salt
2 teaspoons cornstarch
1¼ cups peanut oil or water
1 tablespoon peanut oil
2 eggs, beaten
1 teaspoon sesame oil
½ teaspoon salt

FOR THE SAUCE

2 tablespoons Thai fish sauce
2 teaspoons Chinese black rice vinegar or
  cider vinegar
2 teaspoons chili bean sauce
2 teaspoons sesame oil
2 teaspoons sugar
1 tablespoon Shaoxing rice wine or dry
  sherry

FOR THE GARNISH

½ cup crushed roasted peanuts
3 tablespoons finely chopped green onions
Sprigs of fresh cilantro

Soak the rice noodles, vermicelli or rice sticks in a bowl of warm water for 25 minutes. Drain them in a colander or sieve. Cut the chicken breasts into strips about 3 inches (7.5 cm) long. Combine them with the egg white, salt and cornstarch in a small bowl; place it in the refrigerator for about 20 minutes.

Heat a wok until it is very hot and then add the oil. When the oil is very hot, remove the wok from the heat and immediately add the chicken pieces, stirring vigorously to keep them from sticking. When the chicken pieces turn white (about 2 minutes), quickly drain the chicken. Drain off all but 2 tablespoons of the oil from the wok.

If you choose to use water instead of oil, bring it to a boil in a pan. Remove the pan from the heat and immediately add the chicken pieces, stirring vigorously to keep them from sticking. When the chicken pieces turn white (about 2 minutes), quickly drain the chicken and all the water from the wok.

Wipe the wok clean. Heat it until it is hot, then add the 1 tablespoon of oil. Mix the eggs with the sesame oil and salt. Immediately, add the egg mixture and stir-fry for 2 minutes or until the eggs have set. Remove and drain on paper towels, cut the eggs into strips and set aside.

Reheat the wok and add the 2 tablespoons of reserved oil (2 tablespoons of fresh oil if you used water before). Add the rice noodles, vermicelli or sticks and stir-fry for 2 minutes, then add the sauce ingredients and bring to the boil. Return the cooked chicken to the pan and stir-fry the mixture for another 2 minutes, coating the pieces thoroughly with the sauce. Turn onto a large warm platter, sprinkle the garnishes over and serve at once, or let it cool and serve at room temperature.

FAMILY-STYLE MUSHROOM RICE WITH TOFU

My mother was an expert at preparing economical and nutritious meals — and quickly. With her wok and a supply of tofu, she had the essentials of such meals. In this recipe, mushrooms add their smoky flavor and unique texture to the tofu and rice. Such a dish indicates how delicious pure vegetarianism can be. It may also be paired with another vegetable platter to make a fully-rounded dinner.

SERVES 4

1¼ cups long-grain white rice
2½ cups water
2 oz (50 g) dried shiitake mushrooms
1¼ cups plus 2 tablespoons peanut oil
8 oz (225 g) firm fresh tofu
2 tablespoons thinly sliced fresh gingerroot
8 oz (225 g) fresh button mushrooms, thinly sliced
2 teaspoons chili bean sauce
1 teaspoon salt
½ teaspoon freshly ground black pepper
3 tablespoons finely chopped green onions

Cook the rice according to the *Steamed Rice* recipe *(see p.210)* at least 2 hours in advance or the night before. Let it cool thoroughly and then put it in the refrigerator.

Soak the dried mushrooms in warm water for 20 minutes. Then drain them and squeeze out the excess liquid. Remove and discard the stems and finely shred the caps into thin strips. Cut the tofu into 1 inch (2.5 cm) cubes.

Heat the 1¼ cups of oil in a deep-fat fryer or large wok until it almost smokes, then deep-fry the tofu cubes in batches. When each batch of tofu cubes is lightly browned, remove and drain well on paper towels. Let the cooking oil cool and then discard it.

Heat a wok or large frying pan over a high heat until it is hot. Add the 2 tablespoons of oil and, when it is very hot and slightly smoking, add the gingerroot and stir-fry for 30 seconds. Then add the button mushrooms and dried mushrooms and stir-fry for 5 minutes. Now add the cool rice and continue stir-frying for 5 minutes. Then add the chili bean sauce, salt, pepper, tofu and green onions. Mix well, turn onto a warm platter and serve at once.

CURRY RICE NOODLES WITH VEGETABLES

This is a vegetarian version of that popular Hong Kong dish called Singapore noodles. These light and subtle rice noodles are an ideal foil for the spicy sauce. A bonus is that it is easy to make. As this is a vegetarian meal, I use a lot of coconut milk to make it really tasty. This recipe is equally delicious served with a fish or meat dish. It is also wonderful cold and makes a lovely and unusual picnic offering.

SERVES 4-6

8 oz (225 g) thin rice noodles

2 oz (50 g) dried shiitake mushrooms

1¼ cups frozen petit pois (peas)

8 oz (225 g) Chinese or Napa cabbage

3 tablespoons peanut oil

3 tablespoons thinly sliced garlic

1 tablespoon finely chopped fresh gingerroot

6 fresh red or green chilies, seeded and finely shredded

1 teaspoon salt

½ teaspoon freshly ground white pepper

6 fresh or canned water chestnuts, sliced

3 green onions, finely shredded

FOR THE CURRY SAUCE

2 tablespoons light soy sauce

3 tablespoons Madras curry powder

2 tablespoons Shaoxing rice wine or dry sherry

1 tablespoon sugar

1 teaspoon salt

1 teaspoon freshly ground black pepper

1 (14 fl oz) (400 ml) can coconut milk

FOR THE GARNISH

Fresh cilantro leaves

Soak the rice noodles in a bowl of warm water for 25 minutes. Then drain them in a colander or sieve.

Soak the mushrooms in warm water for 20 minutes. Then drain them and squeeze out the excess liquid. Remove and discard the stems and finely shred the caps into thin strips.

Put the peas in a small bowl and let them defrost. Finely shred the cabbage.

Heat a wok or large frying pan over a high heat until it is hot. Add the oil and, when it is very hot and slightly smoking, add the garlic, gingerroot and chilies and stir-fry the mixture for 30 seconds. Then add the salt, pepper, water chestnuts, mushrooms, cabbage and green onions and stir-fry for 1 minute. Then add the rice noodles and peas and continue to stir-fry for 2 minutes. Now add all the sauce ingredients and continue to cook over a high heat for another 5 minutes or until most of the liquid has evaporated. Turn the noodles onto a large warm platter, garnish with the cilantro leaves and serve at once.

VEGETARIAN HOT BEANTHREAD NOODLES

Beanthread, or Cellophane, noodles are delightfully light. They make a great vegetarian noodle dish with other vegetables. They are also quite easy to prepare and go well with almost any kind of vegetables. The noodles provide a wonderful satiny texture to the entire dish. The spicy seasonings in this recipe give the noodles body and character, and I think it makes an excellent dish for lunch or a light supper.

SERVES 4

6 oz (175 g) beanthread (transparent)
   noodles

4 oz (100 g) carrots

4 oz (100 g) firm fresh tofu

8 oz (225 g) Chinese flowering cabbage or
   bok choy

1 tablespoon peanut oil

2 tablespoons coarsely chopped black beans

3 tablespoons finely chopped green onions

2 tablespoons coarsely chopped garlic

1 tablespoon finely chopped fresh gingerroot

1¼ cups water

2 tablespoons Shoaxing rice wine or dry
   sherry

1½ tablespoons chili bean sauce

1 tablespoon whole yellow bean sauce

2 tablespoons light soy sauce

2 teaspoons dark soy sauce

½ teaspoon salt

½ teaspoon freshly ground black pepper

2 teaspoons sesame oil

FOR THE GARNISH

2 teaspoons finely chopped green onions

Soak the noodles in a large bowl of warm water for 15 minutes. When they are soft, drain them and discard the water. Cut them into 3 inch (7.5 cm) lengths using scissors or a knife.

Peel and finely shred the carrots. Drain the tofu on paper towels and carefully shred it. Finely shred the Chinese cabbage or bok choy.

Heat a wok or large frying pan over a high heat until it is hot. Add the oil and, when it is very hot and slightly smoking, add the black beans, green onions, garlic and gingerroot and stir-fry quickly for 15 seconds. Add the carrots and stir-fry for 2 minutes, then add the tofu and vegetables. Carefully mix together without breaking up the tofu. Then add all the rest of ingredients, except the sesame oil and cook the mixture over a gentle heat for about 2 minutes. Now add the drained noodles and sesame oil and cook the mixture for another 3 minutes. Ladle some noodles into individual bowls or into one large serving bowl, garnish with the green onions and serve at once.

MALAYSIAN-STYLE RICE NOODLES

One of the most exciting aspects of visiting Malaysia is eating at all the food hawkers' stalls. Here you can find all manner of food that is skillfully prepared and extremely savory and tasty. The strong aromas of garlic, ginger and chilies permeate, it is a food lovers' paradise. A favorite of mine is made with rice noodles. The Chinese influence can easily be detected in the use of the Chinese sausages, which are rich and sweet. This recipe is substantial enough for a one-dish lunch or makes a delightful addition to other dishes.

SERVES 2-4

8 oz (225 g) broad flat dried rice noodles

8 oz (225 g) raw prawns

6 oz (175 g) Chinese sausages or ham

4 green onions

2 eggs, beaten

2 teaspoons sesame oil

A pinch of salt

½ teaspoon freshly ground black pepper

3 tablespoons peanut oil

2 tablespoons coarsely chopped garlic

3 fresh red or green chilies, seeded and finely chopped

2 small onions, thinly sliced

3 tablespoons light soy sauce

3 tablespoons oyster sauce

2 tablespoons Shaoxing rice wine or dry sherry

2 teaspoons chili bean sauce

Scant ½ cup *Chicken Stock (see p. 56)*

6 oz (175 g) fresh bean sprouts

Handful of fresh cilantro leaves

Soak the rice noodles in a bowl of warm water for 25 minutes. Then drain them in a colander or sieve. Peel the prawns and discard the shells. Using a small sharp knife, remove the fine digestive cord. Wash the prawns and pat them dry with paper towels. Slice the sausages on a slight diagonal to about 1 inch (2.5 cm) thick, and do the same with the green onions.

Combine the eggs with the sesame oil, salt and half the pepper and set aside.

Heat a wok or large frying pan over a high heat until it is hot. Add 1 tablespoon of the oil and, when it is very hot and slightly smoking, add the egg mixture and stir-fry for 2 minutes or until the egg has set. Remove it and place it on a platter. When it is cool enough to handle, chop it lengthwise and set aside.

Reheat the wok over a high heat and, when it is very hot, add the remaining oil. Then add the shredded green onions, garlic, chilies and onions and stir-fry for 2 minutes. Add the prawns and sausages and stir-fry for 1 minute. Then add the rice noodles, soy sauce, the rest of the black pepper, the oyster sauce, Shaoxing rice wine or dry sherry, chili bean sauce and stock and continue to stir-fry for 2 minutes. Finally, add the bean sprouts and cooked egg and continue to cook for 2 minutes. Stir in the fresh cilantro leaves for 30 seconds. Transfer to a warm platter and serve at once.

INDONESIAN-STYLE FRIED RICE

This is my version of the famous nasi goreng — a one-meal rice dish inspired by the imaginative chefs of the Grand Hyatt Jakarta. Their opulent version uses much more meat than may be found in the traditional recipe. It is garnished with satay (meat on skewers), fried chicken and prawns, along with a fried egg. The rice dish itself has prawns and additional chicken meat. I have taken some of the best features of the Grand Hyatt's creation and have incorporated them into my version of that delectable rice dish.

SERVES 4-6

1¼ cups long-grain white rice

2 eggs, beaten

2 teaspoons sesame oil

½ teaspoon salt

8 oz (225 g) boneless, skinless chicken thighs

6 oz (175 g) raw prawns

2 tablespoons peanut oil

2 tablespoons coarsely chopped garlic

1 small onion, finely chopped

2 teaspoons finely chopped fresh gingerroot

1 tablespoon shrimp paste

½ teaspoon salt

½ teaspoon freshly ground black pepper

1 tablespoon chili bean sauce

1 tablespoon oyster sauce

2 teaspoons dark soy sauce

FOR THE GARNISH

3 tablespoons finely chopped green onions
Handful of fresh cilantro

Cook the rice according to the *Steamed Rice* recipe *(see p.210)* at least 2 hours in advance or the night before. Let it cool thoroughly and then put it in the refrigerator.

Combine the eggs with the sesame oil and salt. Cut the chicken into ½ inch (1 cm) dice.

Peel the prawns and remove the fine digestive cord. Cut them into ½ inch (1 cm) pieces.

Heat a wok or large frying pan over a high heat until it is hot. Add the oil and, when it is very hot and slightly smoking, add the garlic, prawns, onion, ginger, shrimp paste, salt and pepper. Stir-fry for 2 minutes. Then add the chicken and stir-fry for 2 minutes. Add the rice and continue to stir-fry for 3 minutes. Finally, add the chili bean sauce, oyster sauce and dark soy sauce and continue to stir-fry for 2 minutes. Add the egg mixture and continue to stir-fry for another minute. Turn onto a platter, garnish with the green onions and fresh cilantro and serve hot or cold as a rice salad.

THAI-STYLE CURRY RICE

The Thais are geniuses with spices — they can transform everyday recipes into glorious and tasty dishes. One I particularly enjoy eating in Thailand is curry rice. This popular platter is perfect for a quick snack which one can enjoy there from sidewalk vendors. It is simple to make and surely makes a change from the ordinary plain rice. In fact, it is a meal by itself.

SERVES 4-6

1¾ cups long-grain white rice

2 eggs, beaten

2 teaspoons sesame oil

2½ teaspoons salt

8 oz (225 g) chicken breasts

2 tablespoons peanut oil

2 tablespoons coarsely chopped garlic

1 small onion, finely chopped

1 tablespoon finely chopped fresh gingerroot

½ teaspoon freshly ground black pepper

1¼ cups diced red bell peppers

¾ cup fresh or frozen corn kernels

1 teaspoon chili oil

1 tablespoon Madras curry powder

FOR THE GARNISH

3 tablespoons finely chopped green onions

Cook the rice according to the *Steamed Rice* recipe *(see p.210)* at least 2 hours in advance or the night before. Let it cool thoroughly and then put it in the refrigerator.

Combine the eggs with the sesame oil and ½ teaspoon of the salt.

Cut the chicken into ½ inch (1 cm) dice.

Heat a wok or large frying pan over a high heat until it is hot. Add the oil and, when it is very hot and slightly smoking, add the garlic, onion, gingerroot, 2 teaspoons of the salt and the pepper. Stir-fry for 2 minutes. Then add the chicken and stir-fry for 2 minutes. Add the rice and continue to stir-fry for 3 minutes. Finally, add the bell peppers, corn, chili oil and curry powder and continue to stir-fry for 2 minutes. Add the egg mixture and stir-fry for another minute. Turn onto a warm platter, garnish with the green onions and serve hot or cold as a rice salad.

FRAGRANT RICE

■■■■■

*R*ice is a cereal grass that is cultivated extensively in Asia and is a staple food throughout the world. It is an adaptable food that blends well with any spices. Here is a tasty Vietnamese-inspired rice dish that is easily made in the wok. The result is a fragrant, tempting rice dish that reheats well. Serve this rice by itself or as a light and delicious side dish.

SERVES 2-4

1¼ cups long-grain white rice

1 stalk fresh lemon grass

2 tablespoons dried shrimps

2 tablespoons peanut oil

8 oz (225 g) onions, coarsely chopped

2 tablespoons coarsely chopped garlic

3 tablespoons thinly sliced shallots

3 tablespoons finely chopped green onions

2 red or green chilies, seeded and finely chopped

2 teaspoons sugar

2 teaspoons salt

½ teaspoon freshly ground black pepper

Cook the rice according to the *Steamed Rice* recipe *(see p.210)* at least 2 hours in advance or the night before. Let it cool thoroughly and then put it in the refrigerator.

Peel the lemon grass stalk to reveal the tender, whitish center and cut into 2 inch (5 cm) pieces. Smash them with the flat side of a cleaver or knife. Soak the dried shrimps in warm water for 30 minutes. Drain well. In a food processor, chop the dried shrimp. Remove and set aside.

Heat a wok or large frying pan over a high heat until it is hot. Add the oil and, when it is very hot and slightly smoking, add the lemon grass and shrimps and stir-fry for 20 seconds. Then add the onions, garlic, shallots, green onions, chilies, sugar, salt and pepper. Stir-fry for 3 minutes. Then add the rice and continue to stir-fry for 5 minutes. Turn onto a warm platter and serve hot or cold as a rice salad.

TAIWANESE PORK CHOPS WITH NOODLE SOUP

Another user-friendly wok recipe, this is a delicious one-dish meal which I have greatly enjoyed at countless food stalls in Taipei, the capital of Taiwan. Tasty pork chops are marinated, then deep-fried and served with a hearty bowl of soup and noodles. It is the type of basic food that is mouth-watering, sustaining and altogether satisfying.

SERVES 2, AS A WHOLE MEAL

2 (6 oz) (175 g) pork chops with bone in

5 cups *Chicken Stock (see p.56)*

8 oz (225 g) wheat or egg noodles, fresh or
   dried

Cornstarch, for dusting

2½ cups peanut oil

FOR THE MARINADE

1 tablespoon light soy sauce

½ teaspoon salt

¼ teaspoon freshly ground black pepper

1 teaspoon five-spice powder

1 teaspoon Shaoxing rice wine or dry sherry

½ teaspoon chili powder or chili flakes

1 tablespoon finely chopped garlic

2 teaspoons white rice vinegar

FOR THE GARNISH

Handful of fresh cilantro leaves

Combine the pork chops with the Marinade ingredients and marinate for 45 minutes.

Bring the stock to a simmer. Then, in a separate pan, cook the noodles for 3-5 minutes in boiling salted water. Drain well, then drop the noodles into the stock. Take the stock and noodles off the heat.

Remove the pork chops from the marinade and dust with cornstarch, shaking off any excess. Save any excess marinade and put it into the stock with the noodles.

Heat a wok or large frying pan over a high heat until it is hot. Add the oil and, when it is very hot and slightly smoking, add the pork chops, reduce the heat to medium and fry the pork chops for 5 minutes. Remove with a slotted spoon and drain well on paper towels. Ladle broth and noodles into individual serving bowls or a large bowl and top with the pork chops. Garnish with fresh cilantro and serve at once.

BEANTHREAD NOODLES WITH CRAB

Beanthread noodles are light and easy to use. They are a good alternative to noodles made with wheat. The silky texture of the noodles is a nice contrast to the rich crabmeat. Be sure to get the freshest crabmeat available. This dish literally takes about 15 minutes to prepare and even less to stir-fry in the wok. Serve with rice or as an unusual first course.

SERVES 4

4 oz (100 g) dried beanthread (transparent) noodles

1½ tablespoons peanut oil

2 tablespoons coarsely chopped garlic

2 teaspoons finely chopped fresh gingerroot

3 tablespoons thinly sliced shallots

8 oz (225 g) fresh crabmeat

3 tablespoons finely chopped green onions

1¼ cups *Chicken Stock (see p. 56)*

1 tablespoon light soy sauce

2 tablespoons oyster sauce

FOR THE GARNISH

Handful of sprigs of fresh cilantro

Soak the noodles in a large bowl of warm water for 15 minutes. When soft, drain and discard the water. Cut the noodles into 3 inch (7.5 cm) lengths using scissors or a knife.

Heat a wok or large frying pan over a high heat until it is hot. Add the oil and, when it is very hot and slightly smoking, add the garlic, gingerroot and shallots and stir-fry for 1 minute. Then add the crabmeat and green onions and stir-fry for 30 seconds. Add the beanthread noodles and stir-fry, mixing well. Finally add the stock, soy sauce and oyster sauce and stir-fry until most of the liquid has evaporated. Transfer the contents of the wok to a warm platter, garnish with the fresh cilantro and serve at once.

GARLIC FRIED RICE

Garlic is one of my favorite seasonings. This is to be expected because, like ginger and soy sauce, garlic is indispensable in Chinese cookery. Without garlic, Chinese food would be something quite other than it is, and not nearly so good. Simply put, garlic makes the most bland food come alive. Here I have paired it with rice to make a special fried rice that is quickly stir-fried in the wok to give it an additional smoky flavor. A simple but delightfully garlicky treat.

SERVES 4

1¼ cups long-grain white rice

2 tablespoons peanut oil

8 oz (225 g) onions, coarsely chopped

3 tablespoons coarsely chopped garlic

2 teaspoons salt

½ teaspoon freshly ground black pepper

2 tablespoons finely chopped fresh cilantro

Cook the rice according to the *Steamed Rice* recipe *(see p.210)* at least 2 hours in advance or the night before. Let it cool thoroughly and then put it in the refrigerator.

Heat a wok or large frying pan over a high heat until it is hot. Add the oil and, when it is very hot and slightly smoking, add the onions, garlic, salt and pepper. Stir-fry for 4 minutes. Then add the rice and continue to stir-fry for 5 minutes or until the rice is heated through. Finally, add the fresh cilantro. Give the mixture several good stirs. Turn onto a warm platter and serve at once.

STEAMED RICE

Steaming rice the Chinese way is simple, direct and efficient. I prefer to use long-grain white rice, which is drier and fluffier when cooked and gives the most authentic results in wok cooking. There are many varieties but I particularly like basmati or Thai fragrant rice which are widely available. Don't use pre-cooked or "easy-cook" rice for Chinese cookery as both these types of rice have insufficient flavor and lack the texture and starchy taste fundamental to Chinese rice.

The secret of preparing rice that is not sticky is to cook it first in an uncovered pan at a high heat until most of the water has evaporated. Then the heat should be turned down to very low, the pan covered and the rice cooked slowly in the remaining steam. As a child I was always instructed never to peek into the rice pan during this stage or else precious steam would escape and the rice would not be cooked properly, thus bringing bad luck.

Here is a good trick to remember: if you make sure that you cover the top of the rice with about 1 inch (2.5 cm) of water, it should always cook properly without sticking. Many packages recipes for rice specify too much water and the result is a gluey mess. Never uncover the pan once the simmering process has begun; time the process and wait. Follow my method and you will have perfect steamed rice, the easy Chinese way.

Most Chinese eat quite large quantities of rice (about 5 oz (150 g) per head, which is more than many Westerners are able to manage). This recipe and that for Fried Rice *allows about 13 oz (375 g) dried weight, of rice for four people. If you want more than that, just increase the quantity of rice, but remember to add enough water so that the level of water is about 1 inch (2.5 cm) above the top of the rice.*

SERVES 4

1¼ **cups long-grain white rice**
2½ **cups water**

Put the rice into a large bowl and wash it in several changes of water until the water becomes clear. Drain the rice and put it into a heavy pan with the water and bring it to the boil. Continue boiling until most of the surface liquid has evaporated. This should take about 5 minutes. The surface of the rice should then have small indentations like pitted craters. At this point, cover the pot with a very tight-fitting lid, turn the heat down to as low as possible and let the rice cook undisturbed for 15 minutes. There is no need to "fluff" the rice. Let it rest for 5 minutes before serving.

DESSERTS

Desserts are not the forte of wok cookery; indeed, desserts are the one weak element in all of Chinese cookery. Hence, with these recipes, I have introduced quick and easy Western themes, but with an East-West or Southeast Asian accent manifest in the emphasis on fruit. These desserts are all extremely easy to prepare and deliciously refreshing. Fruits are versatile, and cleanse the palate nicely after the more complex Asian flavorings and seasonings of earlier courses.

There are a few steamed dessert recipes too, such as the Fluffy Steamed Cantonese Cake, *or* Thai-style Steamed Pumpkin Custard, *which are easy to make in the wok. You should, however, use a non-reactive wok (such as a good non-stick one) for desserts like* Stewed Pineapple *because the acid in the fruit will react with a carbon steel wok.*

FLUFFY STEAMED CANTONESE CAKE

*O*ur family had a typical Chinese kitchen, that is, one that was small and compact. We did have a small oven in our Chicago apartment, but my mother used it for storing extra pots and pans. In the traditional Chinese home, ovens are a rarity because they are too bulky and so expensive to use. Commercial bakers were resorted to when necesssary for a banquet or family celebration.

At home, we relied on the ever-useful wok for all our cooking needs. Instead of baking a cake in the oven, my mother steamed cakes in the wok. The result was a light, fluffy cake that was absolutely delicious, and still remains one of my favorite childhood memories. I recall very clearly waiting by the wok for the cake to be done, always ready for that first slice.

Here, I have added to my mother's recipe my own touches of butter, lemon zest and vanilla extract. This cake is delicious served warm or cold.

SERVES 4-6

2 tablespoons butter

1¾ cups all-purpose flour

2 teaspoons baking powder

½ teaspoon baking soda

A pinch of salt

5 eggs, separated

Generous ¼ cup sugar

⅔ cup skimmed or semi-skimmed milk

2 teaspoons vanilla extract

1½ tablespoons finely chopped lemon zest

Vanilla ice-cream to serve

Generously butter an 8 inch (20 cm) cake pan. Sift the flour, baking powder, baking soda and salt together.

In a bowl, beat the egg yolks with the sugar for 5 minutes until they are well incorporated. Add the milk, vanilla extract and lemon zest. Mix well and add the sifted ingredients. Continue mixing well until you have a smooth mixture.

In a separate bowl, beat the egg whites until they are stiff with soft peaks. Fold the egg whites into the cake mixture. Pour the cake mixture into the prepared pan.

Next set up a steamer or put a rack into a wok or deep pan and fill it with 2 inches (5 cm) of water. Bring the water to the boil over a high heat. Put the cake onto the steamer or the rack. Turn the heat to low and cover the wok or pan tightly. Steam for 25 minutes or until a toothpick inserted into the center of the cake comes out clean.

Remove the cake from the steamer. The cake should be light and springy to the touch. Unmold the cake onto a platter, slice and serve. It is delicious with plain vanilla ice cream.

POACHED GINGER PEARS

In Chinese culture, pears are a traditional symbol of longevity and fidelity. Moreover, their appeal extends beyond the grave, to the dead who cannot forget the pleasure they brought. Thus, I was told as a child never to bring home pears on the fifteenth day of the seventh month, for at that time ghosts were roaming the earth seeking pears, among other things. So, on that day the pears might contain ghosts who would bring bad luck into the house. It was quite believable to me at the time.

Pears also traditionally bring happiness, and this means that they should be eaten whole, never divided. Chinese pears are quite different from Western ones, being round and crisp like apples, rather than the soft and pear-shaped fruit with which we are most familiar.

In Chinese cuisine, the pear is most often cooked and served as part of a soup. In this French-inspired recipe, however, the pears are poached with ginger, resulting in a delicious, refreshing dessert. For a richer dessert, serve it with cream or a compatible ice cream.

In using a wok to make this dessert, switch to a non-reactive one, that is, a non-stick wok. A basic carbon steel wok will react to the acid from the lemon and may lose its seasoning.

SERVES 4

4 firm pears

1 lemon

6 tablespoons Chinese rock sugar or sugar

2½ cups water

1 vanilla bean, split in half

8 slices fresh gingerroot

Peel the pears and cut them in half. Remove the core and seeds. Cut the lemon in half, squeeze the juice on the pears and mix well. Combine the sugar, water, vanilla bean and fresh gingerroot in a non-stick wok and boil the mixture together until the sugar has completely dissolved. Add the pears, cover and simmer over a low heat for 20-25 minutes or until they are tender. The cooking time will depend on the ripeness of the pears.

When the pears are cooked, remove them with a slotted spoon together with the vanilla bean and gingerroot slices. Over a high heat, reduce the liquid to a syrup by boiling it fast. Discard the gingerroot slices, but keep the vanilla bean and, when it dries, put it in a jar of sugar to keep for future use.

Pour the syrup over the pears and serve at once. Alternatively, you can let the mixture cool, cover it with plastic wrap and chill until you are ready to serve it.

WARM BERRY COMPOTE WITH BASIL

This dessert is inspired by the English summer pudding I have enjoyed many times. It works to perfection only when berries are at their peak of flavor. It is a refreshing and simple dessert to make and is delicious served warm as well as cold. The touch of basil adds a piquant accent which balances the slight acidity of the berries. Any combination of berries in season will work well, and the more variety the better. I love it with cream or vanilla ice cream. Again, if you use a wok, make sure it is a non-stick one so that the acid of the berries does not react with the carbon steel.

SERVES 4

½ cup sugar
⅔ cup water
1 vanilla bean, split in half
6 oz (175 g) strawberries
6 oz (175 g) raspberries
6 oz (175 g) blueberries
2 tablespoons unsalted butter
3 fresh basil leaves, finely shredded

Using a non-stick or coated wok, bring the sugar and water to a boil, add the vanilla bean and simmer for 10 minutes. Remove the vanilla bean and save for future use.

Add the berries and butter and simmer for 2 minutes, just enough to warm and not to cook them. Remove from the heat, add the basil and stir gently. Transfer to a warm bowl and serve at once.

THAI-STYLE STEAMED PUMPKIN CUSTARD

I n Thailand, I have many times enjoyed this delectable and unusual dessert. It is a custard steamed inside a small pumpkin. The pumpkin is gently cooked in hot vapors which keeps it extremely moist while its rich sweet flavors suffuse the pudding.

I have changed it slightly so that you may serve this in ramekins. This dessert can be served hot or cold which makes it ideal for entertaining. If you are serving the desserts cold, you could serve them with some heavy cream.

SERVES 6

1 lb (450 g) cooked pumpkin or squash
5 eggs, beaten
¾ cup sugar
½ teaspoon salt
1 (14 fl oz) (400 ml) can coconut milk

Purée the cooked pumpkin or squash in a food processor or blender. Add the eggs, sugar, salt and coconut milk and continue to purée until it is well mixed. Pour into individual ramekins or small dishes.

Next, set up a steamer or put a rack into a wok or deep pan and fill it with 2 inches (5 cm) of water. Bring the water to the boil over a high heat. Carefully place the ramekins or dishes into the steamer or onto the rack. Turn the heat to low and cover the wok or pan tightly. Steam gently for 20 minutes or until the custard has set. Remove the ramekins and serve at once or leave them to cool and serve later.

WATERMELON SALAD

The watermelon is the fruit of a vine that originated in Africa. How it made its way to Asia is uncertain but there is no doubt about the popularity of its sweetness, coolness and rich colors. Watermelon is the perfect dessert for Asian meals, which are so often spicy and aromatic.

SERVES 4

⅔ cup water
3 tablespoons sugar
2 tablespoons lime juice
1½ lb (675 g) fresh watermelon cubes

Start by making the syrup. Bring the water and sugar to a boil in a wok over a high heat. When the sugar has melted, add the lime juice. Leave the syrup mixture to cool thoroughly.

Remove the watermelon rind and discard it. Cut the watermelon into 1 inch (2.5 cm) pieces. In a large bowl, gently combine the syrup mixture with the watermelon. Let it sit for 10 minutes, then serve at once.

STEWED PINEAPPLE

Pineapples are a New World fruit. Columbus brought some samples back to Europe in 1493, giving Europeans their first taste of the fruit. Despite its long history, the pineapple is still thought of as being an exotic fruit. Used extensively in Asia for savory specialties as well as simple dishes, its tart taste is always welcome as a refreshing end to any meal.

When pineapples are cooked briefly, their tartness is mellowed and the texture softens. They are transformed into a luscious cooked fruit. For a lighter dessert, omit the ice cream or heavy cream.

SERVES 4

1½ lb (675 g) fresh pineapple
1 vanilla bean
1¼ cups water
½ cup sugar
Vanilla ice cream or heavy cream, to serve

Peel the pineapple and cut it into thick pieces, discarding the tough core. Split the vanilla bean in half lengthwise.

In a large, non-reactive wok, combine the vanilla bean, water and sugar. Simmer for 10 minutes. Then add the pineapple and simmer for 5 minutes. Serve warm with either ice-cream or heavy cream.

PINEAPPLE FRITTERS

This is a delectable way to enjoy pineapple. The crispy coating makes a nice contrast to the soft sweetness of the fruit. Quick and easy, it is always pleasing.

SERVES 4

1 lb (450 g) fresh pineapple
2½ cups peanut oil for deep-frying

FOR THE BATTER

½ cup potato flour or cornstarch
¼ cup all-purpose flour
1 teaspoon baking powder
1 teaspoon baking soda
A pinch of salt
2 teaspoons peanut oil
⅔ cup of water

Peel the pineapple and cut it into thick pieces, discarding the tough core.

Mix the batter by combining the potato flour or cornstarch with the all-purpose flour, baking powder, baking soda, salt, oil and water. Blend until you have a smooth batter.

Heat a wok or large frying pan over a high heat until it is hot. Add the oil and, when it is very hot and slightly smoking, turn the heat down to moderate.

Dip the pineapple pieces into the batter mixture using a slotted spoon and drain off any excess batter. Deep-fry them for 2 minutes or until golden brown. Remove with a slotted spoon and drain on paper towels. Repeat the process until you have fried all the fruit. Serve at once.

EXOTIC FRUIT SALAD

My favorite dessert is a simple one, consisting of mixed fresh fruits: nutritious, colorful, soothing and fresh-tasting. The combinations are endless, but here is a rather exotic example I often enjoy.

SERVES 4-6

1 lb (450 g) fresh pineapple
1 lb (450 g) papaya
2 bananas
Juice of 1 lime
2 tablespoons sugar

Peel the pineapple and cut it into thick pieces, discarding the tough core. Slice the papaya in half lengthwise and remove the seeds. Peel away the skin and cut the flesh into slices. Peel and slice the bananas. Combine all the fruit in a large bowl, add the lime juice and sugar and mix well. Serve at once.

BANANAS IN SWEET COCONUT MILK

Asian bananas are of a different variety from the ones found in Europe. They tend to be quite small and are best when very ripe. In Thailand, they are slowly cooked in coconut milk and the result is a sweet, wonderful dessert, resembling a light pudding. This is a simple, unusual and very satisfying dessert that works just as well with Western bananas.

SERVES 4

1 lb (450 g) fresh, ripe bananas

1 (14 fl oz) (400 ml) can coconut milk

⅔ cup water

3 tablespoons sugar

¼ teaspoon salt

Peel the bananas and cut them into bite-size pieces.

Combine the coconut milk, water, sugar and salt in a non-reactive wok. Bring the mixture to a simmer. Add the banana pieces and simmer for 2 minutes. Remove from the heat and serve at once.

REFRESHING GRAPEFRUIT SALAD

Cultural traditions are very difficult to overcome. In the West in general, grapefruit is a "morning" fruit, a way to begin the day, but in China it is most often served as a refreshing dessert.

Grapefruit works especially well after aromatic and flavorful courses as it pleases as well as cleanses the palate, making the perfect close to a fine meal. I have added strawberries for color and the candied ginger for a special bite.

SERVES 4

4 grapefruit

2 tablespoons lemon juice

2-4 tablespoons sugar

8 oz (225 g) fresh strawberries, hulled and cleaned

2 tablespoons finely chopped candied ginger

Peel and slice the grapefruit into segments. Combine the grapefruit segments and strawberries in a large serving bowl, sprinkle with the lemon juice and sugar and toss in the candied ginger. Cover the bowl tightly in plastic wrap until you are ready to serve the fruit.

INDEX